# ENGLISH IN PRINT

*from Caxton to Shakespeare to Milton*

# ENGLISH IN PRINT

*from Caxton to Shakespeare to Milton*

VALERIE HOTCHKISS
& FRED C. ROBINSON

UNIVERSITY OF ILLINOIS PRESS

URBANA AND CHICAGO

CATALOG OF AN EXHIBITION OF MATERIALS FROM
THE COLLECTIONS OF THE RARE BOOK & MANUSCRIPT
LIBRARY, UNIVERSITY OF ILLINOIS AT URBANA-CHAMPAIGN,
AND THE ELIZABETHAN CLUB, YALE UNIVERSITY, HELD AT
THE GROLIER CLUB, MAY 14 – JULY 26, 2008

© 2008 by the Board of Trustees
of the University of Illinois
All rights reserved
Manufactured in the
United States of America
1 2 3 4 5 C P 5 4 3 2 1
∞ This book is printed on acid-free paper.
Library of Congress Cataloging-in-Publication Data
Hotchkiss, Valerie R.
English in print from Caxton to Shakespeare to Milton /
Valerie Hotchkiss, Fred C. Robinson.
p.   cm.
Includes bibliographical references and index.
ISBN-13: 978-0-252-03346-9 (acid-free paper)
ISBN-10: 0-252-03346-9 (acid-free paper)
ISBN-13: 978-0-252-07553-7 (pbk. : acid-free paper)
ISBN-10: 0-252-07553-6 (pbk. : acid-free paper)
1. Printing—England—History—Exhibitions. 2. Early printed
books—England—16th century—Bibliography—Exhibitions.
3. Early printed books—England—17th century—Bibliography—
Exhibitions. 4. Incunabula—England—Bibliography—
Exhibitions. 5. England—Imprints—Exhibitions.
I. Robinson, Fred C. II. Grolier Club. III. Title.
Z151.H68     2008
686.2074'7471—dc22     2007044081

*For*
*Kyle Weng Robinson*
*and Samuel Price Hotchkiss,*
*great lovers of books*

# CONTENTS

# PREFACE

This survey of early English printing draws upon the collections of the University of Illinois at Urbana-Champaign and the Elizabethan Club at Yale University. These libraries hold two of the most remarkable English Renaissance collections in America. The Elizabethan Club, founded in 1911, contains over three hundred outstanding volumes of sixteenth- and seventeenth-century literature, including the first four folios of Shakespeare, the Huth Shakespeare quartos, and first or early quartos of all the major dramatists. Early English holdings at the University of Illinois are broad and deep, including tens of thousands of fifteenth- through seventeenth-century English works of literature, history, philosophy, religion, science, politics, and culture in general. The collaborative nature of this work—preparations for which included many happy and instructive "show and tell" sessions in each other's vaults—has allowed us to do more than either institution could have done on its own. Even when both libraries held the same rarity—a First Folio of Shakespeare or Ben Jonson, for example—we gained new insights by getting to know another copy of a great book.

The "Englishing" of books begins very early. Already in the late ninth century, King Alfred supported the distribution of books in English and even undertook important translations himself. Once printing got underway in England in the early 1470s, English language, history, and literature could be disseminated more widely through books. This book and the exhibition it is designed to complement look at the history of early English books, exploring the concept of putting English into print, with close study of the texts, the formats, the audiences, and the functions of English books. Its coverage nearly mirrors that of Pollard and Redgrave's famous *Short-Title Catalogue* (1475 – 1640). Our bookends are William Caxton, England's first printer, and John Milton, the language's most eloquent defender of the freedom of the press in his *Areopagitica* of 1644. Shakespeare, neither a printer nor a writer much concerned with publishing his own plays, nonetheless deserves his central place in our title because Shakespeare imprints, and Renaissance drama in general, not only are well represented in the collections of both the University of Illinois and the Elizabethan Club, but also provide a fascinating window on the world of English printing in the period between Caxton and Milton.

Our survey is divided into six sections on the themes of early English printing; the role of printing in the development of modern English as a language; regulation and censorship in English printing; the place of translation in early English printing; play publishing; and, as a kind of coda, the technical aspects involved in the making of English books. Fred Robinson's introductory essay covers the historical and topical themes of the exhibition and offers an overview of the history of printing and publishing in England. This is followed by item descriptions that place each book or manuscript in its historical context and offer item-specific information on such aspects as former owners, bindings, printers' biography, and marginal notes. Among the highlights of the exhibition are English incunabula printed by Caxton and his contemporaries; the earliest recorded schoolbook in English; first editions of several English Bibles; first editions of Jonson, Chapman, Milton, and others; early English newsbooks; the first four folios of Shakespeare; numerous quartos of Elizabethan and Stuart plays, including the only surviving perfect copy of the 1604 quarto of Hamlet; examples of early printed music and maps; and several examples of English bookbinding. Our selections include many monuments of English culture alongside lesser-known but interesting works that help us elaborate upon the story of English printing, while giving the reader and visitor a sense of the extraordinary collections at Illinois and Yale.

The English language remains a work in progress, and the English represented in this survey reflects the variety and vagaries of orthography, style, and typography in Renaissance England. When quoting from exhibition items, we have transcribed the text as it appears in the source, preserving the consonantal *i* and *u,* the vocalic *v* and *j,* and the occasional *vv* for *w.* We trust that the modern reader can adjust easily to this and will appreciate a closer connection to the original. For titles, we have generally followed the practices of the *English Short Title Catalogue.* References are given to standard bibliographic works and to shelfmarks for both Illinois and Elizabethan Club copies, as well as to pertinent secondary literature for further reading. Biographical dates (taken from the *Oxford Dictionary of National Biography* or the Library of Congress authority record) are given for the first mention of a name, and again in the index. References to items on display are provided within the narrative to help both the visitors to the exhibition and the readers of this book understand the many connections between the books and manuscripts discussed. The binomial reference indicates chapter and item number.

We are grateful to the the Grolier Club in New York for hosting this joint exhibition. In particular, we thank Eric Holzenberg, Arthur Schwarz, Megan Smith, and Robert J. Ruben for helping with the details of this project. Stephen Parks and the Board of Governors of the Elizabethan Club have been enthusiastic supporters of this joint venture from the beginning and we appreciate their encouragement and goodwill. Our heartfelt gratitude goes to Ellen and Nirmal Chatterjee, who have generously supported this publication and the costs associated with mounting the exhibition. Support for research and transportation costs also came from the Arnold O. Beckman Research Award of the University of

Illinois at Urbana-Champaign. We would also like to express our appreciation to Jeff Love, our accurate and ever-cheerful research assistant; to Fred Sand and Wanda Smith, who read early drafts; to Noah Pollaczek and Rebecca Bott for the photography; and to Willis Regier, Cope Cumpston, and Carol Betts for their efforts in making this book a beautiful example of printing in English. We thank Earle Havens and William Stoneman for their informed and insightful comments on our text. And we acknowledge the staff of the Rare Book and Manuscript Library and Conservation Laboratory at Illinois for the assistance they provided in preparing many of the items for exhibition, especially Alvan Bregman, Christopher Cook, Renee Hough, Laura Larkin, Dennis Sears, Jane Somera, and Jennifer Hain Teper. Finally, we are indebted to David Price and Helen Robinson for their intellectual and moral support during the long course of this project.

# ABBREVIATIONS

| | |
|---|---|
| Alston | Alston, R. C. 1965– . *A Bibliography of the English Language from the Invention of Printing to the Year 1800*. To be complete in 22 vols. Leeds: E. J. Arnold. |
| BMC xi | *Catalogue of Books Printed in the XVth Century Now in the British Library*. Part xi, England. 2007. The Netherlands: Hes and De Graaf. |
| DMH | Herbert, Arthur Sumner, T. H. Darlow, and H. F. Moule. 1968. *Historical Catalogue of Printed Editions of the English Bible: 1525–1961*. London: British and Foreign Bible Society. |
| *ESTC* | *The English Short Title Catalogue*. Online cooperative database maintained by the British Library at http://estc.bl.uk. |
| Faye and Bond | Faye, C. U., and W. H. Bond. 1962. *Supplement to the Census of Medieval and Renaissance Manuscripts in the United States and Canada*. New York: Bibliographical Society of America. |
| Goff | Goff, Frederick Richmond. 1964. *Incunabula in American Libraries: A Third Census of Fifteenth-Century Books Recorded in North American Collections*. New York: Bibliographical Society of America. |
| Greg | Greg, W. W. 1939–59. *A Bibliography of the English Printed Drama to the Restoration*. 4 vols. London: Bibliographical Society. |
| *GW* | *Gesamtkatalog der Wiegendrucke*. 1925– . Stuttgart: A. Hiersemann; New York: H. P. Kraus. |
| *ISTC* | *Incunabula Short Title Catalogue*. 1980– . London: British Library. Electronic database, www.bl.uk/catalogues/istc/index.html. |

| | |
|---|---|
| *ODNB* | *Oxford Dictionary of National Biography.* 2004. Edited by H. C. G. Matthew and Brian Harrison. Oxford: Oxford University Press. Electronic version (www.oxforddnb.com), 2004–7. Cited with name entry and author for reference to either paper or electronic resource. |
| *STC* | Pollard, Alfred W., and G. R. Redgrave. 1976–91. *A Short-Title Catalogue of Books Printed in England, Scotland, and Ireland, and of English Books Printed Abroad, 1475–1640.* 2nd ed. 3 vols. Revised and enlarged by W. A. Jackson, F. S. Ferguson, and Katharine F. Pantzer. London: Bibliographical Society. |
| UIUC | University of Illinois at Urbana-Champaign. |
| Wing | Wing, Donald Goddard, et al. 1972–98. *Short-Title Catalogue of Books Printed in England, Scotland, Ireland, Wales, and British America and of English Books Printed in Other Countries, 1641–1700.* 2nd ed. 4 vols. New York: Modern Language Association of America. |

# ENGLISH
## IN PRINT

*from Caxton to Shakespeare to Milton*

ENRY THE.VIII.BY
THE GRACE OF GOD KYNG
of England, Fraûce, and Jreland, de=
fendour of the feith, and of the church
of England, and alfo of Jrelande, in
erth the fupzeme hed, to al schoolemai=
sters and teachers of grammer within this his realm
gretynge. Emong the manifolde buſynes and moſt
weighty affayzes, appertaining to our regall aucto=
ritee and offyce, we fozgette not the tendze babes, and
the youth of our realme, whoſe good education and
godly bzinging vp, is a greate furniture to the fame
and caufe of moche goodneſſe. And to the intent that
hereafter they may the moze readily and eafily atteine
the rudimentes of the latine toung, without the great
hinderaunce, which heretofoze hath been thzough the
diuerfitee of grammers and teachinges : we will and
commaunde, and ſtreightly charge al you fcholemai=
sters and teachers of grāmer within this our realme,
and other our dominions, as ye intende to auoide our
difpleafure, and haue our fauour to teache and learne
your fcholars this englyſſhe introduction here enfu=
ing, and the latine grammer annexed to the fame,
and none other, which we haue caufed foz your
eafe, and your fcholars fpedy pzeferment
bziefely and plainely to be com=
piled and fette fozth. Fayle
not to apply your fcho
lers in lernynge
and godly e=
ducation.

# INTRODUCTION

This exhibition explores the history of the book in England from the time of the introduction of printing to the mid-seventeenth century. The books displayed are intended to show the stages by which the printed book evolved from early handpress volumes, which in most respects imitated the characteristics of medieval manuscript books, to the books from the mid-seventeenth century, whose appearance is in most respects like that of books produced today. (There are a few differences, however; for example, modern books lack signatures and catchwords and are printed on paper that is by and large inferior in quality to the durable rag paper used in earlier books.) The exhibition also exemplifies the individual printers who produced the books and suggests their distinctive characteristics and contributions to the development of the English printed book. Consideration of the qualities of the individual printers moreover raises the question of why the work of English printers is for the most part notably inferior to that of their contemporaries on the Continent. We shall be further concerned to show what genres were particularly popular with printers — such as primers, grammars, and dictionaries — and the important role that translation played in the development of the early English book. Since the early years of printing in England coincide with the flowering of English drama, we shall consider the circumstances under which plays went from stage to page. Another significant factor in the early history of the book is the attempt by some groups, most important the government, to control and censor book production. John Milton's response to these efforts in his *Areopagitica* (item 3.14) and Charles II's 1660 proclamation suppressing two of Milton's books (item 3.15) mark the chronological terminus for the exhibition. The present essay giving a running account of the first century-and-a-half of English printing provides historical context for the exhibition's review of the makers, materials, subjects, and early progress of the English printed book.

Since the earliest printed books were planned, produced, and sold in conformity with the traditions and procedures that had been established during the later centuries of the preceding manuscript culture,[1] it will be helpful to begin with a few brief observations about the books hand produced by scribes in England during the fourteenth and fifteenth centuries. In the early Middle Ages the majority of books produced by scribes were religious in content and were predominantly in Latin. While books of this kind continued to characterize much of the scribal output in the fourteenth and fifteenth centuries, the rise of humanism and increasing use of the English vernacular broadened the range of books' contents as the age of print drew near. Another feature of late medieval books is that they were often collections or anthologies of diverse texts rather than a single work by a single author. The content of manuscript books was of course determined by the person who instructed the scribe to produce the book—typically an abbot in a monastery or a person of means in the secular world. This close association between a book's production and the person who commissioned it established a pattern that would not for some years give way to the system of producing masses of books to be put on sale to a general public. As for the physical form of books, paper was used increasingly during the fifteenth century, although vellum continued in use on certain occasions even after the introduction of printing. Manuscript books differed from modern books in not having title pages; they often did not even have titles, and scribes normally remained anonymous. Illustrated books and manuscripts with historiated initial letters were collaborative projects, the scribe leaving empty spaces for an illuminator to fill as instructed.

The incunables (books published before 1501) printed by England's first printer, William Caxton (c. 1415 / 24 – 1491 / 92), and his competitors at first resembled quite closely the manuscript books that had preceded print. Indeed, printers not uncommonly used manuscripts as the exemplars from which they set type, and so it was inevitable that some standard features of manuscript books would be carried over into early printed books. Like manuscripts, early printed books had no title pages or running heads and were unpaginated. Just as scribes did not normally sign the books they copied, so early printers often did not identify themselves in their books or give the date and place of printing. Where illustrations or historiated initials were required, the printer left blank spaces for illuminators or rubricators to fill in by hand, just as scribes had done. (Where uncolored illustrations were needed, however, early printers sometimes used woodcuts.) Just as the output of late medieval scribes in England was increasingly in the vernacular, so was it with early printed books: although many Latin books were printed, continental printers supplied enough Latin books to meet the needs of most English readers, and therefore English incunables were more likely to be in the vernacular. (Well more than 60 percent of Caxton's books are in English.) This predominance of vernacular texts among English printers contrasts strikingly with continental printers' heavy output of Latin texts. The types that printers used were imitations of manuscript hands. Caxton, for example, used a typical Gothic typeface for liturgical and religious works and for vernacular books a font based on the bâtarde characters used by Flemish scribes. Again, like manuscript codices, the incunables of Caxton and others were often anthologies of various items rather than single volumes devoted to single texts (item 1.3). The continuity of manuscript culture and print culture is further attested by the fact that scribes were sometimes hired to make copies of printed books.[2] Also collectors often made no distinction between printed books and manuscripts, printed books sometimes being bound together indiscriminately with manuscripts. (At least two of Caxton's books survive in copies bound together with manuscripts.)[3]

While the handpress printing of books was a landmark in the history of the book, it may be worth noting that it was only the last of four revolutionary changes in the form books have taken over their long history. (1) The first books were the papyrus rolls of the ancient Egyptians, Greeks, and Romans, but near the beginning of the Christian era papyrus rolls were replaced by the codex, a development that made books far more accessible and manipulable than they had been before. (2) When around the same period vellum rather than papyrus became the material from which books were made, books became far more durable than they had previously been. (3) When paper began to replace vellum (in England, soon after the beginning of the fourteenth century), makers of books had a material that was not more durable than vellum but which was far more plentiful and affordable, and this plenitude and affordability proved to be major enhancements of the impact made by the last revolutionary change in the history of the book: (4) the invention of printing with movable metal types. The mass production of books that printing on paper inaugurated has changed the character of our civilization in ways that are almost incalculable.[4]

Johann Gutenberg (born Johannes Gensfleisch zum Gutenberg c. 1400) is usually credited with the invention of printing with movable metal types in the West (the Chinese had printed with wooden blocks from at least the fifth century C.E.), although none of the books thought to have been printed by him bears his name. Still, according to more than one fifteenth-century source he began experimenting with printing around 1440, and in the period 1452–55 produced the magnificent "Gutenberg Bible," around 35 copies being printed on vellum and some 150 more on paper. The press that Gutenberg invented is essentially the same machine as that used later by Caxton in England and, indeed, this press continued in use essentially unchanged until around 1800, when the Stanhope iron press was introduced. The operation of the handpress was described by Joannes Comenius (1592–1670) in the seventeenth century:

> The Printer hath Copper Letters in a great number put into Boxes. The Composi-tor taketh them out one by one, and (according to the Copy, which he hath fastened before him in a Visorum [a device formerly used by compositors to hold copy and mark the line being set]) composeth words in a composing-stick, till a Line be made, he putteth these in a Galley, till a Page be made, and these again in a Form, and he locketh them up in Iron Chases [quadrangular frames], with coyns [fastening wedges], lest they should drop out, and putteth them under the Press. Then the Presse-men beateth [applies ink, inks] it over with Printers-ink by means of Balls [cushions used for inking type], spreadeth upon it the papers, put in the Frisket [frame with strips that keep the sheet in place while printing], which being put under the Spindle, on the Coffin [part of printing press on which form of type is laid], and pressed down with the Bar he maketh to take Impression.[5]

From Gutenberg's press in Mainz printing spread with remarkable speed throughout German-speaking lands. Less than fifty years after the appearance of the Gutenberg Bible there were printing presses in more than sixty German towns. Printing spread quickly

Image of a print shop from the 1672 English translation of Comenius's *Orbis sensualium pictus,* 190–91.

to Italy, where during the late fifteenth century it flourished impressively. The Venetian publisher Aldus Manutius (1449 / 50–1515) was especially innovative and influential, printing editions of many Greek and Latin classics in italic and roman types as well as Greek letter. (See item 4.3, his edition of Ovid's *Metamorphoses*.) After 1500 supremacy in printing passed to France, where both Paris and Lyons had major publishing centers. It was from this florescence of continental printing that Caxton, the father of printing in England, emerged.

William Caxton was an Englishman (born in Kent) who moved to Bruges as a young man and for the next thirty years was a prosperous merchant and (after 1463) governor of the "English nation in the Low Countries"—that is, the English merchants in and around Bruges. Around 1471 he retired from the business world and entered the service of Edward IV's sister, Margaret Duchess of Burgundy (1446–1503). This more leisurely career allowed him to indulge his literary interests, and he began to translate the French *Recueil des histoires de Troye,* a collection of what he called "many strange and meruayllous historyes." He also studied the art of printing (at Cologne, according to Wynkyn de Worde) and bought a press around 1473, and on it he printed his translation, *The Recuyell of the Historyes of Troye* (1473 / 74), the first book ever to be printed in English. Like late medieval manuscripts produced by scribes, it was a collection of texts, in the vernacular, produced at the behest of his patron (Margaret Duchess of Burgundy, who "largely rewarded" him for it), and provided with no indication of where or by whom it was produced. He printed a few other books in Bruges (both French and English), and then in autumn 1476 he returned to England and set up his press at Westminster, the seat of the court and of parliament as well as of Westminster Abbey, next to which he located his printing house. Here he enjoyed convenient proximity to his patrons—Edward IV and Henry VII and their families; the lords Arundel, Hastings, Oxford, and Rivers; and wealthy merchants, who either subsidized directly the production of individual books or agreed beforehand to purchase substantial quantities of a run of books, probably for use as gifts.

It is in a way unfortunate that Caxton set up his first press in Bruges, which had become something of a cultural backwater by the time he lived there. Had he modeled his work on the more advanced printing then being done in Italy, France, and some German-speaking towns, the quality of print and typography that he introduced into England might have been higher.[6] "Although he is known to have produced about a hundred books during his fifteen years as a printer, most of which show evidence of careful workmanship, none are more than adequate considered as examples of printing."[7] In contrast with the history of printing in Germany, which saw the early production of a masterpiece of printing—the Gutenberg Bible—the history of printing in England is a story of modest beginnings and slow progress, with the English printers only gradually coming up to the standard of their contemporaries on the Continent. It is startling to note that when Stanley Morison, Cambridge University Press's eminent typographical designer, provided 272 plates showing outstanding examples of the printer's art in his *Four Centuries of Fine Printing*, the earliest English example he could find was published in 1702.[8]

But if Caxton (and his followers) were not up to fine printing, it should be noted that Caxton was as much a literary figure as a printer, being himself the translator of twenty-two of the books he published and showing a wide knowledge of the literature of his day both in England and abroad. Indeed, it has been suggested that he is "among the most cosmopolitan of English literary figures."[9] His *Recuyell of the Historyes of Troye* was the first of the series of translations that he made and printed (1473/74). Caxton produced his 1481 edition of Cicero's *De senectute* for Edward IV (item 1.3), and at the request of other royalty he translated and printed Christine de Pisan's *Fayttes of Armes* (1489). He translated from the Dutch *Reineke Fuchs*, printing his translation under the title *Reynart the Foxe* in 1481. *Eneydos* (1490?), another of his translations from the French, is provided, like many of his translations, with a charming and elegant prologue by Caxton himself. *The Dictes or Sayengs of the Philosophres* (1477), probably the first book in English to be published in England, was translated by his friend and patron Anthony Woodville, the Earl Rivers (c. 1440–83), although Caxton added to it his own translation of some supplementary material. In the last year of his life Caxton translated the *Vitas Patrum*, which his assistant and successor Wynkyn de Worde (d. 1534/35) printed after Caxton's death (item 4.2). Besides his translations Caxton was a conscientious editor and printer of the most important English literature of his day. He printed Geoffrey Chaucer's *Canterbury Tales* (1476–77), and then, having discovered that he had not used the best manuscript for his exemplar, he printed a later edition (1483) using a better manuscript. He also published editions of Chaucer's *Parliament of Fowls* (1477), *House of Fame*, and *Troilus and Criseyde* (1483). John Gower's *Confessio Amantis* (1483), John Lydgate's *Temple of Glass* (1477), and Thomas Malory's *Morte Darthur* (1485) came off his press as well. The most massive volume he produced was *The Golden Legend* (1483–84), for which he says he drew upon English, French, and Latin sources. This was one of a number of Caxton's editions that were provided with illustrations; it contains seventy-two woodcuts.

Caxton's importance as a literary figure and as a preserver of the canon of Middle English writings was indeed great, but his lasting impact on the development of the English language—and specifically on English spelling—was even greater. In his prefaces he expresses much concern over the "dyversite and chaunge of langage,"[10] by which he means the variety of English dialects and the absence of consistency in spelling as well as the phonological and lexical changes in English that he noticed taking place in his lifetime. Although himself a Kentishman, he adopted the dialect of London and the court for the most part in his prefaces, translations, and other books, and this is the dialect that by and large becomes modern standard English. At the time he was writing and printing, English as a whole was undergoing one of the most momentous internal changes in its history—the great vowel shift. Before this vowel shift the vowels of English were pronounced in roughly the same way as the same vowels in the continental languages — Spanish, Italian, French, German, and so on. After the vowel shift, English pronounced the vowels differently. The "broad A" that one hears in the Spanish *estado,* Italian *stato,* French *état,* German *Staat,* and Middle English *state* (all of which are derived, like English *state,* from the Latin *status,* which also had the broad A) in English comes to be pronounced "ay" as in the modern English *state.* And similar changes in pronunciation take place in the other English vowels. In many fifteenth-century writings (such as the Cely letters and the Paston letters) signs of these and other changes begin to show up in the way people spelled.

What is remarkable in Caxton is that he retained for the most part the spelling of the late Middle English manuscripts from which he printed many of his books, especially as that spelling was codified and somewhat normalized in the Chancery Standard of documents emanating from Westminster. These conservative spellings represent the way English was pronounced before the great vowel shift. They also preserve letters like the *k-* and the *-gh-* of *knight,* consonants that were probably ceasing to be pronounced in the late fifteenth century. Caxton's spelling, then, represents Middle English rather than his own early modern English pronunciation, and since his printing press produced books in the thousands, all spelled the same way, he and the printers who followed him went a long way toward making his spelling system standard throughout England. For the chaotic variation in spelling that prevailed among manuscript scribes to begin to be replaced with a uniform, standard spelling system was a positive development, but the fact that the spelling that was standardized represented not English as it was spoken in early modern times but rather the pronunciation of an earlier day means that English today has one of the most inefficient spelling systems in the world, a spelling system full of silent letters and multiple ways of spelling the same sound (e.g., *meat, mete, meet*). One wonders whether the adoption among printers of a spelling system so far removed from the English then being spoken might not be in part the result of the presence of many foreigners among the early printers in England. These printers would be inclined simply to follow Caxton's example in spelling the language rather than trying to devise an efficient phonetic spelling system for what was to them a foreign tongue.

It should be emphasized that while Caxton and his fellow printers determined that English spelling would be based upon late Middle English orthography (a fateful decision for the future of English spelling) and made a beginning toward standardization of spelling, complete standardization lay far in the future. As Richard Mulcaster in 1582 and Charles Butler in 1634 complain, spelling in their day was still chaotically variable (see items 2.3 and 2.4). It would not be until the late eighteenth century that English spelling would settle into a truly standardized (late Middle English) system, deviation from which

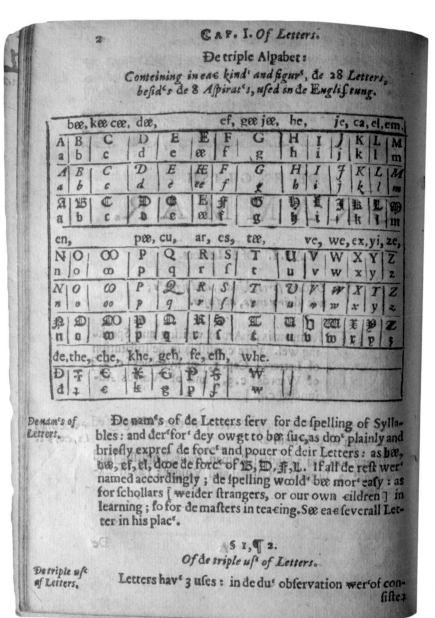

Butler's proposed alphabet for improving English spelling (1634), item 2.4, A1[r].

would be henceforth characterized as "misspelling." It is significant that the *Oxford English Dictionary*'s earliest attestation of the word *misspell* applied to English occurs well into the eighteenth century.

We have noted that Caxton's decisions about what to print went a long way toward establishing the canon of what was then English literature. His selection of books to print was not based simply on personal whim, however; there were external influences at work, and we should ask what these external influences were and also how he financed his publications. To a considerable extent the answer to both questions is patronage—a carryover from the days of handmade manuscripts when scribes were commissioned by people of status or means to produce specific volumes.

As we have seen, Caxton had commenced printing with royal encouragement, and he had had aristocratic support from Earl Rivers for three volumes. For a number of his works supported by patrons we have only the shadowy "requeste of dyverce gentilmen," or of "a noble lady which hath brought forth many noble and fayr daughters," or of "a gentyl and noble esquyer," which he tells us encouraged him to put them in print. The last ten years of his career, however, saw at least ten new publications expressly put forth at the request of a named patron. Royalty, the aristocracy, and rich citizens of London all made use of his services.[11]

It was precisely because of his dependence on patronage that Caxton had set up his press at Westminster in proximity to the court and aristocratic patrons rather than in London. And yet he had his eye on London too, as Bennett describes:

> Hugh Bryce, Alderman of London, asked him to translate *The Mirrour of the World* (1481) at his "coste and dispense," so that he could present the work to Lord Hastings, the Lord Chamberlain. Then "an honest man, and a specyal frende of myn, a Mercer of London named William Praat . . . delyvered to me in frenshe a lytel book named the book of good maners . . . and desyred me instantly to translate it in to englyssh." At much the same time he translated *The Royal Book* for another "worshipful marchaunt and mercer of London." Although Caxton does not say as much, save in speaking of Hugh Bryce, we may imagine that all three citizens underwrote to some extent the cost of these books, as did the Earl Rivers and many other aristocratic patrons.[12]

A more modest but perhaps more reliable source of income for Caxton was jobbing—taking orders for things like handbills, broadsides, church indulgences, and the like. David R. Carlson has suggested that rather than printing books for patrons, "the logic of profit allots pride of place to jobbing in the development of early English printing."[13] Printing for patrons and jobbing are of course similar in that both provide prior assurance of payment before the printing is done.

In addition to printing for patrons and to jobbing, Caxton apparently also had a sense that there might be a market for books among general readers. (Although the number of literate Englishmen was limited, it was growing.) *Reynard the Fox,* he tells us, is meant "for all good folk"; *Blanchardyn and Eglantine* appeals to "all vertuouse yong noble gentylmen and wymmen for to rede therin as for their passe tyme"; *The Order of Chyvalry* "is not requysyte to every comyn man to have, but to noble gentylmen that by their vertu entende to come and entre into the noble ordre of chyvalry."[14]

Caxton's attempt to target a market of general readers for some of his books did not escape the notice of Wynkyn de Worde, although De Worde did not act on that perception at first. Caxton died in 1491 / 92, and in the immediately ensuing years De Worde was occupied with completing the projects that Caxton had left unfinished. Since De Worde lacked Caxton's literary talents and his contacts with aristocrats and the wealthy, he did not launch major volumes comparable to Caxton's more ambitious efforts supported by patronage. It was Caxton's nascent perception that there might be a market for books among general readers that held the most promise for De Worde. And so he decided to leave Westminster and set up his printing house in the City of London. Carlson's comment on this development is noteworthy:

A more significant date than 1476 (Caxton's establishment in England) for the history of printing in England may be 1500, the year in which Caxton's heir, Wynkyn de Worde (d. 1534 / 35), and Wynkyn's still greater co-industrialist, Richard Pynson (c. 1449–1529 / 30), both moved shop from Westminster into the City of London. These moves embody a recognition of the proper nature of the only foundation on which a local printing industry could be securely built, that is, on book publication aimed at the (relatively) mass markets of book-using professionals, of the sort attracted to the city first of all, not the court.[15]

Wynkyn de Worde was a businessman who saw a bourgeois market for moderately priced, utilitarian books as his most promising source of income. Therefore the nature of his output was quite different from that of Caxton—both in format and in subject. "If the characteristic work of Caxton is the large folio, running to hundreds of pages, the typical volume of De Worde is the quarto of 24 or 32 pages."[16] In deciding which books to print, De Worde had his eye on the grammar school curriculum, which provided a captive market for books like Robert Whittinton's series of Latin grammars (he produced 155 editions of it) and John Stanbridge's grammatical primers (77 editions). About 40 percent of his output was of this kind.[17] (Caxton had printed only three or four such books.) The market for liturgical books being lucrative as well, De Worde printed missals, psalters, breviaries, and the like in large numbers. Once in London, De Worde became "the first publisher and printer to popularize the products of the printing press."[18] Quantity rather than quality was the hallmark of De Worde's books. Bennett's "Handlist of Publications by Wynkyn de Worde, 1492–1535" numbers 828 volumes.[19]

Another important printer working in London in the first decades of the sixteenth century was Richard Pynson, who, like De Worde, was an astute businessman. He specialized in religious and legal books, which constituted about two-thirds of his total output.[20] His lock on the market for legal books became especially strong after 1506 when he began to call himself Printer to the King and was charged with the publication of statutes. The quality of work from Pynson's shop was somewhat superior to that of De Worde's, and he introduced features like pagination and catchwords. He also published a few books of a more literary cast like Alexander Barclay's translation of *The Ship of Fools* (1509) and the play *Everyman* (after 1509), but it was legal and religious books that earned him his greatest profits. Pynson died in 1530 and De Worde in 1534 / 35; the two of them were the dominant printers in England in the early sixteenth century.

But they were not the only printers of incunables and early sixteenth-century books in England. Starting around 1478 Theodoric Rood was printing scholastic texts in Oxford; he and his partner Thomas Hunt published a total of seventeen books. In 1480 John Lettou (joined later by William de Machlinia, the printer who in 1490 printed a book with the first known title page in English) set up a printing house in London. They produced mainly theological treatises, law books, and scholastic texts. Another press printing scholastic texts was an establishment at St. Albans, the proprietor of which is unknown. On the whole, printing was slow to develop in England. In 1500 when there were but five printers in London, in Venice there were well over one hundred printers at work.[21] It is also noteworthy that most of the printers who produced incunables in England were foreigners. Wynkyn de Worde was probably Dutch, and Theodoric Rood was German, William de Machlinia was from Mechelen in Brabant, Richard Pynson was French (as was another printer from this period named William Faques, who called himself "printer at the king's command" from 1504 to 1507), and John Lettou was probably Lithuanian. Relying heavily on printers who had been trained on the Continent and lacking the technical resources of other countries, England in the earliest years of its printing history produced only modest specimens of the craft of bookmaking.

As the sixteenth century progressed, Englishmen increasingly took charge of the printing presses in England, although the foreign presence did not completely disappear. (Thomas Berthelet, a Frenchman, became the King's Printer in 1530, succeeding the Frenchman Pynson, and went on to print, among many other books, the first Latin Bible to appear in England [1535].) Diversification of typefaces was one concern of the printers. The earliest books were all printed using a variety of black-letter types. In 1509 Richard Pynson introduced roman types in England, and in 1524 Wynkyn de Worde used italic type, which had been pioneered by Aldus Manutius (item 4.3). He also imported Greek, Hebrew, and Arabic typefaces. All these fonts were of continental origin, typecasters in France and the Low Countries typically filling the needs of English printers. In 1566, however, appeared a book printed with a font cut by an Englishman, probably in England. John Day (1521/22–1584), at the behest of his patron Archbishop Matthew Parker (1504–75), created types that imitated the distinctive lettering used by Anglo-Saxon scribes writing vernacular manuscripts. Day used these types for printing a sermon by the Anglo-Saxon abbot Ælfric discussing the nature of the Eucharist (*A testimonie of antiqvitie, shewing the auncient fayth in the Church of England touching the sacrament of the body and bloude of the Lord* [item 6.3]). Parker wanted the sermon printed because he thought Ælfric's discussion proved that the English church founded by Henry VIII was a return to the pristine state of Christianity in England before the introduction of later papal corruptions. To Parker and Day it seemed that the Old English language of Ælfric had to be printed in characters resembling those of the Anglo-Saxon manuscript, and Anglo-Saxon types continued to be used whenever Old English texts were printed for many years to come.

It was characteristic of English printers to try to match typefaces to subject matter or function. Often in a single book English was printed in black letter while Latin was in roman (e.g., in Golding's translation of Ovid and in Lily's grammar). In Peter Levens's dictionary, English headwords are in black letter, Latin definitions in italic, and modern English commentary in roman (item 2.8). In Ælfric's *Testimonie of antiqvitie* (item 6.3) the Old English text is printed from Day's Anglo-Saxon types, translations are in large italic, biblical references and marginal notes are in small italic, and Latin words are printed in roman. In a book published in 1558 (*The Quenes maiesties passage*) Richard Tottel (c. 1528–93) uses black letter for the English prose text, reduced black letter for English verse, italic for Latin verse, and roman for quoted titles.[22] The earliest printing of the King James Bible, in 1611 (item 4.17), uses black letter for the scriptural text and roman and italics for glosses and ancillary text. Later editions replaced the black letter with roman (following the example of the Geneva Bible of 1560 [item 6.4], the first English Bible printed in roman type), and after this roman becomes standard for most books in England, although black letter continued in use for works such as law books, proclamations, and licenses as late as the eighteenth century.

Turning from the typographical habits of early printers in England to the subjects of the books they printed, we find that an extraordinary number of their publications were

Day's Anglo-Saxon typeface (1566?), item 6.3, K8ᵛ–L1ʳ.

translations. During the fifteenth century the virtual monopoly on education previously enjoyed by clerics was drawing to a close as universities expanded and a rising middle class constituted an increasingly large reading public.[23] The medieval and clerical tendency to equate literacy with reading and writing Latin was in decline. Aware of the classical texts to which humanists were giving prominence and of books in foreign languages that were increasingly in circulation, the new reading public wanted access to these works in the vernacular language that they could read (items 1.3 and 4.4–7, for example). The market for books that this craving for translation created was considerable. A large portion of Caxton's publications were translations, many of them done by him, and the English printers who followed him continued to print translations from both classical and contemporary foreign authors. Religious books were assured a good sale, while translations of the Bible proliferated as the Protestant Reformation grew in strength (items 3.1, 4.14–17, 6.4). Works in Italian, French, and other foreign languages dealing with literature, culture, and current events (items 4.9, 4.10, 4.13) were popular with the reading public, and translations of scientific works were in increasing demand (items 4.5, 4.10, 4.11).

Since the printing press gave these translations an unprecedentedly wide circulation, the translators' style and language had a major impact on the way the English language developed. During the Middle Ages in England, French and Latin were by and large the languages in which Englishmen discoursed about theological, philosophical, civic, and scientific subjects. Accordingly, over the years the native English (i.e., erstwhile Anglo-Saxon) vocabulary for dealing with such matters fell into disuse. And so when sixteenth-century translators began broadscale rendering of classical, scientific, and theological texts into English, they found there were no words for many of the concepts and technical details that they encountered in the texts they were translating. How best to fill these gaps in the vocabulary became the subject of heated debate in the sixteenth and seventeenth centuries. Basically there were three potential sources of words to meet deficiencies in English: old words could be revived (a practice especially popular with Edmund Spenser), or new words could be made up out of existing English vocabulary (e.g., rendering Latin *resurrectio* with *gainrising* or *superscriptio* with *onwriting*), or foreign words could simply be borrowed into English (*resurrection, superscription*).[24] The most spirited debate focused on the third option. Those who favored taking foreign terms into English regarded this practice as "enrichment" of the vernacular; those opposing it stigmatized foreign borrowings as "inkhorn terms."

One major proponent of borrowing foreign words was the printer John Rastell (c. 1475–1536), and another was Sir Thomas Elyot (c. 1490–1546), Henry VIII's ambassador to the Emperor Charles V, who fervently advocated taking words "out of greke, latyn or any other tonge into Englysshe" in order "to augment our Englyshe tongue."[25] But others objected to "the translatours of thys age, whych . . . do marre and misframe our Englysshe tounge through theyr termes unnedefullye borowed of other languages" (Peter Betham in *The preceptes of warre* [1544]) and condemned "inkhorne-termes (as they call them) which the common people, for lacke of latin, do not understand" (Peter Ashton, *A shorte treatise vpon the Turkes chronicles* [1546]).[26] Similarly, Sir Thomas Hoby (1530–66) in his very popular translation of Baldassare Castiglione's *The Courtier* denounced "borowing of other tunges" (item 4.12). Despite such protests, it is in fact borrowing from foreign languages (primarily Latin, French, and Greek) that became the standard means of expanding the English vocabulary, making English the language it is today—a tongue in which over 70 percent of the vocabulary is of foreign origin. And the most important single source of foreign borrowings was the spate of translations made and printed from Caxton's time through the seventeenth century.

How did the printers decide which foreign works should be translated? In the earliest years of printing, and especially in printing by Caxton, more often than not the books to be translated were determined by patrons' requests. Such requests implied a commitment to subsidizing the printer's investment in translating a book (or securing a translation by another) and then printing it or else by assuring the printer of a substantial sale of the book. Later, as De Worde and Pynson moved their presses to Fleet Street hoping to support themselves from book sales to the public, the printers had to make their best guess as to which foreign books would, if translated, have the best potential market. Translations of religious books such as Caxton's printing of *The Doctrinal of Sapyence* (item 4.1), a manual of popular theology, or the ever popular *Imitation of Christ*, which both Pynson and De Worde printed, would be assured of a good sale. (Forty-seven English editions of *The Imitation of Christ* appeared before 1650.) Classical works that had appeal as both narratives and moral instruction, like Plutarch's *Lives* (item 4.6) or Pliny, had a good chance of finding a market. Also the fifteenth century and after showed "a remarkable zeal for vernacular works of information, and the coming of print stimulated this desire. There are few topics of this kind that were not provided for by translations from Latin, French, German, Italian or Spanish sources. The art of warfare, the treatment of horses, the preparation of medicinal waters, or the ways of the stars were made plain in translation, as were treatises on medicine, chiromancy, surgery, navigation, and foreign travel [items 4.8–11]. Authorities, ancient and modern, were ransacked, and often ruthlessly adapted to provide a cheap handbook on astronomy, dietary or popular medicine."[27] And of course any book that might wind up as a textbook in the schools was a very promising candidate for translation and printing.

A special chapter in the history of translation in the early years of printing is the production of translations of the Bible.[28] William Tyndale (c. 1494–1536) translated the New Testament (1525 / 26), the Pentateuch (1530), Jonah (1531), and Joshua to 2 Chronicles (published in 1537) from Greek and Hebrew versions into English, but these had to be published in Germany since English law at that time forbade the circulation of any part of the Bible in English. After Henry VIII separated the English church from the papacy, however, circulation of English versions of the Bible became legal, and Miles Coverdale's version, largely a translation from the German and Latin, was issued first by a continental printer in 1535, and then a second edition, published in London by James Nicholson in 1537, received "the king's most gracious license." In the same year (1537) appeared the "Matthew Bible," a Tyndale translation from the original languages that now finally appeared in England legally (item 4.14). The editing of this version is attributed on the title page to "Thomas Matthew" but it was most likely produced by John Rogers (c. 1500–1555), a disciple of Tyndale's. Later, Miles Coverdale (1488–1564) was authorized to revise the Matthew Bible, and the result was the Great Bible of 1539 (item 3.1), a massive volume that Henry VIII ordered set up in every church in England. As successive editions of this translation appeared and comparisons were made with other translations and with Greek and Hebrew originals, defects in the Great Bible's renderings were detected. Accordingly, Queen Elizabeth's archbishop of Canterbury, Matthew Parker, proposed a new translation for which he would enlist the cooperation of the bishops of the realm. He farmed out various sections of the Bible to various bishops, providing them with instructions as to how to proceed. Upon completion, the bishops' translations were submitted to him for final revisions, and in 1568 the Bishops' Bible was published and presented to the queen with her portrait on the title page accompanied by fulsome tributes to her. The printer, Richard Jugge (c. 1514–77), produced a revised edition in 1572 (item 4.15) and thereafter more than forty editions ensued.

After the publication of the Bishops' Bible and before the publication of its great successor, the King James Version, two other English Bibles that are worth note appeared. One is a scholarly curiosity. Under Matthew Parker's patronage John Foxe (1516 / 17–1587) edited an eleventh-century translation of *The Gospels of the fower Euangelistes* into the West Saxon dialect of Old English. The book was printed in 1571 by John Day, using the Anglo-Saxon types he had had cut for his printing of *A testimonie of antiqvitie* (item 6.3). Like *A testimonie*, the *Gospels* were part of Archbishop Parker's program to demonstrate that the Church of England was not a "new reformation of thinges lately begonne,"[29] but a return of the church to its pure and original state.

The other English Bible published between the Bishops' Bible and the King James Version was the Douai-Rheims Bible produced by English recusants (Catholics who defied the Act of Uniformity of 1571 requiring English Catholics to disavow the papacy and join the Church of England) who were in exile in France. Gregory Martin (1542?–82) was the primary author of the translation, which was published in two stages—the New Testament in Rheims in 1582 (item 4.16) and the Old Testament in Douai in 1609–10. The Catholics were conflicted over translating the Bible into English. The Council of Trent (1546) had declared St. Jerome's Latin Vulgate the only and sufficient Catholic version of the Bible, and Catholics deplored the vernacular versions that began appearing after the Reformation. But Catholics gradually became aware that Protestant preachers who were able to quote Scripture in English and invite their congregations to read the Bible themselves in their own tongue had a considerable advantage over Catholic priests. They resolved eventually to permit a translation, but only one that adhered closely to the Vulgate text. In the interest of remaining faithful to the Latin Vulgate, they imported many of the Latin terms into their English translation—for example, *advent, anathema, calumniate, catechize,* and *commessation.* Gregory Martin included at the end of his translation a list of those words "not familiar to the vulgar reader" with explanations of their meanings (item 4.16, Eeeee2ʳ). Martin's list did not prevent the Protestants from accusing the Catholics of introducing obscure Latinate words with devious intent, "deliberately trying to nullify the value of their translation and to withhold from the unlearned that which they were ostensibly seeking to impart."[30] William Fulke (1536 / 37–1589) published a vociferous *Confutation* (1589) in which he printed in parallel columns the Bishops' Bible and Martin's translation for the Catholics and pointed out the unfamiliar, Latinate terms in the latter and refuted the polemical notes in Martin's version with his own polemical notes. Ironically, the Catholic translation, which was banned in England, became familiar to Englishmen through Fulke's *Confutation* and would even be consulted by the King James translators.

Although the Bishops' Bible enjoyed something like official status among English Protestants (the Convocation of Canterbury decreed in 1571 that every cathedral and church in England should have a copy), it was uneven in quality, the dozen or more bishops who produced it having had varying degrees of skill as linguists and prose stylists. Also, advances in biblical scholarship led readers to realize that the Bishops' Bible, like other available English translations (such as the Great Bible and the Geneva Bible), was in many passages "not answering to the original."[31] It was therefore suggested to King James I in 1604 that a new translation of the Bible was needed, one that would supersede the various English translations then in circulation and provide a uniform biblical text for the realm. James, a monarch uncommonly learned in languages and theology, soon announced the appointment of fifty-four men of learning to form six translation teams. The group included several professors of Hebrew and of Greek as well as clerical scholars of the stature of Lancelot Andrewes (1555–1626). The first of fifteen rules for the translators instructs them to make the Bishops' Bible the base-text for their rendering. Other rules ensure that the fifty-four translators will collaborate intimately and will constantly review and revise one another's work so that the final version will be uniform in style as well as more accurate than its predecessors. The result became a landmark of English literature—the Authorized Version of 1611 or, as it is more commonly called in the United States, the King James Version (item 4.17).

The King's Printer, Robert Barker (c. 1568–1646), was entrusted with the production of the book, and he devoted careful attention to the format. As was mentioned above, the text proper is printed in the traditional black-letter type, but words supplied or loosely rendered by the translators are printed in roman. The columns of text are surrounded by rectangles whose lines separate the text from the few marginal notes, which are printed in italic type. (By order of the king these are exclusively textual and not polemic, as had been notes in earlier English Bibles.) Despite the care that Barker took, there were misprints and omissions in the 1611 Bible, but in the course of time these were corrected in later editions, one in 1613 printed by the Oxford University Press, another by Robert Barker in 1616, and subsequent printings in 1629 and 1638, all with revisions and corrections. New editions continued to appear throughout the seventeenth, eighteenth, nineteenth, and twentieth centuries, each one making corrections where needed and discretely modernizing some archaisms, but without losing the stately cadence and restrained eloquence of the 1611 King James Bible.

The fact that Bibles, primers, grammars, and dictionaries made up such a large part of the early English printers' output is understandable in the context of contemporary society. Church services required both Bibles and liturgical books, and this created a huge market. Indeed, the need for liturgical books was so great that the printers in England were unable to meet the demand, and "not less than sixty percent of all breviaries, . . . primers, manuals, missals, etc. printed before 1557 came from overseas presses, despite the restrictions on the importation of books printed abroad from time to time."[32] Private devotionals were also encouraged and widely practiced, and this explains the large market for Books of Hours (or primers) (item 3.2). The convulsed state of Christianity in this period with Reformation, Counter-Reformation, disputes over Bible translation, and so on led to extensive publications of religious controversy. It is not surprising that more than 45 percent of Caxton's and Berthelet's publications and about 40 percent of Wynkyn de Worde's and Richard Pynson's dealt with religious and devotional subjects.[33] Two other printers who entered this booming trade were Richard Grafton (c. 1511–73) and Edward Whitchurch (d. 1562). Grafton was originally a member of the Grocers' Company and Whitchurch a member of the Haberdashers' Company. In 1537 the two of them paid to have copies of the Matthew Bible imported from the Continent, and they secured a royal license to sell the Bible in England. This led to their going into the printing business full time, and in 1543 they received the royal privilege to print all the service books to be used in England—a most lucrative patent. With the accession of Edward VI in 1547, Grafton was appointed King's Printer with exclusive rights to print all acts and statutes. He lost this appointment when, on Edward's death, he rashly published a proclamation of accession for Lady Jane Grey in July 1553, signing it "Printer to the Queen." When Lady Jane's reign ended nine days after her accession, Grafton was fined, briefly imprisoned, and deprived of his title. Whitchurch, known as a reformer, was also in disgrace during Mary's reign and died four years after Mary's death. The monopoly that the royal privilege granted for a time to Grafton and Whitchurch was by no means unique. John Wayland (c. 1508–71 / 73), for example, held a patent for the sole printing of all primers and manuals of prayer during Mary's reign (item 3.2), while Grafton's successor as King's Printer, John Cawood (1514–72), held a patent for the printing of Greek, Latin, and Hebrew books.

As for grammars and other books used in the schools, their proliferation in this period is explained in part by the fact that the sixteenth and seventeenth centuries in England were an epoch of remarkable educational expansion. Lawrence Stone has referred to "The

Educational Revolution in England 1560–1640."[34] One factor contributing to this growth in schooling was the religious ferment of this period. Protestants saw literacy as a religious imperative since the Christian's ability to read the Bible was helpful, if not requisite, to his salvation. Richard Baxter (1615–91) spoke for generations of Protestants when in his *Christian Directory* of 1673 he says, "By all means let children be taught to read, if you are never so poor and whatever shift you make, or else you deprive them of a singular help to their instruction and salvation."[35] But other factors as well served to promote expanding education and literacy, one of them being the introduction of printing itself. The sudden availability of a vast amount of reading material in the vernacular tongue at prices people could afford was bound to stimulate the growth of reading. In 1527 the printer John Rastell observes with satisfaction that since Henry VII's reign "the universal people of this realm had great pleasure and gave themself greatly to the reading of the vulgar English tongue."[36] And in 1534 Robert Whittinton adds, "I se many yonge persones . . . very studyous of knowledge of thynges, and be vehemently bente to rede newe workes, and in especyall [those] that be translated into the vulgare tonge."[37]

There is debate among historians as to just how many English people were schooled readers in the sixteenth and seventeenth centuries. Some think that, as Rastell's observation suggests, "the universal people" or at least a broad segment of the urban population were literate. Others wonder whether a small elite who increasingly bought and read books were not giving us the impression of an educational revolution and widespread literacy. One scholar suggests that "a reasonable guess might place male illiteracy around 80 percent and female illiteracy close to 95 percent at the time of the accession of Elizabeth."[38] Whatever the case, there can be no doubt that education and literacy grew after schooling ceased to be an exclusive preserve of the church and books were no longer precious rarities produced one at a time by scribes toiling for weeks or months to produce a single volume. That there was keen interest in educating English people in this period is demonstrated by publications like Sir Thomas Elyot's *Boke named the Governour* (1531), Richard Mulcaster's *Elementarie* (1582), Francis Bacon's *The Advancement of Learning* (1605), John Milton's *Of Education* (1644), and the publications during the Commonwealth of the Moravian immigré Joannes Comenius. In higher education this period saw a marked expansion of the universities. At Cambridge the foundation of Christ's College (1505), St. John's College (1511), and Trinity College (1546) and at Oxford the founding of Trinity and St. John's (both in 1555) stand out, as do the founding of "the College of Edinburgh" by charter of James VI in 1582 and the founding of Trinity College, Dublin, in 1592. Booksellers, of course, were active around the universities, and printers came there early as well, although university printers were slow to develop.

In a period of educational expansion schoolbook grammars like those of William Lily (1468?–1522/23) (see item 2.2) and Robert Whittinton (c. 1480–1553?) (whose Latin grammars Wynkyn de Worde and others printed and reprinted to supply the needs of schools) had a built-in clientele and a continuing sale. Indeed, Lily's Latin grammar continued in use at Eton until 1860. Actually several people contributed to this grammar (Dean Colet, Erasmus, and a royal commission that revised it in 1540), which, as the title states, was printed at the behest of the king, who, in a preface, exhorts all "scholemaisters and teachers of grammer within this our realme" to use this textbook (item 2.2, A1$^v$, shown opposite page 1). It is not surprising, given this royal support, that Robert Whittinton's grammars, after enjoying a brisk sale for a time, succumbed to the competition from Lily's grammar and passed out of use. But Whittinton's works, three-quarters of which were printed by Wynkyn de Worde, received a wide circulation in the early sixteenth century and were a commercial success for De Worde.

Richard Mulcaster's *Elementarie* (item 2.3) was intended to include a grammar of English, but it never got beyond a discussion of English spelling ("right writing") and a patriotic defense of the English tongue ("I honor the *Latin,* but I worship the *English*"). R. F. Jones has with great persuasiveness argued that Mulcaster in his discussion of spelling and of other aspects of English, such as loanwords, was "the sanest and most comprehensive" of Elizabethan commentators on the English language.[39] He was also far ahead of his time in his call for an English dictionary: "It were a thing verie praiseworthie in my opinion, and no lesse profitable then praise worthie, if som one well learned . . . wold gather all the words which we vse in our English tung, whether naturall or incorporate [i.e., borrowed], out of all professions, as well learned as not, into one dictionarie, and besides the right writing, which is incident to the Alphabete, wold open vnto us therin, both their naturall force, and their proper vse."[40] One hundred thirty-nine years would pass before this clarion call would, with the publication of Nathaniel Bailey's *Universal Etymological English Dictionary* (1721), be answered. But, as the following paragraphs explain, the slow beginnings of progress toward an English dictionary do get underway in the early years of printing.

The primitive starting point of the English dictionary can be glimpsed in the glossed manuscripts of the Middle Ages. A Latin text will often contain translations here and there of a Latin word into the vernacular, a reader or readers having concluded that future readers might need help understanding these words. Such brief explanations of the meanings of individual words (called "glosses") constitute the earliest stage of the lexicographical impulse in English. As certain manuscripts acquired large numbers of glosses, an abbot or other person of authority would sometimes instruct a scribe to copy out onto separate sheets of parchment all the glossed Latin words with their vernacular equivalents, thus creating a glossary. In order to facilitate access to the items in the glossary, the glossed Latin words would be arranged in alphabetical order, like these entries in a fifteenth-century glossary:

| Difficilimus | hard |
| Dignosus | worthy |
| Domina | a lady |
| Dominus | a lord |
| Dominatus | a lordship |
| Dulcor | swetness |

Such lists may be said to constitute the rudiment of the modern bilingual dictionary.

Among many such bilingual glossaries surviving from the Middle Ages one compiled around 1440 by a Dominican friar from Norfolk stands out as a particularly advanced form of this proto-dictionary. This is the *Promptorium parvulorum sive clericorum,* or "treasury for young scholars" (item 2.5), and the book is indeed a treasure trove for English-speaking pupils learning Latin. Rather than entries being in the usual order Latin–English, the *Promptorium* has the English term first and in alphabetical order, thus:

Abasshment.
> *Terror. roris. Pauor. uoris. Ambo ma. ge. tercie de. Formido.*
> *is. fe.ge. ter. de.*

Abatement or a withdrawyng of weyte or mesure.
> *Subtractio. nis. fe. ge. ter. decli.*

Abbey.
> *Abacia. e. femi. gene. prime declina.*

The first entry tells the student that the Middle English noun *Abasshment,* "fear, dismay," has not one but three equivalents in Latin—*terror, pavor,* and *formido*—and (like modern Latin dictionaries) explains how to form the genitive of each noun. The entry then explains that the first two nouns are masculine of the third declension, while the last is a third-declension feminine noun. With this information at his disposal the student should know how to use the noun he chooses. There are approximately twelve thousand English entries in the *Promptorium,* and on average there are two Latin terms in each entry, these terms being drawn from a range of sources—for example, Alexander Neckam (1157–1217), John of Garland (c. 1195–1258), and Hugo of Pisa (d. 1210)—who are identified in *preambula* that appear in some of the surviving manuscripts.[41] The popularity of the *Promptorium* is attested by the fact that six manuscripts of it survive and five early editions of it were made, the earliest being Richard Pynson's edition of 1499 (item 2.5). (Pynson gave the author's name as Galfridus Anglicus, and others have called him Galfridus Grammaticus, but the evidence supporting both names is slight, and the Dominican friar remains anonymous.) Julian Notary (c. 1455–c. 1523) printed the *Promptorium* in 1508, and Wynkyn de Worde printed editions of the *Promptorium* in 1511, 1512, 1516, and 1528. In his preface "Ad Lectorem," De Worde calls the reader's attention to another bilingual dictionary printed by him in 1500, the *Ortus Vocabulorum,* or Garden of Words, in which Latin words are given first followed by English equivalents. By using the two dictionaries together, De Worde says, even a child can "serche for ony latyn or englysshe worde."[42] De Worde based the *Ortus Vocabulorum* on a fifteenth-century manuscript called *Medula Grammatica,* or Marrow of Grammar, which survives in many manuscript copies. De Worde produced several editions of it, this and the *Promptorium* being the kind of book he especially liked printing since they would have a continuing sale among generations of schoolchildren learning Latin.

The large market for these bilingual glossaries led to further, expanded compilations, a notable one being Sir Thomas Elyot's (item 2.6), which introduces the word *dictionary* in its title. A moral and political philosopher as well as a lexicographer, Elyot took the bilingual dictionary in a direction very different from that of the *Promptorium* and the *Ortus Vocabulorum.* The latter two works, as we have seen, had roots in the Middle Ages, coming as they did out of the medieval manuscript tradition and drawing their Latin words from medieval authors like Alexander Neckam and John of Garland. Elyot was attuned to the humanist revival of classical authors, and the Latin elements in his dictionary are extracted from authors like Cicero, Galen, Livy, Martial, Plautus, Pliny, Quintilian, Salust, Terence, and Virgil. He did not necessarily mine these authors' works himself but made considerable use of previous compilers of dictionaries and reference books, especially the Italian author Ambrosius Calepinus's *Dictionarium* for his (Elyot's) 1538 edition and the French lexicographer Robert Stephanus's *Thesaurus* (and his later dictionaries) and others for his later editions. He expanded the scope of his *Dictionary* beyond what is now thought to be the province of a dictionary, including aphorisms (mostly taken from Erasmus's *Adagia*), biographical sketches, personal reminiscences, and mythology.

The first edition of Elyot's Latin–English *Dictionary* (published by Thomas Berthelet, who had also published Elyot's *Boke named the Governour*) is something of a jumble. This is because Elyot first submitted the book for publication (although not altogether satisfied with it), and Berthelet began typesetting it, when Henry VIII, who had heard of Elyot's project, praised his work and gave him access to books in the Royal Library. Elyot had Berthelet stop work on the book so that he could make use of the king's books to augment

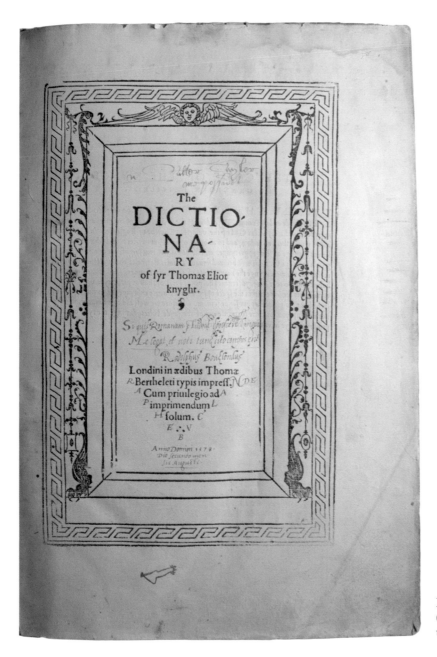

Elyot's *Dictionary*
(1538), item 2.6,
title page.

and improve his text. The result is that when the typesetting of the book was resumed and completed and the book then printed, half the sections for various letters of the alphabet are followed by "Addicions" that provide supplementary material out of alphabetical order. In subsequent editions (1542, 1545) these "Addicions" are for the most part integrated with the main text and properly alphabetized. Also, after the first edition the book was entitled *Bibliotheca Eliotae: Eliotis Librarie*. After Elyot's death in 1546 Berthelet continued to publish editions in 1548, 1552, and 1559 augmented and improved by Thomas Cooper (c. 1517–94, scholar and later vice-chancellor of Oxford and bishop of Winchester). Cooper continues Elyot's emphasis on classical authors, drawing heavily on later editions of Stephanus's dictionaries as well as other compilations.

Richard Huloet's *Abcedarium Anglico-Latinum* (item 2.7), like the *Promptorium,* is an English–Latin rather than a Latin–English dictionary. The arrangement of its entries apparently owes something to Robert Stephanus's French–Latin dictionary. For its contents it draws heavily on Elyot's *Bibliotheca Eliotae,* although Elyot's material is completely rearranged. Huloet seems particularly concerned to provide schoolchildren with a broad range of Latin synonyms for English words, enabling them to compose Latin sentences with that becoming variety required by the teachers of the day. This concern grows in the 1572 revision of Huloet by the poet and compiler John Higgins, who adds more synonyms and also provides at the end of his entries the relevant French words (probably taken from Stephanus), thus giving the revised *Abcedarium* a trilingual dimension. For example:

> Combate and to fighte. *Batuere, Confligere, Conflictare, Depugnare, Dimicare, Praelium edere, Præliari, Pugnam capessere, Certamen conserere, Contrahere certamen, Belli fortunam tentare vel experiri.* Combatre & battailer. (I5ᵛ)

Huloet's *Abcedarium* (1552) and Higgins's revision of it (1572) were not greatly successful, especially after John Baret's *Alvearie* (item 2.17) entered the competition (1573). But its innovations left a lasting impression on the English lexicographical tradition.

Peter Levens's *Manipulus vocabulorum* or "handful of words" (item 2.8) begins with a "Preface to the Reader" that seeks to justify the publication of yet another English–Latin dictionary: "So many Dictionaries of Latin and English (gentle Reader) have now beene of late by divers sundrye writers set forth, that except some kind of Noueltie should bring delite to the peruser . . . , it should be but a vaine thing, and counted but as lost laboure" (¶1ᵛ). Levens's "Nouelties" include some special uses of accents and, most notably, the backward alphabetization of his English headwords. That is, he arranges headwords according to their final syllables, words with identical endings being grouped together. Both of these features have provided valuable evidence to modern historians of early English pronunciation. Here is a representative excerpt:

> A ante B. . . .
>
> | | |
> |---|---|
> | vnstáble | *instabilis, æ.* |
> | vnáble | *inualidus, a. impotens.* |
> | dúrable | *durabilis, e.* |
> | mútable | *mutabilis, e.* |
> | túneable | *symphonicus, a.* |
> | sáyleable | *nauigabilis, e.* (Aiʳ) |

| | | | |
|---|---|---|---|
| a garð of a garmét | fimbriale is, hæ | a pilcharðe | gerres is, halecula á |
| larðe | lardum i | a pótcharðe | teſta æ, rudus, eris |
| A ſharðe | teſta, rud° eris, hoc | ý rerewarðe | poſt, principia |
| a warðe, pupill | pupillus i | a regárðe | reſpeƈtus, us |
| a warðe, priſon | cuſtodia æ | a rewárðe | mun° eris, donú, hoc |
| to carðe woll | carminare, peƈtere | a ſáuegarðe | ſecuritas, tutamétú |
| to garðe | communire | a ſcábarðe | vagina æ |
| to warðe | tutare, protegere | a ſheparðe | opilio, cuſtos, odis |
| harðe | durus a | a ſluggarð | deſes idis, ſonulent° |
| an awárðe | arbitramentum i | ſpikenarðe | aſarum, ſpica æ |
| a báſtarðe | ſpurius a | a ſtéwarð | procurator, œcono- |
| a ſtandarðe | ſignum, vexillum i | a tábarðe | timpanum   (mus |
| a bóggarðe | ſpeƈtrum i | a tánkarðe | amphora, cathar° i |
| a búſtarð | buteo, picus i | a wýſarðe | augur uris, hic hæc |
| a cówarðe | cohardus, timid° a | to awárðe | arbitrari, adiudi- |
| a báſtarðe | idem | to ióparðe | periclitari   (care |
| a ðiſarðe | pantomimus, ſannio | to rewárð | remunerare |
| a ðúllarðe | hebes etis, tardus a | to regárðe | curare, æſtimare |
| backwarð | retrorſum | frówarde | prauus a |
| fórward | antrorſum | tówarð | ingenuus a |
| ðownewarðe | deorſum | inwarðe | intrinſecus a |
| vpwarðe | ſurſum | óutwarðe | extrinſecus a |
| ſpðewarðe | lateraliter | vnhárð | mollis e |
| a baʒelarðe | enſis, gladiolus | hytherward | huc |
| a cúſtarðe | artogala æ | thytherward | illuc |
| a gurnarðe, fiſh, | capo onis, hic | whitherwarðe? | quorſum? |
| an haſkarðe | proletari°, ignobilis | a farðle | ſarcinula æ |
| ý haʒarð play | alearum ludus | a harðle | crates, caula æ |
| an hopparðe | lupuletum i | a ðwarfe | nanus, homuncio |
| a lybarðe | leopardus a | a quarfe | portus us, hic |
| a lýſarðe | lacertus a | ðarſe, ſtubborn. | pertinax, obdurat° |
| a Lumbarðe | longobardus | **In arge.** | |
| a málarðe | anas atis, hic | a barge | cimba æ, remulcus i |
| múſtarðe | ſinapium i | a charge | cura, mandatum |
| a niggarðs | parcus i | large | largus, amplus, a |
| an órcharðe | pomarium | to charge | mandare |
| | | C ij. | a ðiſ. |

Levens's rhyming dictionary (1570), item 2.8, C2ʳ.

Aside from Levens's "Nouelties," the *Manipulus* is largely derivative both of the *Promptorium* (whose English–Latin order of words in entries it follows) and of Huloet's *Abcedarium*. The printer, Henry Bynneman (c. 1542–83), uses black letter for English words, italic for Latin, and roman for commentary. Essentially, the *Manipulus* is a combination of an English rhyming dictionary (the first of its kind) and an English–Latin lexicon.

John Baret's *An Alvearie or Triple Dictionarie, in Englishe, Latin, and French* (item 2.17) has English headwords arranged alphabetically but two indexes at the end—one Latin and one French—which make it serviceable as a Latin dictionary and a French dictionary as well as English. The title *Alvearie*—"Beehive" (Latin *alvearium*)—refers to the method of composition. In "An Address to the Reader" Baret explains that when he was teaching at Cambridge University he had his students "gather a number of fine phrases out of Cicero, Terence, Caesar, Liuia, &c. and to set them vnder seuerall Tytles, for the more ready finding them againe at their neede. Thus within a yeare or two they had gathered togither a great volume, which (for the apt similitude betweene the good scholars and diligent Bees in gathering their wax and hony into their Hiue) I called then their Aluearie" (*5ʳ). Some years later Baret, with the help of others, reduced the gathered material to English entries arranged alphabetically, and Henry Denham (fl. 1556–90) printed it. The Latin and English words seem not to have been gathered from the original authors Baret lists but rather were taken from Elyot's *Bibliotheca Eliotae* as revised by Cooper and from other reference works such as Cooper's *Thesaurus,* which Cooper compiled after revising Elyot. It is less clear where the French words come from, but many show striking parallels with Robert Stephanus's *Dictionarium Latino-Gallicum* (1538, 1552, 1561) and other dictionaries by Stephanus.[43] Like Huloet, Baret supplies copious synonyms:

> Abundance or plenty. Abundantia. Affluentia, Feracitas, Redundantia,
> Fertilitas, Vbertas, Profluentia, Copia.
> *Abondance, foyson.* (C3ʳ)

After Baret's death in 1578 an antiquary and poet named Abraham Fleming brought out a revision of the *Alvearie* (1580) in which he added aphorisms (from Erasmus's *Adagia*), etymological information, and other features.

For the English reader interested in French, an important book is John Palsgrave's *Lesclarcissement de la langue francoyse* (item 2.13), the last volume set by Pynson. It was, in fact, completed by Pynson's son-in-law, the printer John Hawkins, shortly after Pynson's death early in 1530. A full treatment of pronunciation, grammar, and idioms with a wealth of illustrative phrases, *Lesclarcissement* was used by Palsgrave in his teaching of French, and in his contract with Pynson he stipulates that the book shall be sold only to persons designated by him—that is, his students and friends. (Apparently he did not want competitors in French-teaching to have access to his book.) A second condition in the contract specifies that Palsgrave has the right to correct proofs of his book. These stipulations are early examples of an author claiming rights over the production and distribution of his work.

A colonist member of the Virginia Company, Richard Perceval (1550–1620), published *Bibliothecæ Hispanicæ* (item 2.16) in 1591, for readers seeking help with Spanish. (Earlier, in 1586, Perceval had used his Spanish to decipher packets containing the first certain information about the Spanish Armada, a feat for which he was rewarded with a pension.) The scholar and lexicographer William Salesbury (c. 1520–c. 1580), who translated the New Testament and other texts into Welsh, issued a *Dictionary in Englyshe and Welshe* (item 2.14) primarily to help Welshmen learn English. In the early seventeenth century, the expanding worldview of the English is reflected in the etymological guide and polyglot dictionary of John Minsheu (1559 / 60–1627), which lists English headwords and their equivalents in eleven different languages (item 2.18).

All the dictionaries discussed above have in common the purpose of giving readers access to foreign words and to English explanations of the meanings of those words. The idea of an English dictionary explaining the meaning and use of all English words (such as Mulcaster proposed in his *Elementarie*) seemed as yet beyond the ken of those publishing English books.

A start toward conceiving of such a dictionary, however, is Thomas Speght's glossary

*The old and obscure words of Chaucer explained,* which he prepared in connection with his edition of Chaucer (1598). Here is acknowledgment that at least some English words — archaisms in Chaucer — are obscure and require explication in English for English readers. Similarly, John Rastell's *The exposicions of the termes of the lawes of England* (1567, with many subsequent editions extending down through 1708) gives proof that there are other English words that English-speaking readers need to have explained to them — in this case, legal terms. But the real impetus for developing an English dictionary came not from the need for explaining archaisms or legal terms but from the welter of foreign borrowings that, as we have seen, swelled the English vocabulary when so many classical and foreign texts were being translated into English in the early years of the printed book. English readers not schooled in the classics or in foreign languages who turned to these translations were confronted by a host of strange terms or "hard words" that the translators had adopted from the foreign texts they were translating.

Robert Cawdrey (1537 / 38 – c. 1604), a schoolmaster and parson from Rutland, addressed the needs of such readers with *A Table Alphabetical, containing . . . hard vsuall English wordes, borrowed from the Hebrew, Greeke, Latine, or French, etc. With the interpretation thereof by plaine English words, etc.* (1604); 120 pages long and containing 2,521 entries, this is the first English dictionary. Subsequent editions appeared in 1609, 1613, and 1617, and other authors began producing similar books. John Bullokar's *An English Expositor* (item 2.9) appeared in 1616 and Henry Cockeram's *English Dictionarie* in 1623. In 1656 Thomas Blount's *Glossographia* (item 2.10) was printed by Thomas Newcomb (1625 / 27 – 1681) and ran through five editions. Comparison of these books with the earlier bilingual dictionaries shows that the former borrowed definitions from the latter, and so there was continuity between the bilingual tradition and the nascent tradition of monolingual English dictionaries.[44] The hard-word dictionaries were in brisk competition with one another, and one way of promoting themselves was for each successive edition of each work to claim that it contained more words than its predecessors. This led some editors of hard-word dictionaries to the dubious practice of taking from Latin–English dictionaries Latin words that had not actually been borrowed into English and adding them with their English definitions to their trove of hard words. (As was mentioned above, the hard-word dictionaries had from the start included definitions drawn from the bilingual dictionaries.) John Milton's nephew Edward Phillips (1630 – c. 1696) published *The New World of English Words* (item 2.11) two years after Blount's *Glossographia* (item 2.10) appeared, and in his fifth edition (1696) he took Blount and others to task for this practice, speaking of "Errors for which *Blunt* and *Cole* are justly to be condemned as having crowded the Language with a World of Foreign Words, that will not admit of any free Denization." Blount in his turn accused Phillips of plagiarizing his *Glossographia* and in 1673 published a stinging pamphlet called *A World of Errors Discovered in the New World of Words* (item 2.12), where he demonstrates clearly that Phillips had cribbed from his *Glossographia*, even incorporating some of Blount's misprints into *The New World of English Words.*

As his title proclaims, Phillips (and before him Blount) included, in addition to (genuine) foreign loanwords, a wide variety of other English words that he thought might be difficult for English readers to understand — technical terms, mythological references, and so on. But the modern concept that a proper English dictionary should include and define *all* the words in the language would not be realized until one year after the seventh and last edition of Phillips's dictionary was printed in 1720: that is, when Nathaniel Bailey's *Universal Etymological English Dictionary* appeared in 1721.

The impulse to regulate the production and distribution of books did not originate with the advent of printing, but printing certainly did raise anxieties throughout Europe over what writings were available to the public. Attempts to limit or control what people could read in England during the late Middle Ages and Renaissance were motivated at various times and sometimes simultaneously by three different interests: ecclesiastical, commercial, and governmental. Pre-Reformation church authorities' perennial anxiety over the prospect of laypeople reading the Bible prompted such measures as the *Constitutions* of Thomas Arundel, archbishop of Canterbury, in 1407–9. Alarmed by the activities of the Lollards (followers of the reformer John Wyclif), who translated into English and widely disseminated manuscript copies of the Bible, Archbishop Arundel decreed "that no one shall in future translate on his own authority any text of holy scripture into the English tongue.... Nor shall any man read this kind of book, booklet or treatise ... under penalty of the greater excommunication.... Whoever disobeys this, let him be punished after the same fashion as an abettor of heresy or error." Five years later a law of 1414 specified that anyone found reading the Bible in English translation would "forfeit land, catel, lif, and goods from their heyres for ever."[45]

After printing was introduced into England, the campaign against reading English translations of the scriptures continues. Copies of William Tyndale's English translation of the New Testament, which Tyndale had completed and published while in exile on the Continent, were finding their way into England, and Cuthbert Tunstall (1474–1559), the bishop of London, ordered that these and other reform-minded works should be destroyed (item 3.4). There were repeated public burnings of Tyndale's New Testament, destruction of this book being zealously advocated by, among others, St. Thomas More (1478–1535).

Prohibitions against English translations of the Bible and against English people's reading such translations ceased after Henry VIII broke with Rome and established the Church of England. He granted specific license for the publication in England of the second edition of the Coverdale Bible, and in 1537 approved, though with restrictions, the Great Bible (item 3.1). Although the Bible in the vernacular ceased to be controversial in England, both ecclesiastical and royal authorities continued to oppose steadfastly the importation of heretical publications (first Luther's, then Calvin's) from the Continent or the writing and printing of such books in England. As early as October 1526, Cuthbert Tunstall had summoned the booksellers of London and given them stern warning against importing or buying from printers books containing Lutheran heresies and further demanded that any books that they imported should be submitted to ecclesiastical authorities for their approval before putting these books on sale. The next year Tunstall again threatened sanctions against the importation of books without first seeking ecclesiastical approval and in addition decreed that no new books could be printed in England without such approval. After the Act of Supremacy in 1534 the king issued proclamations against the circulation of heretical material and in July 1546 forbade his subjects to read all works by reformers. With the accession of Edward VI in 1547 restrictions against printers and booksellers continue to be imposed. In 1549 and 1551 proclamations are made demanding that nothing be printed without prior approval by the Privy Council or its agents. "Popish books" as well as writings by reformers are interdicted, at least until Mary becomes queen in 1553

Bishop Tunstall's 1526 list of prohibited books in Foxe's *Book of Martyrs* (1563), item 3.4, 450–51.

and begins the reestablishment of Roman Catholicism in England. Royal restrictions on the circulation of works by reformers are then intensified, and in June 1555 a proclamation declares that anyone found to be in possession of "wicked and seditious books" should be "executed for that offence according to the order of martiall law."[46] Later that month a proclamation names specifically the heretics whose works are forbidden, among them being Martin Luther, Philipp Melanchthon, John Calvin, Miles Coverdale, and William Tyndale. Books relating to the church service as it was conducted during the reign of Edward VI are also to be seized and their owners punished.

With the accession of Elizabeth (1558) and the restoration of the Church of England, efforts to repress books of dubious theological content both Catholic and Puritan resume. Nonetheless, both Puritan extremists and Catholics managed to maintain secret, unlicensed presses in England. Robert Waldgrave (c. 1554–1603 / 4) produced the notorious Martin Marprelate tracts defaming specific prelates and episcopacy in general until he was driven into exile. And there was a Jesuit press with which Edmund Campion (1540–81) was associated. After the distribution of Campion's *Decem Rationes* against the Anglican Church in June 1581, he was arrested, convicted of treason, and executed, but the press continued to operate for a time. Such unwanted activities continued despite a royal injunction against heretical and seditious books in 1559 (item 3.7) followed by further ordinances in 1566 giving notice to "every stationer, printer, bookseller, merchant, using any trade of book printing, binding, selling or bringing into the realm" that penalties for failing to observe restrictions on book importation and printing would be severe. These injunctions culminate in the Star Chamber decrees "for orders in printing" in 1586. Since "abuses and enormities are nothing abated: but . . . do rather daily more and more increase," these decrees specify limits on the number and location of printing presses in England and require all printed matter to be approved by the archbishop of Canterbury and the bishop of London "or one of them"; permit searches and seizures wherever books are stored; limit the number of apprentices that printers, booksellers, and bookbinders may hire; and assure "breakers and offenders" that they will receive severe punishment.[47] This comprehensive regulation of book production and dissemination was more effective than previous ordinances had been, but it was not completely successful.

The restrictions on printing and the importation of books in this period extend beyond ecclesiastical regulation of the content of what Englishmen read, for now the government took an increasingly larger role in controlling printing and other book-related trades.[48] Besides determining which authors and which subjects the public was allowed to read in print, the government at various times also limited the number of foreign printers working presses in England, specified where presses could be located, restricted (as in the Star Chamber decrees) the number of apprentices who could be hired, required strict reporting of the number of presses each printer was operating, forbade (at certain times) all importation of foreign books for marketing in England, and even imposed restrictions on the binding of books. Many of these government regulations were perceived by printers and book dealers as being primarily of commercial importance. Many English printers were delighted to see foreign imports of books restricted and welcomed limits on the number of foreigners who could legally compete with them in England. The practice of government licensing of printers—especially common during the reigns of Edward VI, Elizabeth, and the early Stuarts—impacted the book trade significantly. When one printer is granted an exclusive right (for a specified number of years) to print Bibles and another receives a patent for all printing in Latin, Greek, and Hebrew and others held monopolies in printing other classes of books, the privileged printers enjoyed lucrative advantages, while smaller printing firms might suffer a disadvantage.

Among those favored with privileges were Thomas Berthelet, on whom Henry VIII in 1538 conferred a royal privilege of six years' duration for printing Sir Thomas Elyot's Latin–English dictionary; Richard Tottel, to whom Edward VI gave the sole right to print law books for seven years; John Day, who held a privilege for printing catechisms and the *ABC* under Edward VI and Elizabeth; Richard Jugge, who had exclusive right to print Bibles in quarto in the 1570s; Thomas Gaultier, who was privileged to print French service books from 1550 to 1553; James Roberts and Richard Watkins, who held a privilege for almanacs (1571, 1578, and 1588–1603); and Thomas Tallis and William Byrd, who held the patent for printing music under Elizabeth. The granting of these privileges (for which the printers paid) increased the government's revenues as well as its control over the production of books. It also impacted dramatically the practical economics of the book trade. Agitation by those lacking privileges against the granting of privileges was intense, but protesting printers were often bought off by being granted privileges themselves, and rebellion against privileges had little effect.

A landmark in the growing role of the government in the history of printing in England was the granting in 1557 of a royal charter for the incorporation of the Stationers' Company of the City of London. This company had grown out of a medieval guild, "the reputable men of the Craft of Writers of Text-letter, those commonly called 'limners,' and other good folks, citizens of London, who were wont also to bind and sell books."[49] The officers of the guild monitored the conduct of its members and the quality of their work. By the time they applied for a royal charter in the middle of the sixteenth century, the "Writers of Text-letter" had been largely replaced by printers, and the guild came to be known as the Stationers' Company. A *stationer* is a bookseller or one engaged in any of the

Thomas Berthelet's patent for Elyot's *Dictionary* (1538), item 2.6, A1ᵛ.

trades dealing with books (including printers) who owns a *station* or a shop (as opposed to an itinerant vendor). By the terms of the charter granted in 1557 the only people in the realm permitted to print and deal in books were members of the Stationers' Company (and hence Londoners) or holders of licenses under royal letters patent. "While the Stationers saw in the charter a means of protecting their craft from unregulated competition, the Crown saw in it the means of controlling the increasingly powerful printing press from which came so many seditious and heretical books."[50]

The Stationers' Company was governed by a master, two wardens, and several senior members called "assistants." The master and warden were granted the right to search the homes and businesses of every bookseller, printer, and bookbinder in the realm and to confiscate any printing press or printed matter that did not conform with the company's regulations and to imprison unqualified printers and others resisting their authority. It was also the intention of the company (and of the Crown) that every book, pamphlet, or broadsheet printed or intended for printing should be entered in the Stationers' Register. In addition to being entered in the Stationers' Register, candidates for printing also had to be licensed either by ecclesiastical or governmental authorities (as had been empha-sized from at least the time of the bishop of London's stipulation of 1526 [item 3.4]). In the early years after the Stationers' Company was incorporated, the incidence of failures to register titles was fairly high. But after the Star Chamber decree of 1586 registration rates rose, and registration increased again after the Star Chamber decree of 1637 with its specific provision that no book should be printed without being licensed and "entered into the Registers Booke of the Company of Stationers" (item 3.12, B2$^v$). Entrance of titles in the Stationers' Register seems never to have become universally practiced, however; some titles not entered in the register were nonetheless licensed and so legal, but other missing titles were unlicensed and illegal. The authors of such publications, if apprehended, were duly fined and could even be imprisoned.

Requiring that titles be entered in the Stationers' Register increased significantly the government's surveillance and control over what was printed in England; it also provided future generations of literary scholars and historians with an invaluable source of informa-tion about what was being printed and the dates of completion or publication of the titles entered.[51]

The reign of Charles I was a period in which restrictions on printers and on others in the book trade became increasingly tight and were vigorously enforced. Besides the Star Chamber decree of 1637 (mentioned above and exhibited as item 3.12), there were more decrees and ordinances strictly limiting the number and location of printing houses, the number of presses that any one printer could own and operate, the number of letter founders who could provide printers with the types they needed, and continuing restrictions on the importation of foreign books. Any carpenter or other craftsman who was hired to build a printing press was required to report this to the Stationers' Company. Later acts specified that when unauthorized publications were discovered, the author, the printer, and the booksellers should all be fined and/or imprisoned and that hawkers or peddlers of such publications should be "whipt as common Rogues." When *Histrio-Mastix*, William Prynne's Puritan attack on Archbishop Laud and the theater, was published (1633), the printers were imprisoned, the publisher was fined heavily (five hundred pounds) and pilloried, and the author was fined, pilloried, had his ears cropped, and was sentenced to imprisonment for life. So apprehensive was the government over the potential threat posed by printing presses that even a person who rented a room or a house to a printer was required to report this to the Stationers' Company.

It was a series of petitions to Parliament by the Stationers' Company for increased restrictions against unlicensed publications and various measures taken to interdict such publications that prompted John Milton (who had failed to register or seek licensing for some of his pamphlets on divorce) to write and publish (unlicensed) *Areopagitica, a speech of Mr. John Milton for the liberty of vnlicenc'd printing to the Parliament of England* in 1644 (item 3.14). Although provoked by specific decrees and regulations, Milton makes only a general observation that "no Nation, or well instituted State, if they valu'd books at all, did ever use this way of licencing" (15). He does not dwell extensively on the details of licensing and of contemporary English restrictions on publication but rather with soaring eloquence

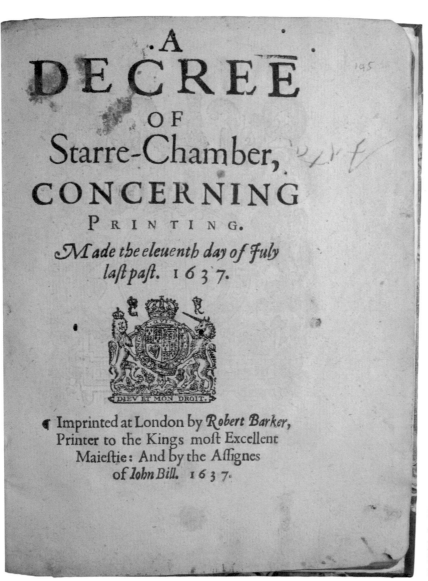

Star Chamber decree to control printing (1637), item 3.12, title page.

mounts a powerful defense of intellectual liberty and freedom of expression in general. Although *Areopagitica* had little effect in its own day and was scarcely noticed by Milton's contemporaries, it stands as our loftiest defense of free expression in the English language. That defense received, however, a caustic retort from the Crown after the Restoration: see the proclamation of 1660 suppressing two of his books (item 3.15).

During the civil wars and the Commonwealth vehement and abusive pamphlets and nascent newspapers were published in abundance, some of them Royalist and some Puritan. The quality of printing and typography was extremely low. The standard of workmanship and the grade of the paper seemed to sink to a level commensurate with that of the crude propaganda contained in these publications. Under the Commonwealth the number of books published dropped, but among those that were published are a few outstanding ones—for example, Thomas Hobbes's *Leviathan* (1651) and Izaak Walton's *Compleat Angler* (1653). Censorship continued, but now it was of course directed against the Royalists. Thus William Duggard was imprisoned, deprived of his printing press, and removed as headmaster of Merchant Taylors' School in punishment for having published Claudius Salmasius's *Defensio Regia pro Carolo I* (1649), which defends both prelacy and monarchy in England and arraigns the Puritan regicides. And in 1655 Oliver Cromwell suppressed all English newspapers except for his own two official gazettes. After the Restoration royal censorship resumes, as is exemplified in item 3.15. It is only after the Glorious Revolution of 1688 that freedom of the press becomes a permanent feature of British culture.

The early history of printing in England runs concurrently with a period of rapid and impressive development in the history of English drama culminating in the glory period of the genre—Elizabethan and Jacobean England. During the years that Caxton was printing, English people were still viewing miracle plays performed on pageant wagons, and morality plays were being written and performed. The morality play's historical successor, the interlude, was also developing. (The two categories are not always easy to distinguish, but in general the characters in moralities are always personified abstractions, while the *dramatis personae* of the interlude are more inclusive.) The first English dramatist whose name is known to us, Henry Medwall (d. 1501), was alive and at work during Caxton's lifetime, and he used a translation (of Buonaccorso's dialogue *De Vera Nobilitate*) that Caxton printed in 1481 (item 1.3) as the source of his interlude *Fulgens and Lucrece*, which was written before 1500 and printed by John Rastell between 1512 and 1516.

The generation of printers following Caxton began printing plays in earnest. As early as 1495–97 Richard Pynson printed an edition of six comedies by Terence, and around 1515 Wynkyn de Worde printed *Hickscorner* and in 1522 another interlude, *Mundus et Infans*. Also in or around 1515 Richard Pynson published the morality play *Everyman*, which must have had a good sale, since he reprinted it ten or so years later. The contemporary printer John Rastell, who was himself a writer of interludes, published in 1520 his *The Nature of the Four Elements* and around 1525 *Calisto and Melebea*, which may have been written for performance in his own house. Besides his own interludes, he published several written by John Heywood (1496/97–c. 1578), Henry Medwall, Thomas More, and other members of his circle. Rastell also printed in 1533 two farces by Heywood, *A mery play between Johan Johan the husbande, Tyb his wyfe, and syr Jhān the preest* and *A mery play betwene the pardoner and the frere, the curate and neybour Pratte*. The titles alone suggest that drama in England was at this time moving away from the allegories and abstractions of morality plays and interludes and approaching a more secular drama.

An important play that was printed for John Rastell by Peter Treveris (fl. 1525–32) around 1530 is John Skelton's *Magnificence*. It is modeled on *speculum principis* or "advice to sovereigns" literature and is thought by some to be a satire on Cardinal Wolsey (1470/71–1530). It is clearly a comment on events and abuses of the day and demonstrates how drama can be an instrument of social or political commentary, something that will stimulate government regulation of theaters and plays in the future. Even more emphatic in using drama as social commentary are the plays of John Bale (1495–1563), an almost fanatical proponent of the English Reformation. His *Tragedye or enterlude manyfestyng the chefe promyses of God unto man* and *A comedy concernynge thre lawes of nature, Moses, and Christ, corrupted by the Sodomytes, Pharysees and Papystes most wicked*, both published by Dirik Van der Straten in 1547–48, vehemently attack ecclesiastical corruption, the selling of pardons, and other abuses and accuse priests and monks of pervasive homosexuality. *A comedy . . . concernyng thre lawes of nature* was reprinted in 1562 (item 5.1), and *The chefe promyses of God* was reprinted by John Charlewood (d. 1593) for Stephen Peele in 1577 (after Bale's death). The English printers evidently thought there would be a market for rabidly anti-Catholic plays in Elizabethan England. Bale's play *King John*, which some have seen as a forerunner of the Elizabethan history play, was apparently not published until the nineteenth century.

The interludes and moralities were performed in a variety of locales—indoors, outdoors, in private homes, in taverns, in Inns of Court, and elsewhere. "[T]he churchwardens of St. Botolph, London, let their parish hall to players between 1557 and 1568, during which years it may have been used a hundred times."[52] Other churches may also have provided space for plays as well. The performers could be family members of the playwright, amateur and semiprofessional actors, children, itinerant companies, or university students.

In 1576 James Burbage had The Theatre erected in Shoreditch—the first building designed explicitly and exclusively for the production of plays. Later in the same year Richard Farrant converted the refectory of the old Priory of the Black Friars into "a continual house for plays." The era of professional theaters was underway. The Curtain (1577) was built in Moorfields, and in subsequent years the Rose (1587), the Swan (1595), the Globe (1599), the Fortune (1600), and others were opened. Most of the theaters were located outside the City of London south of the Thames in the domain of Surrey and hence not under the City's control. Civic authorities did not look kindly on theatrical performances because of the rowdy throngs that they attracted and because of the danger of such crowds' spreading the plague.

In the last quarter of the sixteenth century actors were licensed by the government and formed into several companies, each under the formal protection of some noble person—the Earl of Worcester's company, the Earl of Leicester's company, the Lord Chamberlain's company (Shakespeare's company, which became the King's Men after the accession of James I), and so on. There were two dozen such acting companies of adults as well as eleven "Boy Companies" and three "international Companies." The queen and later Kings James and Charles were generally well disposed toward acting companies and theaters, Elizabeth being especially fond of plays. But Puritan opposition to theaters was always strong, and when the Puritan Parliament closed the theaters on 2 September 1642,

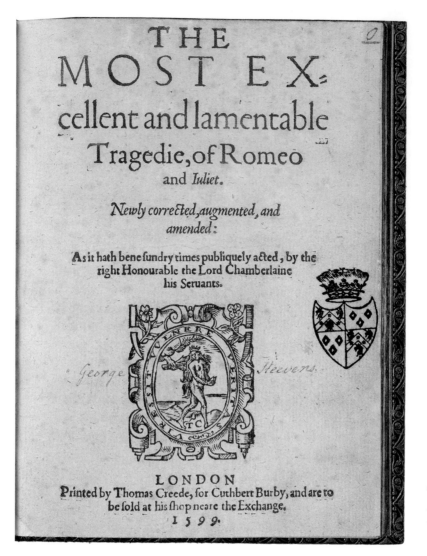

Title page of
*Romeo and Juliet*
(1599), item
5.17.

and especially after the Roundheads prevailed in 1649, the public theaters were, for the duration of the interregnum, finished.

With the erecting of public theaters and the formation of professional acting companies, the printing of plays enters a new era. Writers of interludes and moralities such as those of Rastell's circle would seem most likely to have conducted their own negotiations with publishers over the printing of their plays, but in Shakespeare's day this was not the case. He wrote his plays on commission from his acting company and sold them to the company, surrendering all rights to them. After the company had performed the play (usually) until it had run its course, it was up to the acting company whether to sell the play to a publisher, who would then pay a printer to print it. Shakespeare received no compensation at this stage and had nothing to do with the printing of the play.

Taking Shakespeare as representative of playwrights in his day, we might inquire a little into the circumstances under which plays were published and printed. Of the thirty-seven plays traditionally attributed to Shakespeare's authorship (entirely or substantially) a number were published as independent quarto volumes, all except for *Othello* (1622), during his lifetime, some of them in several successive editions. The remaining eighteen plays survive only because they were included in the posthumous collection of his plays published by his actor friends in 1623 to honor his memory. The quarto editions are printed rather carelessly on the whole (not having been seen through the press by their author or an agent of his) using mediocre materials. Play texts were generally regarded as ephemeral popular literature unworthy of the kind of care a printer would devote to more elevated poetry or serious prose. It has been estimated that they were usually sold for about sixpence a copy. The question arises as to why some of the plays were published and some were not.

In the case of two of the plays—*Hamlet* (item 5.10) and *Romeo and Juliet* (item 5.17)—the motivation for having them printed can be inferred from comments on their title pages ("Newly imprinted and enlarged . . ." and "Newly corrected, augmented, and amended"). Both plays were popular when they were performed, and so unscrupulous hucksters, apparently, acquired illicit copies of the plays and sold them to publishers or printers for their own profit, thereby defrauding the acting company that owned the play. (As the editors of the Shakespeare Folio of 1623 [item 5.29, A3$^r$] put it, the reading public was "abus'd with diuerse stolne, and surreptitious copies, maimed, and deformed by the frauds and stealthes of iniurious impostors.") The texts of both *Hamlet* and *Romeo and Juliet* that the "impostors" got were very incomplete and badly mangled ("maimed and deformed")—as if they had been reconstructed from one or two actors' imperfect memories of the plays or hastily jotted down in shorthand during a performance. When the members of the acting company learned that their plays had been stolen and published in corrupt copies, they sold their authentic texts of the plays to a publisher so that these proper versions could be sold as "true and perfect" copies, perhaps undercutting the sales of the pirated copies.

The emergent circumstances under which these two plays were apparently published do not explain why quarto editions of other plays were sometimes published and sometimes not. For a long time scholars tended to generalize from the cases of *Hamlet* and *Romeo and Juliet*, assuming that the publication of a quarto edition of a play was usually the result of the acting company's being under some kind of pressure, financial or otherwise. It was thought that acting companies were in principle reluctant to see plays go into print, believing that this was bad for playhouse business. E. K. Chambers alluded long ago to this widely held view:

> It is generally supposed, and I think with justice, that the acting companies did not find it altogether to their advantage to have their plays printed. Heywood, indeed, in the epistle to his *English Traveller* (1633) tells us that this was sometimes the case. Presumably the danger was not so much that readers would not become spectators, as that other companies might buy the plays and act them; and of this practice there are some dubious instances, although at any rate by Caroline times it had been brought under control by the Lord Chamberlain.[53]

Recently, however, scholars have rethought this matter. Peter W. M. Blayney has suggested that acting companies would have welcomed publication of play texts as advertisements for performances.[54] Plays, to be sure, were in general not printed all that often. Blayney writes, "In the two decades before the accession of James I . . . the average number of new plays published each year was 4.8. In the next two decades it was 5.75, and in the last two decades . . . exactly 8.0."[55] He adds that plays were not particularly profitable items on the book market, but this conclusion has been questioned.[56] Even so, the old notion that "players reluctantly (if at all) released a manuscript only once a play had lost its drawing power on stage" no longer seems convincing, and it is more likely that "published playbooks may well have recommended plays to theatergoers."[57] Thomas Middleton's *Game at Chess* (item 3.11), for example, was rushed to print at the height of its popularity; whereas John Webster published *The White Devil* (item 5.24) in hopes of gaining readers for a play that had not been successful as a stage performance. It has also been suggested that publication of a play text might have seemed especially expedient when an acting company was planning a revival of that play; reminding the public what a good story was about to be performed may have stimulated them to attend a performance. As to the question why an acting company left some plays unpublished, the answer may be that the financial incentive was slight. A publisher would probably pay an acting company little more than thirty shillings for a play manuscript.[58] Considering these and other factors, at least one scholar has even disputed the scenario suggested above for the circumstances of *Hamlet*'s and *Romeo and Juliet*'s second editions.[59]

It was long assumed that dramatists like Shakespeare who wrote plays on commission and sold their work to acting companies, surrendering all rights to their plays, had no personal interest in seeing their plays published, especially since there is evidence that many people regarded plays as little more than ephemeral popular entertainment. But there is counterevidence to suggest that plays were in fact written to be read as literature as well as to be performed on the stage (see item 5.25). Throughout our period Senecan tragedies were often written more for the study than the stage, and there is ample evidence that closet dramas were written for and read by Puritans as well as Royalists despite the Puritans' inveterate antipathy for the stage performance of plays.[60] Milton's *Samson Agonistes* (1671) is a prime example of a Puritan closet drama. Plays continued to be printed after the closing of the theaters, some of them bearing on their title pages the words "never acted." The epochal moment in the history of English closet drama, one might say, is the publication of *The workes of Beniamin Jonson* in 1616 (item 5.26), in which Jonson boldly included among his literary works nine stage plays (for which he was derided by those who still believed that this genre was subliterary). It is important to notice that he revised his plays for publication, the play *Poetaster*, for example, being quite clearly changed from a performance text to a reading text. Jonson having set this example, there was little demurrer when Shakespeare's actor friends Heminge and Condell published in 1623 a folio collection of his plays to honor his memory (item 5.29). Also, the question has been asked, why did Shakespeare, like Jonson, consistently write plays that were much too long for performance during "the two hours traffic of our stage" (which Shakespeare specifies in the prologue to *Romeo and Juliet* [item 5.17, A2ʳ]) and would have to be cut by the actors presenting the play? It has been suggested that the playwrights envisioned two ultimate versions of their plays—a shortened one for performance and a full version to be read at leisure. Heminge and Condell in their preface addressed "To the Great Variety of *Readers*" repeatedly admonish "reade him." The collected plays of both Jonson and Shakespeare seem clearly to be books designed to be read, not potential promptbooks for an acting company.

Stage plays performed by acting companies are the dramatic form emphasized in this exhibition, but there were other kinds of performances taking place over the time covered here. University plays (item 5.3) and plays performed at court or in the homes of people of rank (items 5.20–22 and 5.25, for example) took place at the same time that the theaters were operating, and less formal kinds of acting such as folk plays, mumming, entertainments, pageants, and masques were also in exercise. Of these the masque requires special attention since many of them were scripted by the same playwrights who were serving the acting companies (e.g., George Chapman, Francis Beaumont, Thomas Campion, and especially Ben Jonson) and many were printed. Both Henry VIII and Elizabeth were notably fond of indoor entertainments as were Edward VI and Mary during their short reigns, and so the masque developed steadily under them and then flourished in the reigns of James I and Charles I.

Masques are not strictly speaking dramatic performances but elaborate shows designed to compliment a sovereign or other person of high station—often in one of their residences—or to honor one of their important guests (items 5.20–22). The masquers,

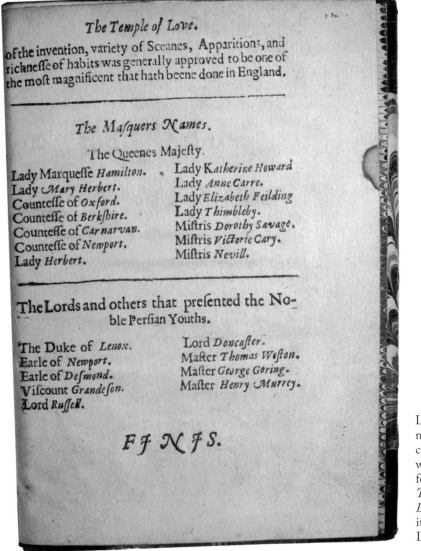

List of nobles and courtiers who performed *The Temple of Love* (1635), item 5.21, D2[r].

who are high-born guests and not professional actors, enter the court or other residence with musicians and torchbearers, all wearing disguises typically, and begin dancing, which is central to the masque. The other guests join in the dance, guest participation being a distinctive characteristic of the masque. There are songs and elaborate props—a castle on wheels, a ship, emblematic artificial animals (such as lions) all adding to the magnificence of the display. The speaking parts are usually performed by professional actors, the masquers themselves remaining mute throughout the entertainment. The circumstances surrounding the performance of a masque can be inferred from the masques incorporated in Shakespeare's *Love's Labour's Lost* or *Romeo and Juliet.* The English masque became increasingly dramatic over time, Ben Jonson's being especially so. His speeches, dialogues, and songs are replete with the learning, eloquence, moral exhortation, and even the satire that characterize his stage plays. Jonson included masques as well as stage plays in his *Workes* (item 5.26). Milton's adaptation of the form (item 5.22), following on Jonson, is highly literary and didactic. It has been said that "all English masques must yield the palm to *Comus.*"[61]

The foregoing discussion of early printed books in England has included some reference to aspects of the physical book in this period—typefaces, quarto and folio formats, woodcut illustrations, and the like. Before closing this general introduction it may be useful to consider in a little more detail the mechanics of producing a book in the sixteenth and seventeenth centuries and the process of preparing copy for printing. To do so will help to explain features of early printed books that might otherwise be puzzling.

The simplest form of printing is the broadside (item 3.15). A client gives a printer a short text—a proclamation, an advertisement, a ballad—that needs to be printed on one side of a sheet of paper, often for posting on a wall. The printer simply sets up the text in types, prints it off, and delivers to his client a stack of printed sheets. This is printing, but it is not printing books. Books require much more planning and involve a more complicated printing process.

The least complicated book format is the folio. A folio is a sheet of paper folded once—or a book composed of such folded sheets. Each sheet contains four printed pages, two on each side of the sheet. The folded sheets are not simply stacked one on the other and sewn together; rather one or two or more folded sheets will be nested inside a covering outer sheet. Such "gatherings" or "quires" can be sewn together more securely into a book than could a mere stack of folded sheets. But the use of gatherings introduces a complication. If the folded sheets are nested one inside the other, then the printer cannot print the pages consecutively. The first leaf of the first folded sheet (the outer sheet) will contain pages 1 and 2 of the gathering, and the second leaf of the sheet will contain the last two pages of the gathering. The folded sheets nested in between the leaves of the first sheet will contain pages 3 and 4, and so on. This means that when a printer plans to print pages on a sheet, he must anticipate where each page will be when the sheets are folded and nested together into gatherings. A popular format for folio books in the early days of printing was the "folio in sixes." This means that three sheets are folded together into a gathering so that each gathering consists of six leaves or twelve pages. This is the format of the Shakespeare First Folio of 1623 (item 5.29) and many of the other large books in this exhibition. When the printer prepared the first sheet for such a volume, he would print pages 1 and 12 on one side of the sheet and 2 and 11 on the other, for when the sheet was folded to form the outer leaves of the gathering, it would form the first two and the last two pages of the gathering. Similar calculations must be made in anticipation of where the pages would occur in the two inner sheets of the gathering.

Figuring out the order in which pages must be printed on master sheets so that the pages will appear in proper sequence once the three sheets are folded into gatherings is not difficult. More complicated is predicting how much text the pages will contain. When the printer sets type for pages 1 and 12 on his first sheet, how does he know which segment of the manuscript (or earlier edition) he is copying from will constitute page 12? Before he begins typesetting, he must go through the entire text from which he is typesetting and mark off each segment of text he expects to fit on each page of the book he plans to print. This process (called "casting off copy") can be difficult when the text is prose. (Verse is easier: he simply determines how many lines of verse each printed page will hold and then marks off units of that number of lines in the text to be printed.) Casting off is based only on an estimate, and yet once he has cast off his copy he is committed to fitting the estimated amount to each page he is printing. Not infrequently he discovers as he sets type that in casting off he estimated too much or too little text for a given page. When this happens, he must resort to various stratagems to make the text fit the page neatly.

An example of one stratagem may be seen if one compares pages 105 and 115 of the First Folio edition of *The first Part of Henry the Sixt*. (See page 38, below.) On page 115 there is ample empty space before and after *Scæna Tertia* and more empty space setting off entrances and exits. Here the printer estimated accurately how much text would fit on the page. But on page 105 there is no empty space following exits, and the act division marked *Actus Tertius. Scena Prima* is jammed in between segments of text with hardly any empty space at all before and after—even though this is a greater break in the play's action than is *Scæna Tertia*. Here the printer had overestimated how much text the page would hold and so has had to eliminate all empty spaces that would normally occur.

Another way of getting a maximum amount of text on a page is to print verse as prose. It is not uncommon when reading a Shakespearean text printed as prose to become aware that the text scans as blank verse. Here the printer was running short of space and simply could not afford the extra space needed to set lines of verse. Conversely when printers have underestimated the amount of text that a page will hold, they sometimes resort to setting prose as if it were verse, thereby using up space. Another device for saving space was the use of turnovers and turnunders at the ends of lines of text. Since spelling was not fixed, printers could also save or waste space by this means, spelling, for example, *rekles* where space is needed and *reckelesse* where space is too abundant. Abbreviations such as the ampersand could also be used as space savers. The latter two stratagems are occasionally used to justify margins as well. The most drastic measure a printer could take in fitting text to page was simply to leave out a portion of the text. In cases where we know that a Folio play text was set from an earlier quarto edition and the two can be compared, occasional instances have been found of a Folio printer simply deleting text when space was short.

Knowledge of how early printers prepared a text for printing and assembled a finished volume can explain other features as well. One such feature is the familiar mark called a "signature." If one turns to the first page of the first play in the Folio (*The Tempest*), one sees in the bottom margin just beneath the second column of text a capital "A." Turning the page, one sees at the bottom of the second leaf (page 3) "A2." At the bottom of the third

That neither in birth, or for authoritie,
The Bishop will be ouer-borne by thee :
Ile either make thee stoope, and bend thy knee,
Or sacke this Country with a mutiny.                    *Exeunt*

---

## Scœna Tertia.

---

*Enter Charles, Burgundy, Alanson, Bastard,*
*Reignier, and Ione.*

*Char.* These newes (my Lords)may cheere our droo-
ping spirits :
'Tis said, the stout Parisians do reuolt,
And turne againe vnto the warlike French.
 *Alan.* Then march to Paris Royall *Charles* of France,
And keepe not backe your powers in dalliance.
 *Pucel.* Peace be amongst them if they turne to vs,
Else ruine combate with their Pallaces.
                        *Enter Scout.*

Shakespeare, First
Folio, item 5.29, 115.

---

And for those Wrongs,those bitter Iniuries,
Which *Somerset* hath offer'd to my House,
I doubt not,but with Honor to redresse.
And therefore haste I to the Parliament,
Eyther to be restored to my Blood,
Or make my will th'aduantage of my good.         *Exit.*

### Actus Tertius. Scena Prima.

*Flourish.  Enter King,Exeter,Gloster,Winchester,Warwick,*
*Somerset,Suffolk,Richard Plantagenet. Gloster offers*
*to put vp a Bill:Winchester snatches it,teares it.*
 *Winch.* Com'st thou with deepe premeditated Lines?
With written Pamphlets,studiously deuis'd ?
*Humfrey* of Gloster,if thou canst accuse,
Or ought intend'st to lay vnto my charge,
Doe it without inuention,suddenly,
As I with sudden,and extemporall speech,
Purpose to answer what thou canst obiect.

Shakespeare, First
Folio, item 5.29, 105.

leaf (page 5) is "A3." The next three leaves have no markings in the margin. After them the next three leaves have the markings "B," "B2," "B3." And so on through the alphabet. These markings or signatures are the printer's instructions to the person who is going to assemble his printed sheets into books. (The person assembling the books could be someone in the printshop, the publisher who paid to have the book printed, the stationer who is going to sell the book, or a binder.) The capital letters indicate that the three sheets bearing each letter belong together in a single gathering. The numerals indicate the order in which the sheets are to be assembled before they are folded into a gathering. The A-sheet is first (the outer sheet), A2 is second, and A3 is third. If the sheets are arranged in the prescribed order and then folded, twelve consecutive pages in proper order will result. And if one assembles all the gatherings in the order indicated by letters of the alphabet, then all the pages of the book will be in proper sequence. If there are more gatherings than there are letters in the alphabet, then the printer can start again with the letter A using some method to indicate that this is a second alphabetic sequence of gatherings. When the printers of the Folio have run through the alphabet, the second sequence of gatherings begins "Aa," "Aa2," "Aa3," "Bb," and so on.

One might wonder why signatures were used rather than simply letting the person assembling the gatherings follow the page numbers. In the first place, books were unpaginated for many years after the introduction of printing. In the second place, the instructions being given are not for the handling of leaves or pages but for the handling of sheets. It should also be remembered that folio format is only the simplest of possible formats. In a quarto format each sheet has not four but eight pages printed on it, and it must be folded twice (see item 6.1). With the octavo each sheet contains sixteen pages and is folded three times. Since possible formats include sextodecimo (folded four times), tricesimosecundo (folded five times), and so on, one can see that trying to keep track of sheets by page numbers (if they are present) would be difficult.

Verbal descriptions of preparing texts for printing and of assembling gatherings become clearer when one sees the materials involved, as visitors to this exhibition can do. For another intimate glimpse into actual printshop practice, see the facsimiles of cast-off copy, signatures, proof corrections, and proofreaders' marks in Roger E. Stoddard's *Marks in Books,* published by the Houghton Library of Harvard University in 1985.

The variety of typefaces that early printers used has been mentioned more than once above, but something more might usefully be said about inferences that some have drawn from printers' use of contrasting typefaces, especially inferences about the readership printers were targeting in the works they were printing. During the period of transition from black letter to roman and italic type, the different types took on certain individual connotations. We have already noted that at one period black letter was seen as most suitable for English vernacular texts while roman or italic seemed appropriate for Latin texts or for commentary on the black-letter English texts. This being the case, elementary education in vernacular literacy would have begun with black letter. Hornbooks used black letter (item 2.1). A hornbook was a sheet of vellum or paper mounted on a paddle-like piece of wood and covered with a thin, transparent sheet of horn. On it were displayed usually the letters of the alphabet and a brief prayer. Children learned their ABCs from a black-letter hornbook, and therefore the lettertype was associated with elementary education, while roman and italic, being the lettertypes suited for Latin, suggested higher learning. This may be why "jestbooks,

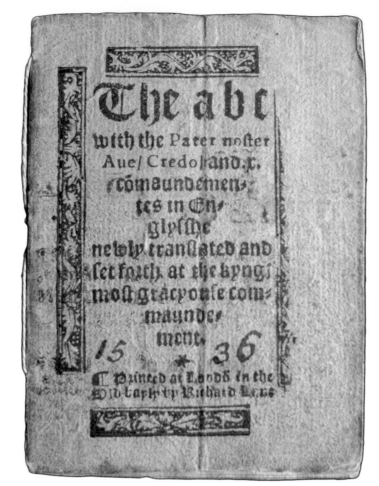

English
*ABC* book,
c. 1536–42,
item 2.1.

works for the instruction and improvement of the young, certain kinds of sensational news pamphlets, and above all, ballads . . . were usually printed in blackletter."[62]

As an article entitled "Blackletter as a Social Discriminator in the Seventeenth Century" suggests, black letter could be taken as an indicator that texts printed in this type belonged to popular culture.[63] The validity of this assumption has been challenged,[64] but one scholar at least thinks that the fact that play texts were not published in black letter after 1605 may indicate that printed plays were expected to appeal more to educated middle-class readers than to the working class.[65]

Part of the history of printing is not simply a matter of the visual representation of words with printed characters but rather involves pictures, maps, and the visual representation of music. The printing of music developed more slowly than the printing of language because music requires a more complicated variety of symbols than just letters of the alphabet. Wynkyn de Worde's edition of Ranulf Higden's *Polycronicon* (item 6.6) contains the earliest known specimen of musical notation printed in England. He set the music by putting together quadrats and rules. Richard Pynson's 1500 edition of the *Missale Sarum* is the first example of music printed from type in England. These specimens involved two or more impressions. The first printing of music by single impression is in John Rastell's

*A new Interlude and a mery of the nature of the iiij elements* (printed between 1526 and 1530). He prints a three-part song "Tyme to pas with goodly sport" (E5ʳ). Eventually it was concluded that movable type was not suitable for the complex task of representing music visually, and engraving was adopted as a more appropriate medium.

Engraving was also used for depicting maps (items 6.8 and 6.9), although woodcutting was an option as well. The earliest printed map of the British Isles appeared in an edition of Ptolemy's *Geographia* published in Bologna in 1477. George Lily (d. 1559), an English Catholic exile at the papal court, showed major progress from the 1477 map toward a recognizably modern map with his new representation of the British Isles published in

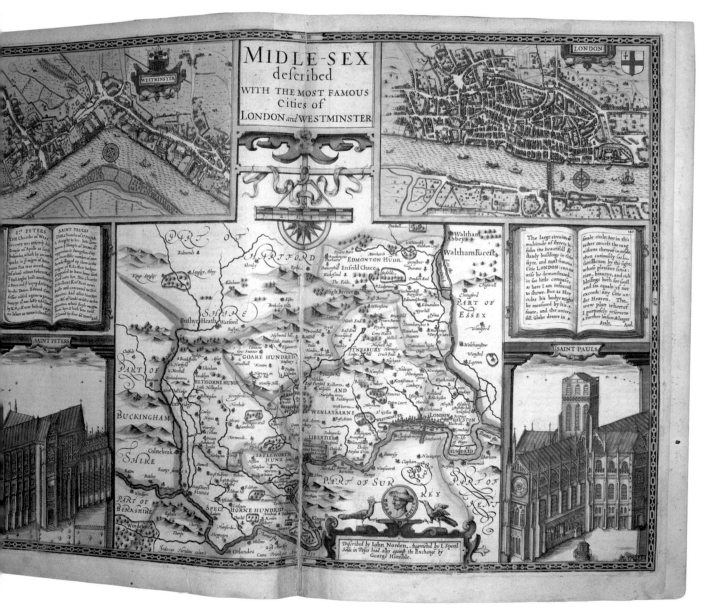

Map of Middlesex with details of London and Westminster (1611/12), item 6.9.

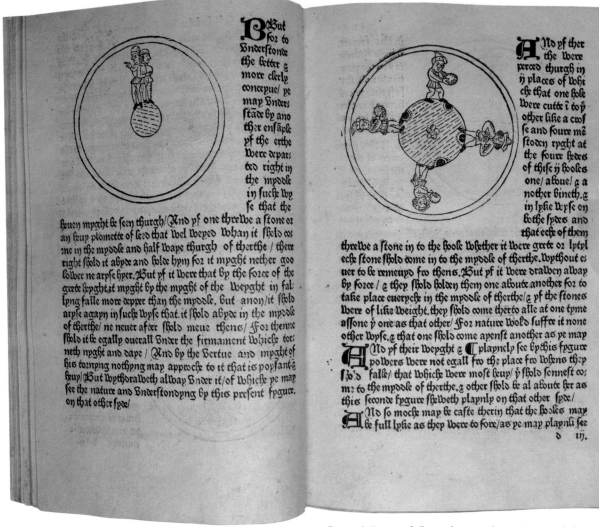

Caxton's "scientific" woodcuts in his *Myrrour of the worlde* (1489–90), item 6.10, D2$^v$–D3$^r$.

1546.[66] Shirley notes, "A major breakthrough occurred with the masterly atlas of Christopher Saxton (c. 1542–c. 1610), published in 1579, and the first ever national atlas."[67] Though most sixteenth-century cartographers in England derived their maps from those of Saxton, John Norden (c. 1547–1625?) based his *Speculum Britanniae* (1593) on his own surveying (item 6.8). His map of Middlesex is the first English county map to mark roads and he introduced locational grids and symbols. John Speed's (1551 / 52–1629) grand atlas, *The Theatre of the Empire of Great Britaine* (1610 / 11), drew upon Saxton and Norden but brought these and other sources together to produce the first set of county maps of England and Wales, most of which include town plans of immense value to historians (item 6.9). Both Norden and Speed were pioneers in the production of English maps.

It has been suggested that picture books enjoy chronological priority over printed books containing texts, since printing of pictures from woodcuts was practiced on the Continent before Gutenberg began printing with movable metal types. In England, however, the printing of pictures from woodcuts was slow to develop. Caxton's *Myrrour of the worlde* (item 6.10) does provide a fairly early example of woodcut illustrations, but according to Colin Clair, "They are of the utmost crudity . . . . The woodcut illustrations used in English books of the fifteenth century are almost devoid of any artistic interest, and in this respect are far inferior to contemporary work in continental Europe. The art of the wood engraver was practically unknown in England before the introduction of printing."[68] As woodcuts were replaced by copperplate engravings for title pages, initials, and other images, the quality of English book illustration improved, as may be seen in items 6.11 and 6.12. But most accounts of early English illustrations in printed books are exercises in unfavorable comparison with continental work of the same period.

The failure of English printers' illustrations to measure up to the more artful work of continental printers is, as we have seen, characteristic of early English printing in general. England's early practioners of printing were primarily commercial entrepreneurs with a utilitarian approach to their trade and few aesthetic pretensions. But if their typography and artwork lagged behind the work of most printers in Europe, they were nonetheless pioneers of predominantly vernacular publishing and served well the needs of a public newly literate and hungry for translations, for religious, scientific, and educational works, and for access to the flourishing literature of Elizabethan and Jacobean England, including dramatic literature. Indeed, English printers were, despite their businesslike stance, intimately cooperative with literary production and have an important place in the literary history of the English Renaissance. Caxton and Rastell, for example, were themselves literary artists as well as printers. The impact of English printers on the English language is also considerable. Through the Stationers' Company and other interactions with government, the early printers helped establish a clearly defined place for printing in English society and cooperated in slow but steady progress toward freedom of the press. If English printing's years of most distinguished work lay in the future, its earliest years were nonetheless an era of great cultural as well as commercial accomplishment.

# CATALOG OF
# THE EXHIBITION

wyth moche honoure and worship aft' his faders deep. ye. xvij. zere of his
regne. Howe arthoure ye sone of Vter was crowned kyng aft' his fa
ders deep. and howe he droue Collogren and ye saxsones. and Cheldryke
of Almayne out of pis londe.    Cap. lxxiij.

Cap. Aj.

Whan Arthoure was made kyng of pis londe. he was but
zonge. of. xv. zere of age. And he was crowned on seynt Siluestrs day
But he was faire and bolde and douztty of body. And vnto meke
folke he was good and curteyse. and vnto proude folke he was stoute
and sterne. And also he was jentyl and curteyse and large of spen
dyng and was welbyloued a mongs al men pere ȳ hit was need
And whan he byganne to regne he swore ȳ ye saxsones neu sthuld
haue pees ne reste til he had dryuen he out of pis londe. And anone
he lete assemble a gret oste and fauztte to Collogren ȳ after tyme
ȳat Octa was ded ye saxsones fledde. and pis Collogren was dis
coumfited and fledde vnto zorke. and toke ye towne and ye helde hi.
And kyng Arthoure byseged hi and ye towne. but he myzt nothing
spede for ye towne was so stronge. and yet to in kept ȳ towne wel
and hardely. and in ye meene tyme Collogren lete ye towne to hi
zsladnd. and flewe hi self to Cheldryke ȳ was kyng of Allmayne
for to haue of hi socoure. and pen ye kyng assembled a gret power
and come and arryued in Scotlond to .v. shippes. And whan Ar
thoure wiste of pis tidyng ȳ he had no power ne strengye ȳ nowe
to fiztten a zenst Cheldryke. he let be ye sege. And went to londoñ
and sent anone his letts in to litel Breteyn to ye kyng. ȳ men cal
led kyng Hole his nevelue. his sisters sone. ȳ he sthuld come to hi
to al ye powere ȳ he myzt. And pan he anone assembled an huge
oste and come in to pis lond and arryued at Souyehamptoñ. ȳ
whan kyng Arthour hit wiste he was glad ȳ nowe and went a
zenst hi and hi receyued to moche honoue. so pat yo two ostes he
assembled and token her wey vnt Azincoll. ȳat Cheldryke had by

# I EARLY ENGLISH PRINTING

1.1 *The Brut.* Manuscript, England, c. 1450.

Matheson 1998, 81, 120. Shelfmark: UIUC Pre-1650 MS 116.


1.2 *Chronicles of England.* [London: William de Machlinia, 1486?]

BMC xi, 261; *ESTC* S121384; Goff C-480; *GW* 6673; *ISTC* ic00480000; *STC* 9993. Shelfmark: UIUC Incunabula 942 C468 1486.

When printed books became available, scriptoria did not close their doors. On the contrary, manuscripts went on being produced—and sometimes preferred by their owners—throughout the fifteenth century. These two copies of the same text, one a manuscript, the other an early printed edition, exemplify the many continuities between early printed books and their manuscript forebears.

Both books present the text of the *Chronicles of England,* also known as *The Brut.* *The Brut* is simple to describe—it is a history of England beginning with its legendary founder, Brutus—but its textual history is complex. The earliest versions, the Anglo-French *Roman de Brut* by Wace in 1155 and the Middle English poetic *Brut* by Layamon (early thirteenth century), stem from Geoffrey of Monmouth's (d. 1154) *Historia regum Britanniae.* Thereafter, the most popular version is the fourteenth-century Middle English prose *Brut,* an anonymous text that survives in some 181 manuscripts. Not surprisingly, the text varies somewhat depending on where, when, and by whom the chronicle was written down or printed. There are *Bruts* with pro-Lancastrian biases and *Bruts* with pro-York biases; there are *Bruts* in Anglo-Norman, Welsh, and Latin, as well as the more common text in English. The history is sometimes updated to the time of its production, resulting in a different terminus ad quem for various manuscript groups or editions. Early modern historians of England such as Edward Hall (1497–1547) and Raphael Holinshed (c. 1525–80) incorporated *The Brut* into their histories, and it continues to serve as a source for historians.

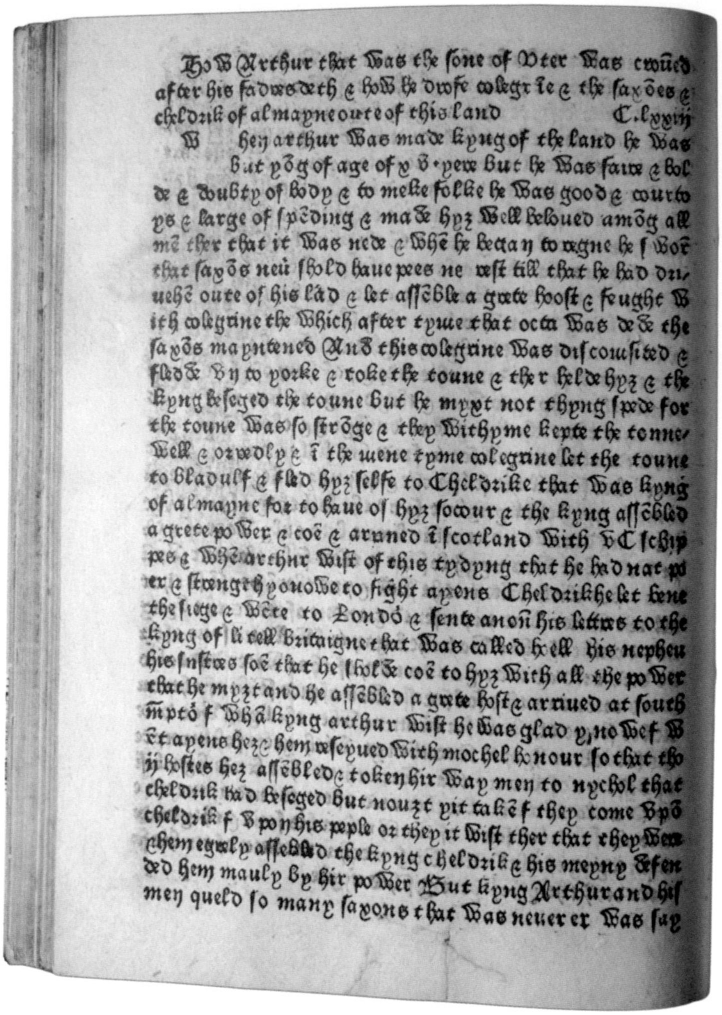

England's first printer, William Caxton, published the editio princeps of *The Brut* in 1480; his version brings the historical account up to the year 1461. Caxton published a second edition in 1482. Thereafter, editions appeared in quick succession from the presses of the St. Albans Printer (c. 1485), William de Machlinia (1486), Wynkyn de Worde (1497), and even from Gerard de Leew in Holland (1493).

William de Machlinia (fl. 1482–90), the printer of the 1486 edition shown here, may have learned his trade from John Lettou, the earliest printer working in the City of London. Lettou was probably not English (his name means "Lithuanian" in Middle English), and De Machlinia was probably from Mechlin in the Low Countries. They collaborated on publishing law books in French and Latin. After 1483, De Machlinia began to print on his own, adding English books to his output and thereby becoming the first printer to produce an English book in the City of London. (Caxton was at Westminster, just outside the City of London.)

Although De Machlinia clearly used Caxton's first edition as his source text, it is nonetheless instructive to compare a manuscript and an incunable of the same text. Early printers imitated the handwriting of medieval scribes with their typefaces and adopted manuscript conventions in designing page layouts. The same passage in the manuscript and the 1486 imprint reveals the similarities in book design, despite some textual differences (the manuscript offering more detail on the coronation and character of King Arthur in this case).

The printed edition belonged to the printer and designer William Morris (1834–96), who found models for his own designs in several magnificent books from the incunabular age.

Literature: Carlson 1993, 123–41; Clair 1965, 31–34; König 1987; Matheson 1998, 1–56.

## 1.3 Marcus Tullius Cicero. *De Senectute. De amicitia.* With the *De vera nobilitate* of Buonaccorso da Montemagno the Younger. [Westminster: William Caxton, 12 August 1481.]

BMC xi, 119; *ESTC* S106523; Goff C-627; *GW* 6992; *ISTC* ic00627000; *STC* 5293. Shelfmark· UIUC Incunabula 871 C7 Ob.Ew.

Printing presses operated in nearly seventy towns on the Continent before William Caxton established the first one in England in 1476, a quarter of a century after Gutenberg. Printing came late to England, and England's first printer came late in life to printing. After a successful career as a merchant, Caxton learned to print in his mid-fifties, probably in Cologne. His motivation may have resulted from his experiences as a merchant. As a member of the Mercers' Guild, he traded in textiles, including not only fabric, but also skins and, by extension, manuscripts, which were written on treated animal skins. According to the epilogue of his first book, *The Recuyell of the Historyes of Troye* (printed in Bruges, 1473 / 74), he learned the art of printing in order to supply multiple copies of a manuscript to "divers gentlemen."

Soon, Caxton became much more than a printer and purveyor of books. He translated popular French literature for his English public, produced English versions of classical texts, and edited and printed the works of Chaucer, Lydgate, Gower, and Malory, among others. England continued to import books from the Continent, of course, but Caxton created a market for English books.

Caxton dedicated these three "bokes of grete wisedom and auctoryte" to King Edward IV. In the prologues, he says that Sir John Fastolf (1380–1459) commissioned the translation of Cicero's *De Senectute* (*On Old Age*) and that John Tiptoft, Earl of Worcester (1427–70), translated the works on friendship and nobility (*De amicitia* and *De vera nobilitate*).[1] Caxton printed Cicero's works on old age and friendship together, he says,

1.3, fol. 13ʳ

## The tale of the maunciple

### Here begynneth the parsons tale

Jer. vj. State super vias
/videte & interrogate de semi-
tis antiquis. que sit via bona
et ambulate in ea. et inueni-
tis refrigeriū aiabz vestris.

Our swete lorde god of heuen. that
no man woll perissh. but woll þ
we torne all to the knowlege of hym. &
to the blisfull lyfe that is perdurable
amonestith vs by the prophete Jeremye
saith in this wyse Standyth vpon
the wayes & seeth. and axeth of olde pa-
thes/ that is to saye/ of olde sentences
whyche is the god waye. & walkyth in
that waye/& ye shall fynde refresshyng
for your soules. &c.¶ Many ben þ wayes espyrytueles that lede folk to our lor-

*marginal note:* what penitence is com sactū Ambrosiū & alios doctores.

de Jesu crist. & to the regne of glory. Of
whyche wayes ther is a full noble way
& a full couenable / whyche maye not
faylle to man ne to woman that thruȝ
synne hath mysgoon fro the ryght way
of Jerusalem celestiall/ And this waye
is called penitence.of whiche man shol
de gladly herkene enquyre wyth all his
herte.to wyte what is penitence.& whi
it is callyd penitence/ And how many
maners ben of accyons/ or werkynges
of penitence.And how many specis ther
be of penitence. and whyche thyngs
apperteyne & behoue to penitence. And
whyche thynges distourbe penitence.✠
Saynt Ambrole saith. þ penitence is
the pleynynge of man. for the gylt that
he hath don./ & nomore to do ony thyge
for whyche hym ouȝt to playne.¶ And
som doctour saith. penitence is þ wayse

## The persons tale

mentyng of man that sorowyth for his
synne. and peyneth hymself for he hath
mysdone.¶ Penitence wyth certey cyr-
custaūces is veri repentaunce of a man
that holt hymself in sorow & other peyne for his gyltes: & for he shall be veri
penitent. he shall frst bewayle synnes
that he hath don. and stedfastly purpose in his hert to haue shryfte of mouth
& to do satisfaccōy.and neuer to do thyge for whyche hym ought more bewayle & or to complene.& contynew in good
werkys/ or elles his repentaunce maye
not auaylle.✠ For as saynt Isyder saith. he is a Japer & a lyar and no veri
repentaunt that eft soone dooth thynge
for whyche hym ought repent. Weppyng
& not for to stinte to do synne may not
auaple/But netheles men shall hope þ
at euery tyme that man falleth.be it neuer so ofte. that he maye aryse thrugh
penaunce/yf he haue grace.but certenly it
is grete dowte. ✠ For as saynt Grego
ri saith. vneth ryseth he out of synne þ
is chargyd wyth the charge of euyl vsa-
ge. And therfore repentant folk þ styn-
te for to synne & leue synne or synne leue them.holy chyrche holdyth them syker of ther saluacōy. And he that syn-
nyth & verily repentyth hym in his last
ende. holy chyrche yet hoppyth his salua
cōy by the grete mercy of our lorde Jhesu crist for his repentaunce.but take the
syker waye.¶ And now syth J haue de-
claryd you what thynge is penitence/
now ye shall vnderstonde that ther ben
thre accōs of penitence. ✠ The frste
is þ a man be baptised after that he haue synned. ✠ Saynt Austyn saith.but
he be penitent for his olde synfull lyfe.
he maye not begyn the newe clene lyf
for certes yf he be baptised wythout penitence of his olde gylt.he retepneth the

marke of bapteme:but not the grace ne
the rempssyon of his synnes.tyll he haue repentaunce veri.✠ A nother defawte is this.that men do dedly synne after
þ they haue receyued baptelme.¶ The
thyrde defawte is this that men fall in
venpall synnes after ther baptelme fro
day to day.¶ Therof saith saynt Au-
gustyn . þ penitence of good & humble
folk is þ penitence of euery day¶ The
speces of penitence ben thre/ That one
of them is solempne. A nother is comu-
ne.And the thirde is pryue.¶ That penaunce þ is solempne is in two maners
As to be put out of holy chyrche in lent
for slaughter of chyldrey.& suche mane-
re thynge.¶ A nother is whan a man
hath synned openly/ of whiche synne þ
fame is openly spoke in the countree/
thenne holy chyrche by Jugement del-
treyneth hym for to do opey penaunce.
¶ Comune penaunce is that prestys en-
ioyne men in certey caas/ as for to goo
parauenture nakyd in pylgrymage/ or
barefote.¶ Pryue penaunce is that yt
men do al day for pryue synnes.of whiche we shryue vs pryuely & recepue pryue penaunce.¶ Now shalt thou vnder-
stond what is behouefull & necessary to
very perfyt penitence.& this stont yn.iij.
thynges¶ Contrycōy of herte.confessi-
oy of mouth.& satilfaccōy.¶ For whiche saith saynt John Crisostomus. penitence distreyneth a man to accept be-
nygnely euery payne þ him is eniorned
wyth contricōy of herte & shryft of mouth wyth satysfaccoy/& in werkynge
of al maner humylyte. And this is fru-
ctfull penitence ayenst thre thynges in
whiche we wrath our lorde Jhesu crist:
This is to saye.by delyte in thinkyng. and by wyc-
kyd synfull werkyng. And ayenst thyse

*right marginal notes:*
The.ij. ac-
coy of pena-
unce
The.iij.ac-
coy of pena-
unce

Of.iij.spe-
ces of pena-
ūce. Of pe-
naūce solep-
ne in two
maneres.
✠ Sciūs
Isidr

Of comu-
ne penaunce
Of pryue
penaunce.
✠ Nōlcom
setu Gre-
goriū
Of.iij.thy-
ges þ be be
houefull to
perfyt peni-
tence.

Johēs Cri-
sostomus

✠ The fr-
ste accōy of
penitence

✠ Sancti
Augustin

p i

1.4, fol. X6ᵛ–Y1ʳ

"by cause ther can not be annexed to olde age a bettir thynge than good and very frendship" ($^2$d4$^v$).

Ultimately, Caxton's goal transcended that of the businessman interested in mass producing a desired commodity. Yet he does not conform to the mold of the scholar-printer that emerged among the second-generation continental printers either. Though he calls himself a "symple persone" in the colophon of this book, Caxton was a cultural activist for English literature, who created an audience for leisure reading in the vernacular. As Nicolas Barker put it, "No other left his mark so strongly, both on the appearance of print and on taste in reading matter, as Caxton did in England."

Literature: Barker 1976, 133; Blake 1973b, 120–25; Corsten 1976; *ODNB* ("Caxton, William" by N. F. Blake); Painter 1976, 111–16.

1.4    Geoffrey Chaucer (c. 1340–1400). *The boke of Chaucer named Caunterbury tales.* Westminster: Wynkyn de Worde, 1498.

BMC xi, 214; *ESTC* S108866; Goff C-434; *GW* 6588; *ISTC* ic00434000; *STC* 5085. Shelfmark: UIUC Incunabula Q. 821 C39c 1498.

1.5    Ranulf Higden (d. 1364). *The descrypcyon of Englonde.* Westminster: Wynkyn de Worde, 1498.

BMC xi, 214; *ESTC* S116801; Goff C-482; *GW* 6675; *ISTC* ic00482000; *STC* 13440b. Shelfmark: UIUC Incunabula 909 H53p:Et 1498.

After Caxton's death, Wynkyn de Worde (d. 1534/35) assumed control over his press, a natural development for him since he had worked for Caxton since the mid-1470s. Although eventually he made his own distinctive mark on English printing, Wynkyn de Worde began his solo career by reissuing a number of Caxton's works, including this edition of Chaucer. Caxton had printed Chaucer's *Canterbury Tales* in 1476–77, followed by another edition a few years later (1483), after he found a manuscript superior to the one used for the first edition.

De Worde was not an Englishman. He probably came from Woerden near Utrecht in Holland. It is possible that De Worde, like Caxton, learned to print in Cologne, but he spent the bulk of his career, some sixty years, in England, first in Caxton's old shop in Westminster and later in London's Fleet Street.

This imprint of *The Canterbury Tales* comes from the period when De Worde was trying to establish himself in the English book market. With this folio, De Worde not only honors his master, but also engages his competition, for Richard Pynson had published the same book soon after Caxton's death. De Worde's is the fourth incunabular edition of Chaucer. It is significant because it seems to be based on an annotated copy of Caxton's second edition as well as a now unknown manuscript of the text. De Worde's Chaucer differs from both Caxton editions in its introduction of more modernized spelling and more frequent captions, paragraph marks, and other textual divisions. The woodcut illustrations were reused from Caxton's second edition. They were used yet again by the printer William Thynne in 1532 and 1542 and copied by Pynson for his edition. This book is noteworthy for its use of paper made at the mill of John Tate (c. 1448 – 1507 / 8), the first—and rather short-lived (1495 – 98)—paper mill in England. (Most English printers imported paper from France.)

In the 1490s, De Worde's program remained similar (in many cases, identical) to Caxton's; like Caxton, he printed folio editions of important works of literature and reference such as Malory's *Morte d'Arthur* (1498), Chaucer's *Canterbury Tales* (1498), Voragine's *Golden Legend* (1493 and 1498), and Higden's *Polycronicon* (1495, item 6.6). De Worde may not have had the elite connections or literary talents of Caxton, but he appears to have had good business sense. He gradually moved away from grandiose imprints such as these to smaller, cheaper, and more practical texts that could find a ready market and plentiful audience. The *Description of Englande,* an excerpt from the larger *Polycronicon* of

1.5, title page

Ranulf Higden, is a reprint of Caxton's 1480 edition. In most copies, it is bound with De Worde's edition of the *Chronicles* (1497–98), but, as this copy shows, it could also be sold separately.

After 1500, De Worde began publishing sermons and other religious tracts (though here he had to exercise caution once the Reformation erupted on the Continent), schoolbooks, law books, and other practical texts, many of which were quartos of fewer than forty pages. Even at the end of his career in the late 1520s, his books remained typographically unsophisticated, with the rough and ready look of an English incunable. But what he may have lacked in quality, he made up for in quantity: in his long and prolific career, De Worde produced more than eight hundred works.

Literature: Blake 1971, 62–69; Clair 1965, 27–31; Moran 1960; *ODNB* ("Worde, Wynkyn de" by N. F. Blake); Partridge 2007; Plomer 1925.

## 1.6    *Dives et Pauper.* [*Riche and Pore.*] London: Richard Pynson, 5 July 1493.

BMC xi, 272; *ESTC* S109783; Goff P-117; *ISTC* ip00117000; *STC* 19212. Shelfmark: UIUC Incunabula 222.16 P22d 1493.

Richard Pynson probably came to England from Normandy and seems to have gotten his start with William de Machlinia (see item 1.2), whose printshop he eventually took over. The fact that Pynson was a foreigner is both unremarkable and noteworthy. From 1476 to 1500, seven printers were active in and around London, only one of whom was English.[2] This makes sense, given that the art of printing comes from the Continent. In 1484, one of the earliest decrees concerning the printing industry expressly allowed foreigners to establish and operate a press in England.[3] While this decree appears to encourage both free enterprise and free speech, foreign workers were generally not welcome in London, and its citizens, unlike its laws, did not make exceptions for printers. Pynson and his workers were even attacked by a mob in 1500.[4] Nor was he the only foreign printer to be harassed. By 1523, the situation had become so volatile that Henry VIII issued an act prohibiting any foreign apprentices and allowing only two foreign journeymen to work in a print shop.[5] Other protectionist legislation followed.

Despite this troublesome business climate, Richard Pynson flourished, printing more than five hundred books from 1492 to 1530. He was named Printer to the King as early as 1506, perhaps an indication of the superiority of his typography over that of his contemporaries. His output includes religious works, law books — especially the *Year Book*, a compilation of common law that he issued in seventy editions — official documents, and a few schoolbooks. He printed many first editions, including Alexander Barclay's translation of *The Ship of Fools* (1509), an English version of the popular *Imitatio Christi* (1503), and Lydgate's *Troy Book* (1513). He also turned out multiple editions of old standbys, including the same texts his competitor Wynkyn de Worde printed. (The concept of copyright was as yet unknown in England.)

Pynson was an innovator in English printing. He was the first in England to paginate, to use catchwords, to print regularly in two colors, and to use roman type. Shown here is the first edition of an anonymous theological work wrongly attributed to a Carmelite monk, Henry Parker (d. after 1504). A lengthy work on every detail and nuance of the Ten Commandments, it is presented as a dialogue between a rich man and a pauper, with the latter taking on the role of the teacher. Woodcut initials are used throughout, marking each commandment and the beginning of each chapter. Particularly interesting is the discussion of religious imagery in which the rich man interprets the commandment against graven images as forbidding representational art in religion, thus broaching an old debate that would become a hallmark of some later Reformation movements. Wynkyn de Worde issued his own edition of *Dives and Pauper* in 1496. His edition includes some typographic errors carried over from Pynson's, indicating that he used the printed edition as his copy text.

Literature: Clair 1965, 34–40; Leadam 1903–11, 1:cxxxvii–cxxxviii and 111–14; *ODNB* ("Pynson, Richard" by Pamela Neville-Sington); Richardson 1934.

1.7    John Holt (d. 1504). *Lac puerorum. Anglice mylke for chyldren.* Antwerp: [Govaert] Bac, [1505? / 1510?].

Goff H-299; *STC* 13606.3; *ESTC* S5113; *ISTC* ih00299000. Shelfmark: UIUC Incunabula 475 H74l.

Not all early English books were printed in England. Indeed, the first book printed in English, Caxton's *The Recuyell of the Historyes of Troye* (1473 / 74), was produced in Bruges, albeit by an Englishman. But continental printers also produced books intended for English audiences, such as the popular *Sarum Missal,* primers and other prayer books, the earliest English Bibles, and even books in English or a mixture of Latin and English, like this charming schoolbook by John Holt.

After graduating from Magdalen College, Oxford, John Holt taught grammar at his alma mater (from 1494 to 1496), as a tutor in the household of Archbishop John Morton (from 1496 to 1500), at Chichester Cathedral School (1501–2), and finally as tutor to Prince Henry (as of 1502), before Holt's early death in 1504. He was a friend and early correspondent of Thomas More, whose first printed poems (which appear in this work) were epigrams in honor of Holt. Around 1500, Holt wrote the only work surviving from his hand, the *Lac puerorum,* or "milk for boys," in which he presents Latin grammar in a simple and straightforward way. In addition to paradigms and grammatical rules, it includes woodcuts as mnemonic aids. The work illustrates the important role that printing played in the expansion of education in early modern Europe. Even beginning students could now have books.

This text for beginners was apparently well received; it was printed at least five times between 1500 and 1520, before a newer crop of Latin grammars and then what came to be called Lily's grammar (item 2.2) supplanted it. Perhaps sensing an underserved market for the schoolbook in England, the Antwerp printer Govaert Bac published this undated edition of the work sometime between 1505 and 1510. In London, both Wynkyn de Worde (c. 1510) and Richard Pynson (1520) printed the *Lac puerorum,* but it is rare in any edition. This Bac imprint exists only in this copy.

Literature: Meersch 1856, 123–29; *ODNB* ("Holt, John" by Nicholas Orme); Orme 1996, 283–305.

¶Of holy pouertie.
The firste chaptre.

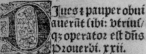

Iues ⁊ pauper obui auerūt sibi: vtriuſ/ q3 operator est dūs Prouerbi. xxii. These ben the wordes of Salo mon this moche to say i englissh The riche and the pore mette to themself/ the lorde is worcher of euireither This texte worshipfulle Bede expowneth thus. A riche man is nat to be worshipped for this cause only that he is riche/ ne a pore man is to be dispysed. bicause of his pouertye. but the werk of god is to be worshippyd in them bothe/ for they bothe been made to the ymage. ⁊ to the lyknesse of god. And as it is writen. Sapiencie. vii. ca. One maner of entring into this worlde/ and a like maner of out wendyng fro this wrechid worlde is to alle men both riche and pore: For bothe riche and pore comen ito this worlde nakyd and pore/ Wepyng and weilynge/ ⁊ bothe they wenden hens nakyd and pore with moche peyne Na thelesse the riche and the pore in their lyuynges in this worlde in many thinges been ful vnlyke For the riche man aboũdeth in tresoure gold and siluer/ ⁊ other richesses He hath honours grete

and erthly delices/ Where the pore creature lyueth in grete penu ry. and for wantyng of richesses suffreth colde and hunger/ and is ofte in dispyte. Pauper. I that am a pore captyf symple ⁊ lytel set by. Bihol dynge the prosperite of them that been riche. and the disese that I suffre and other pore men like vnto me am many a tyme sterpd to gruteche. and to be wery of my lyf. But thanne renen to my mynde the wordes of Salomon bifore re hersyd/ howe the lorde made as wele the pore as the riche. And therto Job witnessith/ that noo thinge in erthe is made withouten cause. Job v. Thanne I suppose within my self/ that by the preuy domes of god that be to me vnknowen/ it is to me profitable to be pore. For wele I wote that god is no nygarde of his giftes. But as the apostle sayth. Rom. viii. To them that been chosen of god alle thinges worchen to gydre into gode. And so sithen I truste throughe the godenes of god to be oon of his chosen/ I can nat deme but that to me it is gode to be pore. Moreouir seint Poule. i. Thy moth. vi. writeth in this maner They that wylle or desire to be made riche falle into temptaci on ⁊ into the snare of the deuyl.
ii a

1.6, fol. A2ʳ

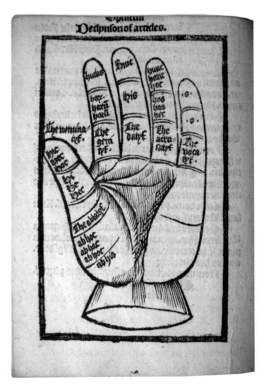

1.7, fol. A3ᵛ

1.8  Gabriel Harvey (1552 / 53–1631). *Commonplace book.*
    Manuscript, England, c. 1584.

Shelfmark: UIUC Pre-1650 MS 150.


1.9  *The crafte of conjureynge and howe to rule the ffierye spiritts of ye planets.* Manuscript, England, c. 1590.

Faye and Bond, 173 (no. 102). Shelfmark: UIUC Pre-1650 MS 102.

Printing did not replace manuscript for certain types of books. Even as a diary still might be handwritten today, so in the fifteenth and sixteenth centuries, after the advent of printing, a manuscript might serve its owner as well or better than a printed book. Cookbooks, diaries, play scripts, and other texts not requiring multiple copies assured that manuscript books continued to be produced in the age of printing.

   An example of a manuscript book that survived the print revolution is the popular commonplace book, a collection of quotations, poems, aide-mémoire, and other snippets

1.8, Commonplace book of Gabriel Harvey, c. 1584

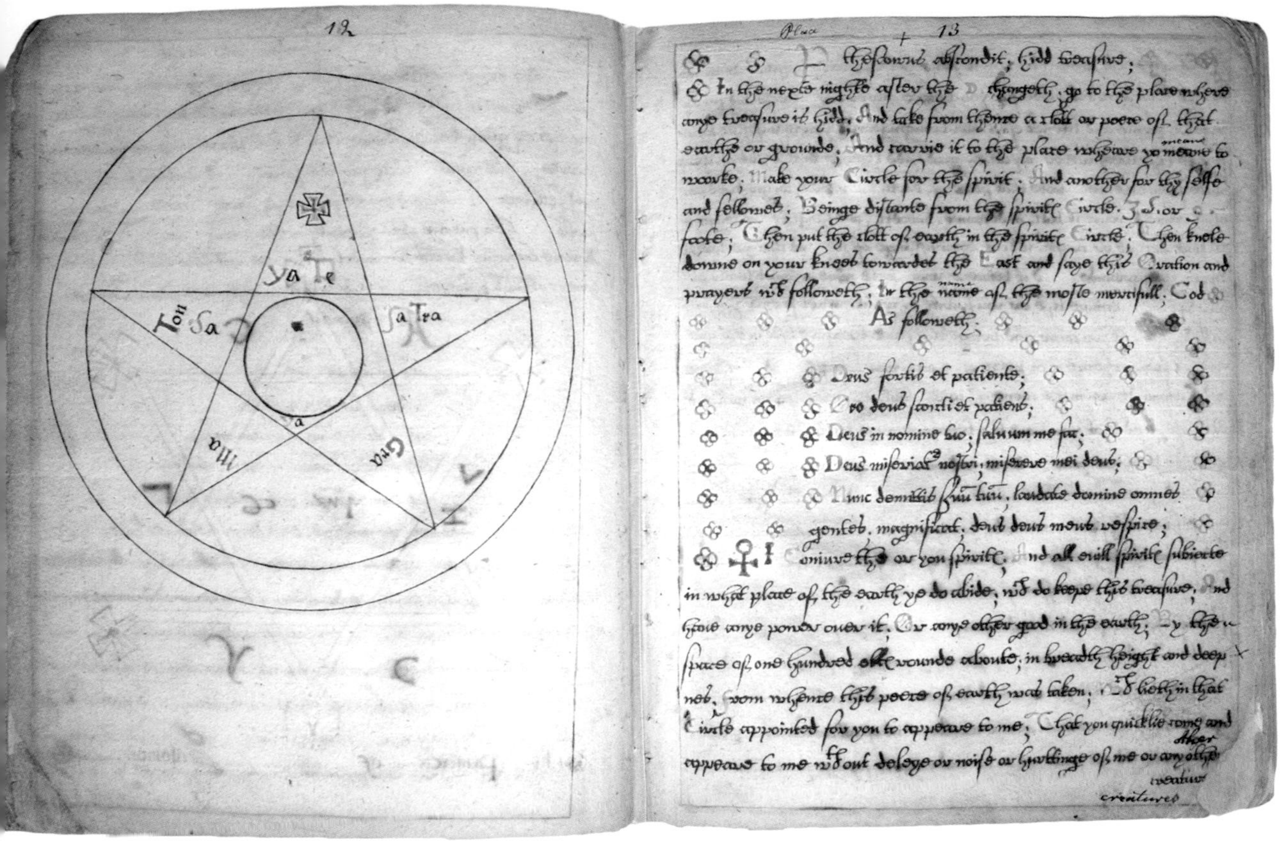

of wisdom jotted down by its owner. Shown here is the commonplace book of Gabriel Harvey, the book collector, literary squabbler, and friend of Edmund Spenser. His "commonplaces" include a poem on vanity, the text of several laws from 1584–85, and passages from Italian, Greek, and Latin sources, such as the Greek phrase "Wise men always live in hope," and the biblical mandate from Genesis 3:19, "In the sweat of your brow shall you earn your bread."[6]

The late-sixteenth-century owner of the second book shown here might have had good reason for preferring manuscript to print. A practical book on magic like this one, full of preternatural recipes and incantations, was best kept to oneself. The book, written in an Elizabethan hand and illustrated with magical diagrams, includes astrological information, advice on how to discover buried treasure, and spells to identify the fate of stolen goods, as well as instructions on conjuring spirits to determine one's ultimate fate. The manuscript adds Christianity to its stock of supernatural powers, regularly invoking God, the Holy Spirit, and Jesus Christ along with demons and spirits such as Beliall, Askariell, and Astaroth. Mystical musings on divinity and the afterlife are also sprinkled throughout this book of practical or "safe" magic.

---

Literature: Biegman 2005; Edwards 1991; Havens 2001; Klaassen 1998; *ODNB* ("Harvey, Gabriel" by Jason Scott-Warren); Stern 1979, 137–243.

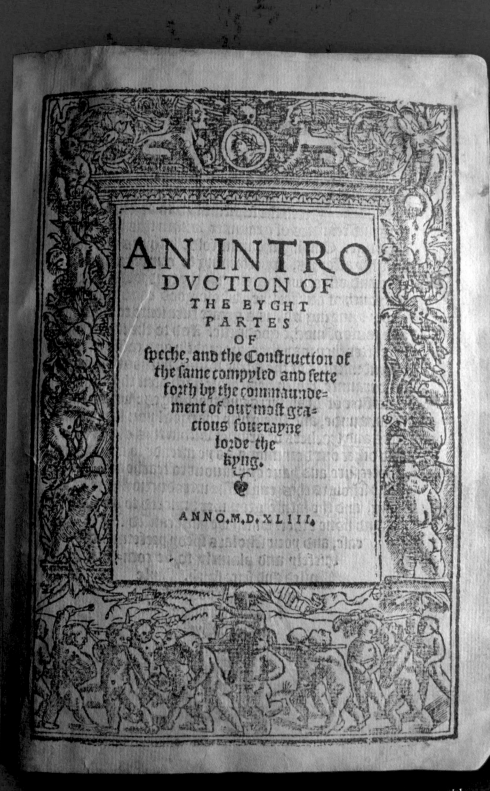

AN INTRO
DVCTION OF
THE EYGHT
PARTES
OF
speche, and the Conſtruction of
the ſame compyled and ſette
foꝛth by the commaunde=
ment of our moſt gra=
cious ſouerayne
loꝛde the
kyng.

ANNO. M. D. XLIII.

2.2, title page

# 2 A WORLD OF WORDS

**2.1**  *The ABC with the Pater noster, Aue, Credo, and .x. com[m]-aundementes in Englysshe newly translated and set forth, at the kyngs most gracyouse commaundement.* London: In the Old Bayley by Richard Lant, [1536 / before 1542?].

*ESTC* S115785; *STC* 19.6. Shelfmark: UIUC 099 Ab3.

This may be the earliest surviving schoolbook written exclusively in English. It is also the only known copy of this pedagogical text for teaching young children their ABCs and simple prayers. These sheets were probably intended to be used for a hornbook since they are printed on only one side.[1] The eight pages of this imprint were long ago pasted together, however, to form a pamphlet of four leaves.

The *ABC* begins with the Sign of the Cross and the alphabet, printed in both roman and black-letter typefaces. Simple prayers in English follow: the Lord's Prayer, Hail Mary, the Creed, the Ten Commandments, and grace for before and after meals. Though, strictly speaking, not a primer—that is, a Book of Hours containing not only more prayers, but also a calendar, almanac, litanies, and offices—this little hornbook served as the first step in an English child's religious education before taking up the more extensive primer. Later, the *ABC* is associated with the primer because they were often printed together.

Even though every English pupil in the sixteenth century began with the *ABC*, not many editions of it survive from before 1545. Fewer than five editions (the others in Latin and English) are extant and each is represented by only one copy. A handwritten date of 1536 appears on the title page of this *ABC*. It is an early hand but does not offer conclusive evidence for its imprint date. We know that the printer, Richard Lant, had his establishment at the Old Bailey between 1537 and 1542, so it must have been printed before 1542. (Butterworth dates the Illinois edition to 1541 or 42.) *ABC* books were probably printed prior to this in the sixteenth century, but no earlier edition survives. The scarcity of the books is explained by their heavy use; they were literally read to death, it seems. Shakespeare alludes to the fact that *ABC* books were learned by rote when he describes the response to a simple question in *King John* (I.i): "And then comes answer like an Absey [*ABC*] booke."

    Another reason for the paucity of early *ABC* books, however, may be their uneasy relation to English primers, which were outlawed in pre-Reformation England because they contained translations of the Bible into English. The Bible in English was illegal from 1408 to 1535. Interestingly, the text of the Lord's Prayer in this *ABC* follows the 1526 translation of William Tyndale, who was executed as a heretic for his work on the English Bible (item 4.14). Despite restrictions against English translations of the Bible, the Lord's Prayer had been printed in English, in different forms, since 1523.[2] The title page of the Illinois *ABC* claims it has been "set forth at the King's most gracious commandment," perhaps indicating the changing religious climate. After all, by 1535, Henry had ushered in his form of the Reformation and allowed Miles Coverdale's Bible to appear in English. English prayers in English–Latin primers and *ABCs* had been tolerated since the mid-1530s, but the first authorized primer did not appear until 1545.

Richard Lant remains a shadowy figure in early English printing. He was made a freeman of the Stationers' Guild in September 1537 and was a charter member when Queen Mary officially established the Stationers' Company in 1557. Lant printed books and broadsides until 1561, but most of his extant works (fewer than ten in number) exist in very few copies; some books that he is known to have printed do not survive at all.

Literature: Birchenough 1938, 182–83; Butterworth 1949, 226–27, 377–78 et passim; Duff [1905] 1948, 88; Simmons 2002, 504; Tuer [1897] 1968; F. Watson 1908, 161–72.

2.2     William Lily (1468?–1522 / 23). *An introduction of the eyght partes of speche, and the construction of the same compyled and sette forth by the commaundement of our most gracious souerayne lorde the kyng.* London: Thomas Berthelet, 1543.

*ESTC* S1112; *STC* 15610.7. Shelfmark: UIUC 475 L62s 1543.

Latin grammars that include English translations and grammatical parallels play an important role in the standardization of English grammar in the Renaissance. John Holt's *Lac puerorum* (item 1.7) is an early example of the mixing of Latin and English in grammatical textbooks. In the next generation, William Lily did the same and the Latin grammar that bears his name (shown opposite page 59) had a profound influence on both Latin and English.

When the humanist John Colet (1467–1519) established St. Paul's School he appointed the grammarian William Lily as its first headmaster (c. 1510). Lily wrote a simple grammar in Latin and English soon afterward, presumably for use in the school. It drew upon the work of others, including ancient grammarians such as Donatus and near contemporaries such as his teacher at Oxford, John Stanbridge. Lily's pedagogical philosophy is indebted to Erasmus, who also contributed a preface to the book. Later, John Colet added to Lily's work his own *Aeditio*, a grammar and primer intended for younger students. In addition, two grammatical poems by Lily had accrued to the text by 1542, the date of the earliest extant edition of the compilation now known as Lily's grammar. Already in 1540, Henry VIII had authorized the text as the sole grammar to be used in English schools. It was also endorsed by Edward VI (1547) and Elizabeth I (1559), and it reigned supreme in English schools for the next three hundred fifty years.

Shakespeare must have learned his "small Latine" from an edition of Lily, for his characters quote from it, as in "'homo' is a common name to all men" (*Henry IV, Part 1*, II.i), and refer to it in *Titus Andronicus* (IV.ii) and *The Merry Wives of Windsor* (IV.i). Indeed, from the 1500s to the late nineteenth century, it rang in the ears of every elementary school child in England. Allusions to Lily appear in works by authors as far removed as Ben Jonson and Edgar Allan Poe. In the 1570s, when, according to the rules of the Stationers' Company, 1,250 copies of an edition could be printed, an exception was made for Lily's grammar, allowing up to 10,000 copies to be printed annually.

Despite the ubiquity of Lily's grammar in English printing, the item shown here is the only known copy of the 1543 edition of *An introduction of the eyght partes of speche*, the part of the grammar for which Lily was directly responsible.

Literature: Baldwin 1944; Flynn 1943; *ODNB* ("Lily, William" by R. D. Smith); Pafort 1946; F. Watson 1908, 243–59.

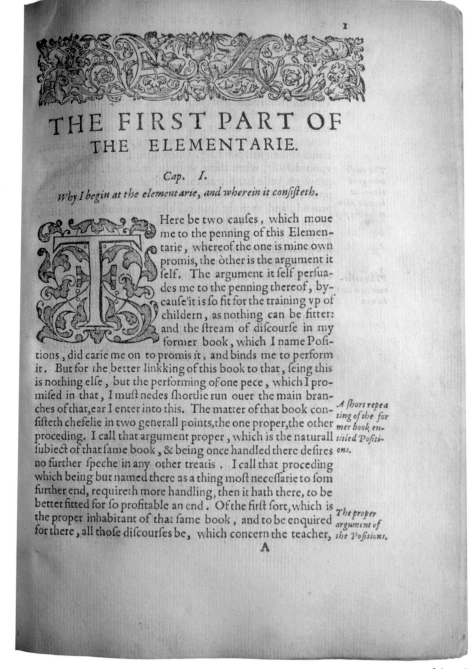

1

# THE FIRST PART OF
## THE ELEMENTARIE.

*Cap. I.*

*Why I begin at the elementarie, and wherein it consisteth.*

Here be two causes, which moue me to the penning of this Elementarie, whereof the one is mine own promis, the òther is the argument it self. The argument it self persuades me to the penning thereof, bycause it is so fit for the training vp of childern, as nothing can be fitter: and the stream of discourse in my former book, which I name Positions, did carie me on to promis it, and binds me to perform it. But for the better linkking of this book to that, seing this is nothing else, but the performing of one pece, which I promised in that, I must nedes shortlie run ouer the main branches of that, ear I enter into this. The matter of that book consisteth chefelie in two generall points, the one proper, the other proceding. I call that argument proper, which is the naturall subiect of that same book, & being once handled there desires no further speche in any other treatis. I call that proceding which being but named there as a thing most necessarie to som further end, requireth more handling, then it hath there, to be better fitted for so profitable an end. Of the first sort, which is the proper inhabitant of that same book, and to be enquired for there, all those discourses be, which concern the teacher,

*A short repeating of the former book entitled Positions.*

*The proper argument of the Positions.*

A

2.3, fol. A1ʳ

2.3 Richard Mulcaster (1531 / 32 – 1611). *The first part of the Elementarie vvhich entreateth chefelie of the right writing of our English tung, set furth by Richard Mvlcaster.* London: Thomas Vautroullier, 1582.

*ESTC* S112926; *STC* 18250. Shelfmark: UIUC IUB00167.

Richard Mulcaster's *Elementarie* represents the first systematic attempt to teach students to read and write in English. Going against the common wisdom of the day, Mulcaster argues that students should spend more time learning English grammar and proper English style before turning to Latin.

In the *Elementarie,* an introduction to an English grammar that was never completed, Mulcaster sets forth a program for elementary education in general. He covers "all those things which young children are to learn of right, and maie learn at ease, if their parents will be carefull, a litle more than ordinarie. The thinges be fiue in number, infinite in vse, principles in place, and these in name, reading, writing, drawing, singing, and playing" (5). This stage of learning, Mulcaster maintains, should have the services of the best-trained and best-paid teachers. There is nothing more important, he claims, for only an educated populace will maintain peace in its country and with its neighbors (247).

The *Elementarie* also includes a call for an English dictionary: "It were a thing verie praiseworthie . . . if som one well learned and as laborious a man, wold gather all the words which we vse in our English tung, whether naturall or incorporate, out of all the professions, as well learned as not, into one dictionarie, and . . . wold open vnto us therin, both their naturall force, and their proper vse" (166). He even appends a "Generall Table" listing about 8,000 familiar English words, albeit without definitions. Many of the words on Mulcaster's list appear later in Edmund Coote's *English Schoole-Master* (1596), a popular primer and English grammar with an etymological dictionary of about 1,500 words, and in Robert Cawdrey's *Table Alphabeticall* (1604), the first true English dictionary. It was not until 1721, however, that an attempt was made—by the lexicographer Nathaniel Bailey—to gather "all the words we vse in our English tung," as Mulcaster had advised.

Mulcaster was headmaster of the Merchant Taylors' School in London and later served at St. Paul's School. His most famous student was Edmund Spenser, who may have used Mulcaster as the inspiration for Master Wrenock in *The Shepherd's Calendar.* Some have proposed him as the source for Shakespeare's pedant Holofernes in *Love's Labour's Lost.* Whether he was a pedant or strict schoolmaster remains unknown, but his curriculum for educating the young certainly seems thoughtful and compassionate.

Without denying the importance of the Renaissance model of education advanced in England by such luminaries as Erasmus and Thomas More, Mulcaster promoted English as a worthy and literary language at an important moment in its development. Mulcaster expressed his position best when he wrote, "I love Rome, but London is better. . . . I honor the *Latin,* but I worship the *English*" (254).

Literature: Charlton 1965, 89–130; DeMolen 1991; *ODNB* ("Mulcaster, Richard" by William Barker); F. Watson 1908, 210–12; Weiss 2003, 46–47.

2.4    Charles Butler (1560–1647). *The English grammar, or the Institution of letters, syllables, and woords in the English tung.* Oxford: William Turner, for the author, 1634.

*ESTC* S106979; Madan I, 176–77; *STC* 4191. Shelfmark: UIUC 425 B97e.

Charles Butler is better known for his important treatises on music (*The Principles of Musik,* 1636) and beekeeping (*The Feminine Monarchie,* 1609), but he also proposed a fairly radical revision of English orthography. He argued for orthographic conventions that might better reflect the spoken language in an attempt to bring some standardization to a situation in which, as he says, four good secretaries, transcribing the same sentence, "differed all, on' from an other, in many letters" (*4ʳ). To this end, he reintroduced the *thorn* and *eth* from Anglo-Saxon and added eight additional "aspirats" to the alphabet. A dead end for English orthography, which remained chaotic for another century at least, Butler's work nonetheless provides interesting insights into seventeenth-century pronunciation in his suggestions for spelling, such as *soon* for son, *caul* for call, *loov* for love, and *woomen* for women. His orthographic proposal is appended to an English grammar, a language he claims has rules "much mor' compendious, than the Grammar-rul's, either of Greek or Latin" (**1ᵛ).

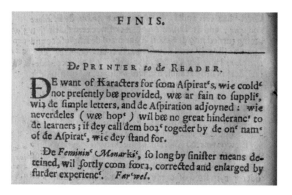

2.4, fol. D2ᵛ (detail)

The printer's note to the reader, shown here, expresses a hint of frustration at the proposed changes to the alphabet, but dutifully does so in Butler's revised fashion.

Literature: *ODNB* ("Butler, Charles" by A. H. Bullen, rev. Karl Showler).

2.5    *Promptorium paruulorum.* London: Richard Pynson, 15 May 1499.

BMC xi, 291; *ESTC* S109932; Goff P-1011; *GW* 10483; *ISTC* ip01011000; *STC* 20434. Shelfmark: UIUC Incunabula 423 G13p 1499.

The *Promptorium parvulorum* is the first dictionary printed in England, the earliest English–Latin dictionary, and the first printed dictionary to contain English words—Middle English, in this case. It lists some twelve thousand Middle English headwords with their Latin equivalents. The work was compiled around 1440 and six manuscripts of it exist from that period. The Pynson imprint shown here is the first printed edition of the *Promptorium.*

Intended as an aid for students learning Latin, this *Promptorium parvulorum*, or "treasury for young scholars," presents an English–Latin wordlist, rather than the more commonly found Latin–English glossary of the Middle Ages.

English words, which are listed in rough alphabetical order, are uniformly defined by their Latin equivalent. The compiler often adds an explanation or synonym in English, however, creating entries that approximate our notion of a "definition" as in the following examples:

Bastard, of gentyl fader and
ongentyle moder.
   *Nothus, -thi; notha, -e.*

Glaren or brightly shyne.
   *Elucido,- das.*

Recorder or witness berar.
   *Testis.*

Schuavynge or scrapynge away.
   *Abrasio, -nis.*

2.5, fol. N3ᵛ

Other entries contain rather elaborate English concepts, followed by a Latin equivalent, as in this entry under I / J: "Joy and myrthe that begynneth with sorow and endeth with gladnesse: Comedia" (I2$^r$).

The Middle English word *prente* (i.e., "print") is included, but the printer Richard Pynson did not feel compelled to update its meaning for post-Gutenberg readers. Its Latin equivalent is merely "signaculum" (seal, mark).

Probably following his manuscript source, but also ushering in the common format for later dictionaries, Pynson prints the entries in two columns. The headwords, however, are not set off in a different typeface, as in later dictionaries. An oddity of this work is the fact that nouns are listed first within each letter, followed by verbs and other parts of speech beginning with the same letter.

The University of Illinois copy of the *Promptorium parvulorum* contains scattered manuscript annotations from the sixteenth century. A note on the flyleaf implies that the book itself was used as collateral for a debt of "tenne poundes of good and lawfull mony of Inglangde" to be paid to a John Falke by a John Arnold of Gurleston. Another early hand has carefully inserted additional words here and there in the alphabetical listings, including "*Burum*, obedient, obediens," "*Bonnair*, meeke, curteous, gentle, mild," and "*A Fixen*, a female fox." The book is open to a page with the addition of "*Quirible*, a treble musicall," as well as a correction of "queen" to "queane," a word meaning "woman."

---

Literature: Knowles and Hadcock 1971, 217; Mayhew 1908, i–xiii; Starnes 1954, 3–23; Stein 1985, 91–97.

2.6     Thomas Elyot (c. 1490–1546). *The Dictionary of Syr Thomas Eliot knyght.* London: Thomas Berthelet, [1538].

*ESTC* S111493; *STC* 7659. Shelfmark: UIUC IUQ03508.

Sir Thomas Elyot not only produced the first Latin–English dictionary reflecting early modern English, but also first used the word *dictionary* to describe his work. This is a quintessentially Renaissance dictionary, one that draws upon classical models, introduces new words and knowledge, and offers almost encyclopedic definitions. In his dedicatory preface to Henry VIII, Elyot explains that he has included medical and legal terms, the names of plants and animals, and "adagia," or proverbs, "whiche I thought necessarie to be had in remembraunce" (A3$^v$). An appended table of terms for various weights and measures represents the first appearance of what later becomes a common feature of English dictionaries.

In order to offer English equivalents for some Latin terms, Elyot often coined new words, usually from Greek and Latin sources. But he also struggled to find English meanings, especially for animal and plant names, as in "Tragoriganon, an herbe whiche I suppose, is callyed Peny royalle, growying wylde" (Dd1$^r$). For concepts not represented in classical Latin, Elyot suggests new meanings for old words, as in "Balista, a crossebowe, or a brake. It may be vsed for a gunne" (B4$^v$).

Elyot's work was soon absorbed into a larger Latin–English dictionary, the *Thesaurus*

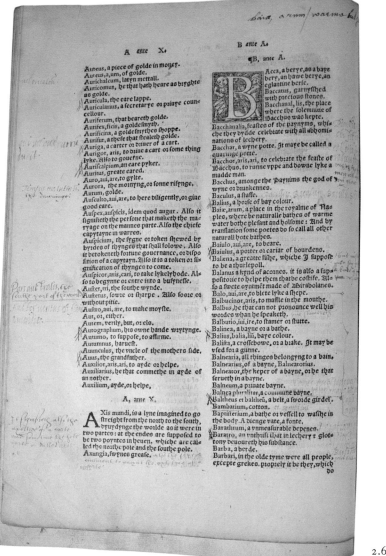

2.6, fol. B4ᵛ

*Linguae Romanae et Britannicae,* compiled in 1565 by Thomas Cooper. As Stein notes, Elyot is the first English lexicographer to measure the greatness of his work by the number of headwords it contained ("a thousande mo latine wordes, than were togither in any one Dictionarie published in the royalme"), thereby ushering in one of the chief marketing strategies of modern dictionary publishers.[3]

Elyot also authored a popular book on good government, *The Book named the Governour* (1531), as well as the *Castel of Helth* (1539), the first medical handbook in the vernacular. All of Elyot's works — some nine altogether — were printed by Thomas Berthelet, who served as the King's Printer from 1530 to Henry VIII's death in 1547.

Literature: *ODNB* ("Elyot, Sir Thomas" by Stanford Lehmberg); *ODNB* ("Berthelet, Thomas" by K. F. Pantzer); Starnes 1954, 45–67; Stein 1985, 140–56.

2.7   Richard Huloet (fl. 1552). *Abcedarivm anglico-latinvm pro tyrunculis.* London: [S. Mierdman] for William Riddel, 1552.

ESTC S117241; STC 13940. Shelfmark: UIUC Q. 423.71 H878a.

Richard Huloet's *Abcedarium* is the first English–Latin dictionary of the sixteenth century. Its importance for English lexicography lies in the fact that English words are systematically defined first in English, followed by the Latin meaning. The inclusion of some twenty-six thousand headwords makes this the largest English dictionary of its day. It is arranged in alphabetical order (though not always carried beyond the third letter within the word). The *Abcedarium* is the first English–Latin dictionary with notes on the letters of the alphabet; in its second edition (1572) it can lay claim to being the first English dictionary to include illustrations, albeit only a few. Huloet also incorporates a number of proverbs and "vulgar" phrases that give the reader a sense of sixteenth-century popular idiom, such as

Borowe of Peter to paye Paule, whyche is a vulgare speach, properly wher as a man doth Borow of one to paye an other.

2.7, fol. G4^v–G5^r

Gramercy to thee, whych is a maner of thankes geuyng amonge the vulgares.

Make a rod for his owne arse. A prouerbe properlye applyed to such as do inuent punishmente for others, hauynge the same them selues.

Ploughemens holidayes, as wakes and such, idle bancquetynge.

Some headwords reflect current events, as in "Anabaptistes, a sort of heretyques of late tyme in Germanye about the yere of our Lorde God 1524."

In his *Peroration to the Englyshe reader* at the end of the dictionary, Huloet apologizes for errors in printing and the quality of the typeface: "I do hartely desyre for the prynter, that thou ne wylt be offended with thys his impression the whiche albeit at thys tyme be ful of faultes: and not of suche good letter as the sayde Prynter woulde haue hadde (yf oportunitie hadde serued)." The pedagogical purpose of Huloet's dictionary is clear in his final note to the reader on the word *Idem*, which, he patiently explains to beginning Latin students, is "not the latten [Latin] worde for those Englyshe wordes" that precede it. Rather, "you must take it and loke in the last kynde of phrase for the Laten" (Nn4ʳ).

The University of Illinois copy of Huloet's dictionary played an important role in the creation of yet another English dictionary. It belonged to the sixteenth-century lexicographer Laurence Nowell (1530–c. 1570), who interleaved and annotated Huloet's work with Anglo-Saxon equivalents while preparing his Old English dictionary, the *Vocabularium Saxonicum*.

---

Literature: Rosier 1977; *ODNB* ("Howlet [Huloet], Richard" by R. W. McConchie); Starnes 1951; Starnes 1954, 147–66; Stein 1985, 181–93; Stein 2006.

2.8   Peter Levens (fl. 1552–87). *Manipvlvs vocabvlorvm. A dictonarie of English and Latine wordes, set forthe in suche order, as none heretofore hath ben, the Englishe going before the Latine, necessary not onely for scholers that wa[n]t varietie of words, but also for such as vse to write in English meetre.* London: Henry Bynneman for John Waley, 1570.

*ESTC* S101107; *STC* 15532. Shelfmark: UIUC IUB00168.

The compiler of this, the first rhyming English–Latin dictionary, takes some pride in his accomplishment, "for the gathering of oure Englishe wordes, and deviding of the same into this alphabet order of the last sillabls, being a trade not of any man afore attempted" (¶3ᵛ). Levens's *Manipulus vocabulorum*, or "handful of words," contains about nine thousand entries, far fewer than Huloet's, which Levens says "is for greter students, [and] them that are richable to haue it." His little work, on the other hand, "is for beginners, [and] them that are pooreable to haue no better" (¶4ʳ).

Perhaps because of his focus on the last syllable of each word, Levens is the first lexicographer to mark stressed syllables. He is also concerned with correct spelling, even attempting to offer some rules. As if conceding the fickleness of English orthography of the day, however, he offers this advice to users of the dictionary in his note on *I ante L:* "ofttimes ble is written for bil; dle for dil; fle for fil. . . . Wherfore, if ye fynd not in the one of these seeke in the other and yee shal not misse" (CI^v).

Despite his aim to provide something less than Huloet, in some ways, Levens provides more. His dictionary is the first to include notes on grammatical concepts such as inflectional morphology and word-formation in the definitions. For example, Levens introduces the entries for *-ing* with a note explaining the grammatical reasons for this final syllable.

Only three copies of this dictionary survive (Illinois, the British Library, and the Bodleian Library). The printer, Henry Bynneman, held the patent for publishing dictionaries "in all tongues," though in the rough and tumble world of English printing, we encounter his name — as both plaintiff and accused — in several disputes about unlicensed printing.

Literature: *ODNB* ("Bynneman, Henry" by Maureen Bell, and "Levens [Levins], Peter" by R. W. McConchie); Stein 1985, 226–44; Stein 1987; Wheatley [1867] 1937, viii–xiv.

MANIPVLVS VOCABVLORVM.

A Dictionarie of English
and Latine wordes, set forthe in
suche order, as none heretofore hath ben,
the *Englishe* going before the *Latine*,
necessary not onely for Scholers
that wât varietie of wordes,
but also for such as vse
to write in English
Poetre.

*Gathered and set forth by P. Leuins.*
ANNO 1570.

For the better vnderstanding of the order of this present
Dictionarie, read ouer the Preface to the Reader,
and the Epistle Dedicatorie, and thou shalt
finde it easie and plaine, and further
thereof thou shalt gather
great profite.

*Imprinted at London by Henrie*
*Bynneman, for John Waley.*

2.8, title page

*Palestricall.* Of, or belonging to wrastling. Also that which is done decently with comely gesture of the body.

*Palinode.* A recantation or denying of an opinion formerly maintained.

* *Palliard.* A Whoore-monger.

* *Palliardise.* Whooredome.

*Palliate.* To cloke, to couer.

*Pallizado.* Great posts set vp in the entry to a Camp for a defence against great shot.

*Palme.* The tree which beareth Dates, growing plentifully in the holy land. There are of these trees found also in some parts of Egypt, but they beare no fruite, or if they beare any it is vnpleasant. The branches of this tree, were wont to be carried as a token of victory, because they are of that nature, that they wil stil shoot vpward, though oppressed with neuer so great weight, & the leaues thereof neuer fall. Of this tree there is male and female: the male beareth only blossomes & no fruit, but the female beares both. In olde times, some people vsed to write with Paper, made of leaues of the Palme tree.

*Palmer.* A poore pilgrime, that visiteth all holy places.

*Palmister.* He that telleth ones fortune by looking in his hand.

*Palmistry.* See Diuination.

*Palpable.* That which may be felt with the fingers: manifest, notorious.

*Pamphlet.* A little booke.

*Pandar.* A base fellow that keepeth or attendeth vpon Harlots.

*Pandect.* A booke treating of all matters: also the Volume of the Ciuill Lawe called *Digests*, is so called.

*Panegyricall.* That which is spoken flatteringly in praise of some great person: Also it signifieth, stately, honorable, magnificent, or a speech made of many great matters together.

*Panther.* A fierce wilde beast, hauing a sweet smel, and a faire spotted skinne, wherewith shee allureth other beastes to looke on her; hiding her head least it should make them afraid, and by this means, getteth her prey more easily. The male of this beast is the libard. The panthers (as is written) haue on their shoulder a spotte, which groweth and waineth like the moon. This beast is so fearfull of the Hyena, that in his presence shee dareth not doe any thing: in so much that if one haue but a peece of the skinne of a Hyena, the Panther will not touch him, and it is sayde, that if both their skins be hanged together, the haire of the Panthers skin will fall of.

*Panyme.* A heathen, a gentile.

*Parable.* A similitude or resemblance made of a thing.

*Paracelsian.* A physition that followeth the method of *Paracelsus*, and his manner of curing, which was by exceeding strong oyles and waters extracted out of the nature of things.

*Paraclete.* A comforter.

*Paradise.* A garden or pleasant place.

*Paradox.* An opinion maintained cōtrary to the common allowed opinion as if one affirme that the earth doth mooue round, and the heauens stand stil.

*Paragon.* A beautifull peece, a louely creature.

*Paragraph.* It properly signifieth any marke set in a margent, to note the different discourses in a booke, or long chapter, wherefore such diuisions in writing, are commonly called Paragraphs.

*Paralipomenon.* Omitted, or not spoken of: There are two bookes in the old testamēt so called, because many worthy histories omitted in the bookes of Kings, are there related.

*Parallels.* Lines running of an equall distance from each other, which can neuer meete, though they be drawn infinitely in length, thus,————.

In

2.9, fol. L6ᵛ–L7ʳ

2.9    John Bullokar (1574–1627). *An English expositor: Teaching the interpretation of the hardest words used in our language.* London: John Legatt, 1621.

Alston 5:6; *ESTC* S115630; *STC* 4084. Shelfmark: UIUC IUA02068.

The first English–English dictionary is Robert Cawdrey's *A Table Alphabeticall*, printed in 1604 by Edmund Weaver (d. 1638), only one copy of which survives.[4] John Bullokar represents the next milestone in English lexicography, offering more detailed definitions in his English–English dictionary and nearly twice as many headwords as Cawdrey, from whom he borrows a great deal.

Bullokar was a doctor, not a schoolmaster or professional lexicographer, and his *English Expositor* was intended for private distribution. Moreover, publishing it might have seemed risky because of the religious stance of its compiler. Bullokar's unwavering allegiance to the Catholic Church caused him enormous hardships. He was charged as a recusant, members of his family were imprisoned for harboring priests, and his son Thomas, a Franciscan, was hanged, drawn, and quartered for celebrating Mass. Perhaps in part for these reasons, the first edition of 1616 is extant in only six copies. The second edition of 1621, shown here, exists in nine copies. And yet its value as an English dictionary should not be judged by its poor survival rate. The *Expositor* contains more detailed definitions than Cawdrey's *Table* and features careful citations of sources and authorities. Bullokar understands the ever-expanding, always-borrowing tendency of the English language and offers a "great store of strange words our speech doth borrow, not only from the Latine and Greeke (and some from the ancient Hebrew), but also from forraine vulgar Languages round about vs" (A3ᵛ), as well as technical terms from the various academic disciplines and "sundry olde words now growne out of vse" (A3ᵛ).

Bullokar's *Expositor* was revised and enlarged after his death, most significantly by Richard Browne in 1707, and remained in print until 1775.

Literature: *ODNB* ("Bullokar, John" by Janet Bately); Starnes and Noyes [1946] 1991, 20–36.

2.10    Thomas Blount (1618–79). *Glossographia or, A dictionary, interpreting all such hard words, whether Hebrew, Greek, Latin, Italian, Spanish, French, Teutonick, Belgick, British, or Saxon; as are now used in our refined English tongue.* London: Thomas Newcomb, to be sold by Humphrey Moseley and George Sawbridge, 1656.

Alston 5:45; *ESTC* R5788; Wing B-3334. Shelfmark: UIUC 423 B62g.

Thomas Blount was a London lawyer who was inspired to compile a dictionary because, as he says in the preface, he often found himself stymied by the language of tradesmen around him and "gravelled in English Books," despite his education in classical languages and French. Collecting difficult words from his readings and encounters, and drawing upon the work of several of his predecessors,[5] including Bullokar, Blount compiled the most comprehensive English dictionary of the seventeenth century. The project consumed some twenty years and he says he feared his "labor would find no end; since our English tongue daily changes habit" (A4ʳ). He does not see this as a weakness, however, and cheerfully acknowledges that English dictionaries must be forever works in progress because of the willingness of the language to expand with neologisms and loanwords.

Blount's *Glossographia* is the first English dictionary that consistently offers etymologies and historical explanations of words. Not all of these explanations are authentic, however, and some are rather far-fetched, as in "Tomboy, a girle or wench that leaps up and down like a boy, comes from the Saxon tumbe, to dance, and tumbod, danced; hence also comes the word tumbling, still in use."

One of the pages shown here (T8ᵛ) includes another interesting etymology, this one for the word *honeymoon*. Huloet had included the word with a long definition, but Blount renders the etymology in a succinct and rather disheartening manner: "Hony-moon, applyed to those married persons that love well at first, and decline in affection afterwards; it is hony now, but it will change as the Moon" (T8ᵛ).

Literature: *ODNB* ("Blount, Thomas" by Ian Mortimer); Starnes and Noyes [1946] 1991, 37–47.

Hony=moon, applyed to those marryed persons that love well at first, and decline in affection afterwards; it is hony now, but it will change as the Moon. *Min.*

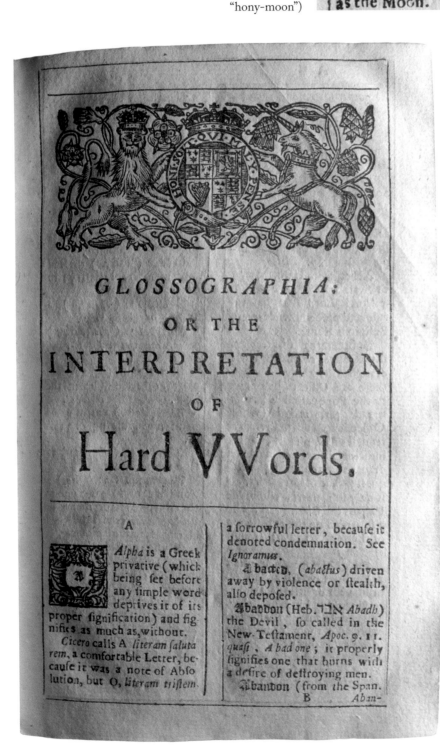

GLOSSOGRAPHIA:

OR THE

INTERPRETATION

OF

Hard VVords.

A

*Alpha* is a Greek privative (which being set before any simple word deprives it of its proper signification) and signifies as much as, without.

*Cicero* calls A *literam salutarem*, a comfortable Letter, because it was a note of Absolution, but O, *literam tristem*, a sorrowful letter, because it denoted condemnation. See *Ignoramus.*

Abacted, (*abactus*) driven away by violence or stealth, also deposed.

Abaddon (Heb. אבד *Abadh*) the Devil, so called in the New-Testament, *Apoc.* 9. 11. *quasi*, *A bad one*; it properly signifies one that burns with a desire of destroying men.

Abandon (from the Span.

B                    Aban-

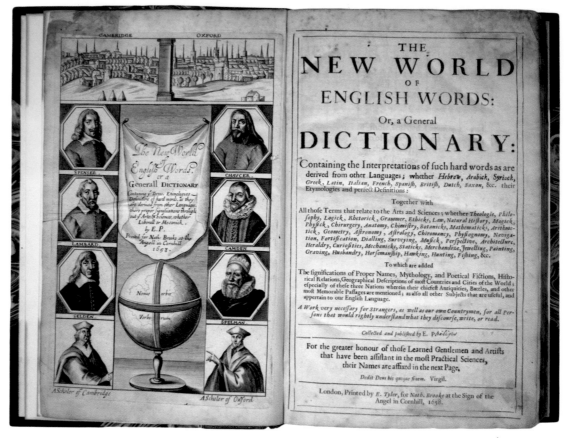

2.11, title page

2.11    Edward Phillips (1630–96?). *The New World of
        English Words: or, a General Dictionary: Containing the
        interpretations of such hard words as are derived from other
        languages.* London: E. Tyler, for Nathaniel Brooke, 1658.

        Alston 5:53; ESTC R14781; Wing P-2068. Shelfmark: UIUC Q. 423 P54n 1658.

2.12    Thomas Blount. *A world of errors discovered in the
        New World of Words, or General English dictionary.*
        [London]: T. N. [Thomas Newcomb] for Abel Roper,
        John Martin, and Henry Herringman, 1673.

        ESTC R18536; Wing B-3345. Shelfmark: UIUC Q. 423 P54nYb.

Edward Phillips was the son of John Milton's only sister, Anne. Milton apparently took an
interest in his nephew's early education. Phillips later went down from Oxford without a
degree and became a clerk to Nathaniel Brook, from some reports, an unscrupulous bookseller in London. Phillips also published several books, including the *Theatrum poetarum* of

1675, which lists the world's great poets, particularly English ones, and includes a prefatory *Discourse of the Poets and Poetry* that is often attributed to his uncle.

Phillips's contribution to lexicography is slight but not without resonance. He gave special emphasis to proper names and claimed to have a staff of specialists as consultants (apparently a false claim, but a characteristic of future lexicography). More important, he borrowed, without acknowledgment, from several sources, but chiefly from Thomas Blount's *Glossographia* (item 2.10).

Blount noticed the egregious plagiarism and published a tirade against Phillips entitled *A World of Errors Discovered in the New World of Words.* Blount charges Phillips with stealing part of his preface, most of his headwords and definitions, and even typographical errors from his *Glossographia.* Appended to this critique is a list of one hundred examples

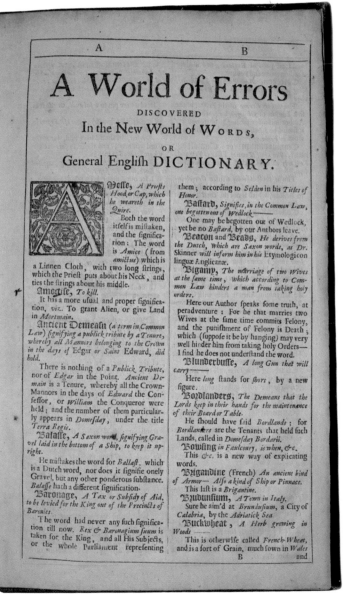

2.12,
fol. B1ʳ

of errors for which Blount readily gives Phillips all due credit, each followed by a sarcastic quip from Blount, as in:

Bowling in Faulconry, is when &c.
*This &c. is a new way of explicating words.*

Convental Church, A Parish Church.
*It is no Parish Church; as most men, except our Author, know.*

Gallon (Spanish), A measure containing two quarts.
*Our Author had better omitted this word, since every Alewife can contradict him.*

To Grown, The Foresters say, a Buck growneth.
*But what it means you must learn elswhere; for this is all he says of the word.*

Despite the blistering condemnation from Blount, Phillips's work enjoyed great success. It went through five editions by 1696. In 1706, it was thoroughly revised and greatly enlarged upon by a better lexicographer, John Kersey (c. 1660–c. 1721).

---

Literature: *ODNB* ("Phillips, Edward" by Gordon Campbell); Starnes and Noyes [1946] 1991, 48–57 and (for more on Kersey's revision), 84–89.

2.13    John Palsgrave (d. 1554). *Lesclarcissement de la langue francoyse compose par maistre Jehan Palsgraue Angloys natyf de Londres, et gradue de Paris.* [London]: Richard Pynson and John Hawkins, 18 June 1530.

*ESTC* S104266; *STC* 19166. Shelfmark: UIUC IUA03513.

2.14    William Salesbury (c. 1520–c. 1580). *A Dictionary in Englyshe and Welshe moche necessary to all suche Welshemen as wil spedly learne the englyshe to[n]gue thought vnto the kynges maiestie very mete to be sette forthe to the vse of his graces subiectes in Wales.* London: [N. Hill for] John Waley, 1547.

*ESTC* S110802; *STC* 21616. Shelfmark: UIUC IUB00169.

2.15    William Thomas (d. 1554). *Principal rvles of the Italian grammer, with a dictionarie for the better understandyng of Boccace, Petrarcha, and Dante.* London: T. B. [Thomas Berthelet], [1550].

*ESTC* S118383; *STC* 24020. Shelfmark: UIUC IUB00189.

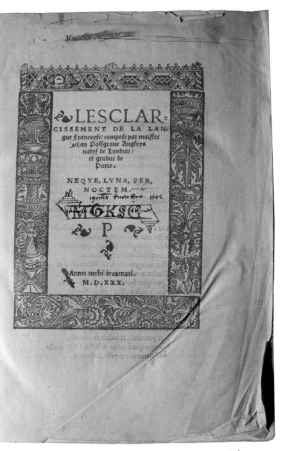

2.13, title page

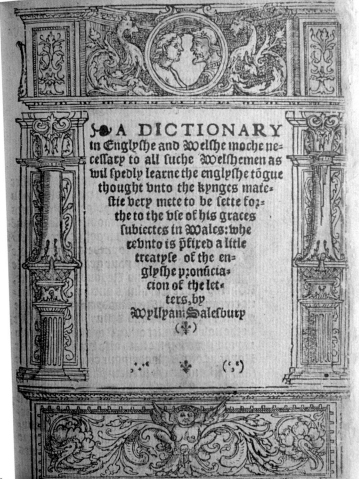

2.14, title page

33

A Dictionarie, taken out of the two bookes in Italian, called Acharisius and Ricchezze della lingua volgare, for the better vnderstandyng of the notable Aucthours in that tongue.

A before B.

Bada, at a baye, in hoope, expectacion, or prolongeyng.
Abbadessa, an Abbesse.
Abbaiare, to barke lyke a dogge.
Abbarbicare, to hange, sticke, or cleaue fast by the rootes, as the Iuie dooeth.
Abbate, an abbotte.
Abbachiera, a maister in Aulgresme, or in castyng of accomptes.
Abbagliare, to bleamishe the sighte, or cast a fygure before the eyes.
Abbaiante, barkyng lyke a dogge.
Abbaiatore, a brawler, or a backebyter.
Abbandonare, to habandone, leaue or forsake.
Abbandonato, habandoned.
Abbandono, the habandonyng.
Abbarbagleare, to darken or bleamishe the sight, vsed most in verse.
Abbassare, to make any thyng decline or stowpe.
Abbattere, to ouerthrowe, or to chaunce sodeinly, to arise.
Abbellire, to make fayre, or to encrease beautie, most properly applied to the peinctyng that women vse on their faces.
Abbeuerare, to geue drinke.
Ablicare, to heape vp.
Abborro, the castyng of the calfe, and therefore somtime

A                                    vsed

2.15, fol. A1ʳ

BIBLIOTHECÆ HISPANICÆ
PARS ALTERA.

CONTAINING A DICTIONARIE IN
SPANISH, ENGLISH, and LATINE:
gathered out of diuers good
Authors : very profitable
for the studious of
the Spanish
toong.

By RICHARD PERCYVALL gent.

Enlarged with the Latine by the aduise
and conference of Master Thomas
DOYLEY Doctor in
Physicke.

Imprinted at London by Iohn Iackson,
for Richard Watkins.
1591

2.16, title page

2.16    Richard Perceval (1550–1620). *Bibliothecæ Hispanicæ.*
        *Containing a grammar; with a dictionarie in Spanish,*
        *English, and Latine; gathered out of diuers good authors:*
        *very profitable for the studious of the Spanish toong.*
        London: John Jackson, for Richard Watkins,
        1591.

        *ESTC* S121971; *STC* 19619. Shelfmark: UIUC IUB00188.


2.17    John Baret (d. 1578). *An Alvearie or triple dictionarie,*
        *in Englishe, Latin, and French.* London: Henry
        Denham, [1573].

        *ESTC* S121929; *STC* 1410. Shelfmark: UIUC IUA00805.


2.18    John Minsheu (1559 / 60–1627). *Ductor in linguas,*
        *the gvide into tongves.* [London: William Stansby
        and Eliot's Court Press, 1617].

        *ESTC* S121927; *STC* 17944. Shelfmark: UIUC Q. 413 M66g.

The inclusion of early foreign-language dictionaries in a study of early English printing may not seem necessary at first glance, but these examples of the earliest printed Welsh–English, French–English, Spanish–English, and Italian–English dictionaries, together with two polyglot dictionaries of the English Renaissance, serve to illustrate the growing importance of vernaculars—and the relation of English to them—in the expanding world of the sixteenth century.

Salesbury and Palsgrave are the first lexicographers in England to work with English and another vernacular, French and Welsh, respectively. Both dictionaries were intended, as Salesbury's title indicates, for people who wanted to learn a language. Palsgrave's is particularly significant because it also includes the first grammar of the French language ever printed—produced by an Englishman in England, no less. It is also the last book printed by Richard Pynson before his death in 1530 (his son-in-law John Hawkins actually finished it). Palsgrave was apparently very particular about the print job, requiring that the seven hundred fifty copies be kept at Pynson's house in a locked room to which Palsgrave had the key, and allowing the book to be sold only to his friends and students and with his permission. This may explain why there are so few copies extant. (The Illinois copy is one of eleven surviving copies.)

The first Italian–English dictionary appeared in 1550, when William Thomas included a glossary in his Italian grammar "for the better vnderstandyng of the notable Aucthous in that tongue" (²A1ʳ). (Thomas was later arrested for plotting against Queen Mary and executed for treason in 1554.) Almost fifty years later, John Florio (1553–1625) compiled his more comprehensive Italian dictionary (1598). Antonio de Corro (1527–91) published

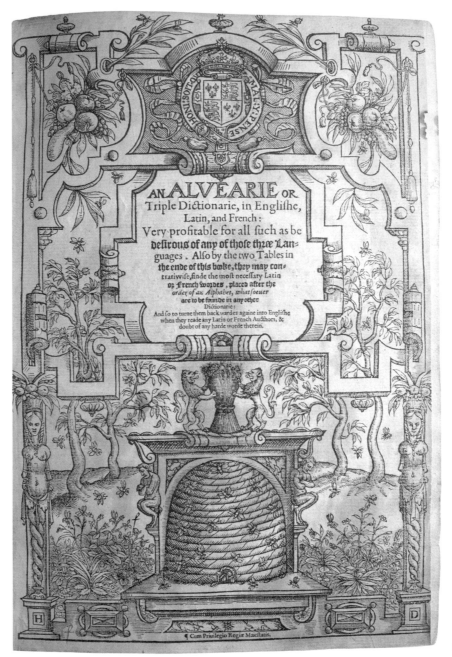

2.17, title page

a Spanish–English Dictionary in 1590, but the first Spanish–English/English–Spanish dictionary appears the following year, compiled by Richard Perceval. Like Palsgrave's and many other Renaissance dictionaries, Perceval's work includes a grammar.

Polyglot dictionaries begin to appear in England in the sixteenth century with works like the *Alvearie,* or "beehive," of John Baret, a triple dictionary of English, Latin, and French, which was later expanded to include Greek as well. In 1617, John Minsheu pub-

2.18, title page

lished a massive polyglot dictionary that included eleven languages. Minsheu's work is also significant in the history of English publishing as the first book printed in England by subscription (not the London Polyglot as is often stated). A list of the subscribers is printed on A6ʳ.

Literature: Kibbee 1987, 181–87; Starnes 1954, 184–217; Stein 1985, 121–39, 157–64, 273–95, and 353–409; Stein 1997.

# By the King.

# A PROCLAMATION

For calling in, and suppressing of two Books written by *John Milton*; the one Intituled, *Johannis Miltoni Angli pro Populo Anglicano Defensio, contra Claudii Anonymi alias Salmasii, Defensionem Regiam*; and the other in answer to a Book Intituled, *The Pourtraiture of his Sacred Majesty in his Solitude and Sufferings*. And also a third Book Intituled, *The Obstructors of Justice*, written by *John Goodwin*.

CHARLES R.

Whereas John Milton, late of Westminster, in the County of Middlesex, hath Published in Print two several Books. The one Intituled, Johannis Miltoni Angli pro Populo Anglicano Defensio, contra Claudii Anonymi, alias Salmasii, Defensionem Regiam. And the other in Answer to a Book Intituled, The Pourtraicture of his Sacred Majesty in his Solitude and Sufferings. In both which are contained sundry Treasonable Passages against Us and Our Government, and most Impious endeavors to justifie the horrid and unmatchable Murther of Our late Dear Father, of Glorious Memory. And Whereas John Goodwin, late of Coleman-Street, London, Clerk, hath also published in Print, a Book Intituled, The Obstructors of Justice, written in defence of his said late Majesty. And whereas the said John Milton, and John Goodwin, are both fled, or so obscure themselves, that no endeavors used for their apprehension can take effect, whereby they might be brought to Legal Tryal, and deservedly receive condigne punishment for their Treasons and Offences.

Now to the end that Our good Subjects may not be corrupted in their Judgments, with such wicked and Traitrous principles, as are dispersed and scattered throughout the beforementioned Books, We, upon the motion of the Commons in Parliament now assembled, doe hereby streightly charge and Command, all and every person and persons whatsoever, who live in any City, Burrough, or Town Incorporate, within this our Kingdom of England, the Dominion of Wales, and Town of Berwick upon Tweed, in whose hands any of those Books are, or hereafter shall be, That they, upon pain of Our high Displeasure, and the consequence thereof, do forthwith, upon publication of this Our Command, or within Ten days immediately following, deliver, or cause the same to be delivered to the Mayor, Bayliffs, or other chief Officer or Magistrate, in any of the said Cities, Burroughs, or Towns Incorporate, where such person or persons so live; or, if living out of any City, Burrough, or Town Incorporate, then to the next Justice of Peace adjoyning to his or their dwelling, or place of abode; or if living in either of Our Universities, then to the Vice-Chancellor of that University where he or they do reside.

And in default of such voluntary delivery, which We do expect in observance of Our said Command, That then and after the time before limited, expired, the said Chief Magistrate of all and every the said Cities, Burroughs, or Towns Incorporate, the Justices of the Peace in their several Counties, and the Vice-Chancellors of Our said Universities respectively, are hereby Commanded to Seize and Take, all and every the Books aforesaid, in whose hands or possession soever they shall be found, and certifie the names of the Offenders unto Our Privy Council.

And We do hereby also give special Charge and Command to the said Chief Magistrates, Justices of the Peace, and Vice-Chancellors respectively, That they cause the said Books which shall be so brought unto any of their hands, or seized or taken as aforesaid, by vertue of this Our Proclamation, to be delivered to the respective Sheriffs of those Counties where they respectively live, the first and next Assizes that shall after happen. And the said Sheriffs are hereby also required, in time of holding such Assizes, to cause the same to be publickly burnt by the hand of the Common Hangman.

And We do further streightly Charge and Command, That no man hereafter presume to Print, Vend, Sell, or Disperse any the aforesaid Books, upon pain of Our heavy Displeasure, and of such further Punishment, as for their presumption in that behalf, may any way be inflicted upon them by the Laws of this Realm.

Given at Our Court at *Whitehall* the 13th day of *August*, in the Twelfth year of Our Reign, 1660.

LONDON, Printed by *John Bill* and *Christopher Barker*, Printers to the Kings most Excellent Majesty, 1660.

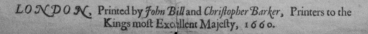

3.15, proclamation against Milton, 1660

# 3 "FOR THE REGULATING OF PRINTING"

3.1      *The Bybc in Englyshe, that is to saye the content of all the holy scrypture, bothe of ye olde and newe testament, truly translated after the veryte of the Hebrue and Greke textes, by ye dylygent studye of dyverse excellent learned men, expert in the forsayde tonges.* [Paris: Francis Regnault] and [London]: Richard Grafton and Edward Whitchurch, Cum privilegio ad imprimendum solum, April 1539.

         DMH 46; *ESTC* S122342; *STC* 2068. Shelfmark: UIUC IUQ00027.

The effort to control the distribution of texts predates printing. In 1401, the *De haeretico comburendo,* an act of Parliament, threatened anyone found with "books or any such writings of wicked doctrine and opinion" (i.e., Wycliffite or Lollard views) with fines, imprisonment, and even death by burning.[1] Henry VIII followed in this tradition, forbidding the Bible in English and all "erroneous," "blasphemous and pestiferous Englishe books" in a proclamation of 1530 (*STC* 7775). Though his views on the Bible and the Reformation may have shifted after his divorce, his interest in controlling the press remained steadfast. In November 1538, Henry VIII issued an act requiring every book printed in England to pass "examination made by some of his grace's privy counsayle, or other suche as his highnes shall appoynte" (*STC* 7790). Significantly, the Act of 1538 transferred the role of censor from the clergy to secular authorities.

3.1, title page

In addition to repeated acts and proclamations concerning printing during the Tudor period, there also arose a system of granting privileges to print particular titles or genres. The practice of granting royal privileges to printers and booksellers might be said to begin under Henry VII, who made Peter Actors Stationer to the King in 1485; the first official Printer to the King was William Faques, so named in 1504. Faques and his successor, Richard Pynson (as of about 1506), printed official state documents (as well as other books) and were permitted to distinguish their imprints with the phrase "cum privilegio regali" (with royal privilege). Soon other printers asked for the privilege to print certain texts, especially profitable ones such as primers, prayer books, Bibles, and law books. In return for a fee to the crown, they might then include the phrase "cum privilegio." The Act of 1538 is also noteworthy because it required even those with printing patents to submit their texts to the Privy Council for review and to add the phrase "ad imprimendum solum" (for exclusive printing) to their statement of privilege.

The first edition of the Great Bible, shown here, is the first book to include this new phrase. There is no doubt it was submitted to the king's Privy Council, for it was produced at the urging of the king's chief advisor, Thomas Cromwell (c. 1485–1540). The text is Miles Coverdale's revision of the Matthew Bible (item 4.14). Like the outlawed Bibles that preceded it, this Bible was to be printed on the Continent. The publishers, Richard Grafton and Edward Whitchurch, arranged for Francis Regnault to print it in Paris. However, the inquisitor-general of France stopped the project, forcing Grafton and Whitchurch to complete the work in London. The Great Bible was the second complete English Bible printed in England, following Richard Taverner's unauthorized Bible of the same year.

The Great Bible went through seven editions between 1539 and 1541. Its large format was required since Henry VIII's Injunctions of 1538 mandated that the Bible be available for public reading in every church throughout England. It is the first "authorized" English Bible.

Literature: Bruce 1978, 67–80; Hotchkiss and Ryrie 1998, item 8.5; Mozley 1953, 201–305; Price and Ryrie 2004, 49–63.

3.2    *The prymer in Englishe and Latine after Salisbury vse set out at length wyth many prayers and goodlye pyctures.* [London]: The assygnes of John Wayland, 1557.

*ESTC* S122886; *STC* 16080. Shelfmark: UIUC IUA02556.

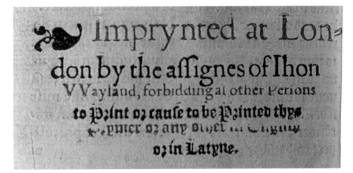

3.2, fol. Dd8ᵛ (detail)

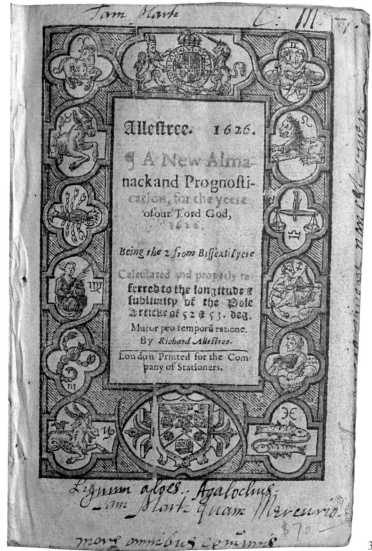

3.3, title page

3.3      Richard Allestree (fl. 1617–43). *A new almanack and prognostication, for the yeere of our Lord God, 1626.* London: Printed for the Company of Stationers, [1626].

ESTC S104378; STC 407.9. Shelfmark: UIUC IUA00187.

The practice of granting rights or monopolies to printers for particular titles or types of books begins in earnest in the early 1540s. Grafton and Whitchurch were granted a joint patent for printing service books in 1541, and this was renewed in 1543 and 1546. They obtained exclusive rights to the official king's primer of 1545. Richard Tottel had the patent for law books, and John Day controlled psalters and almanacs, among other titles. John Wayland received the lucrative monopoly for primers in 1553 when Queen Mary revoked the privilege from William Seres (d. 1578 / 80) and John Day (both Protestants who were imprisoned). It was a right that Wayland guarded with the rather threatening colophon exhibited here: "Imprynted at London by the assignes of Ihon VVayland, forbidding al other Persons to print or cause to be printed thys Prymer or any other in English or in Latyne."

"Assigns" describes any printer with whom the patent holder contracted to do the work. Thus, the holder of a royal patent for printing no longer needed to be a printer himself. Indeed, both Day and Seres worked for Wayland as assigns and Wayland probably never printed a primer himself. Printing rights were sold, shifted, and stolen. Although Queen Mary established the Stationers' Company in 1557 as a regulating body, inequities remained as printers jostled for work. Beginning printers and printers without luck or the necessary influence to gain a patent suffered under such a system. Ostensibly in an effort to rectify the situation, James I, in 1603, revoked the royal patents for some of the most valuable stock, such as primers, psalters, almanacs, and certain schoolbooks. He assigned control over this so-called English Stock "to the whole Companie of Stacioners for the benefit of the poore of the same."[2] In reality, James merely nullified the patents granted under Elizabeth and resold them at great profit to the Stationers' Company, which thereafter controlled the monopolies, doling out print jobs without substantially bettering the circumstances of poorer printers.

The *Almanac* of Richard Allestree, like all almanacs, became part of the English Stock. This example from 1626 gives the lie to the view that the anonymous printers of the Stationers' Company's stock were hacks. On the contrary, this little book is well printed in red and black, with an attractive woodcut border showing the signs of the zodiac. An owner of the almanac has used it, as we might use our calendars, as a place for jotting down "commonplaces," little phrases he or she might want to remember, such as "mors omnibus communis" ("death comes to all") or a note about the aloe plant; other notes in the same hand appear on the back of the title page and the last leaf.

---

Literature: Arber [1875–94] 1950, 1:111; Blagden 1960; Clair 1965, 132–33; Clegg 2001, 39–50; *ODNB* ("Wayland, John" by Elizabeth Evenden).

## 3.4    John Foxe (1516/17–1587). *Actes and monuments.* London: John Day, 20 March 1563.

*ESTC* S122006; *STC* 11222. Shelfmark: UIUC IUQ03509.

The first edition of John Foxe's influential *Acts and Monuments*, or *The Book of Martyrs*, as it is more commonly called, prints an English translation of Cuthbert Tunstall's 1526 order calling for the destruction of all copies of William Tyndale's translation of the New Testament. Tunstall was the bishop of London and a staunch opponent of the Reformation—until nudged the other way by Henry VIII's new policies in the 1530s. Appended to the order is a list of other forbidden books. Interestingly, Tunstall explicitly granted his friend Thomas More special permission to read many of these heretical books in order to refute them—a task More took up with gusto. The list includes many titles by the leading reformers, including Tyndale, Luther, Melanchthon, Zwingli, and Oecolampadius. There is

3.4, p. 449

evidence that Tunstall's order hampered the importation of such books from the Continent and checked any plans for printing the texts in England. Nonetheless, printers occasionally ran afoul of the authorities, as when Wynkyn de Worde published John Ryckes *Ymage of Love* in 1525 only to be forced by Tunstall to recall all copies at the printer's expense. Thomas Berthelet appeared before the authorities in 1526, not because his publications

3.4, 1570 edition
of Foxe's *Book of
Martyrs,* p. 2151

were seditious or heretical, but because he failed to receive an official imprimatur before
printing them. Other printers and distributors of books suffered worse fates for ignoring
censorship guidelines, including imprisonment, fines, mutilation, and, rarely, even execution. In *The Book of Martyrs,* Foxe recounts several of the more severe cases under both
Henry VIII and Mary. For example, according to Foxe, the reformer Thomas Hitton was
executed in 1530 for distributing William Tyndale's New Testament, and the publisher of
the Matthew Bible (item 4.14), John Rogers, died at the stake in 1555, the first martyr of
Queen Mary's reign. Books also went to the pyre, as the image of the woodcut from the
second edition of 1570 edition shows (p. 2151).

Clearly, Henry's goal in the 1520s was to prevent the Reformation from spreading
to England. In his *Assertio septem sacramentorum aduersus Martin Luther,* written in 1521,
Henry attacked Luther as one who "so undervalues customs, doctrine, manners, laws,
decrees and faith of the church (yea, the whole church itself) that he almost denies there
is any such thing as a church, except perhaps such a one as himself makes up of two or
three heretics, of whom himself is chief."[3] For this support of orthodoxy, Henry received
the title Defender of the Faith from Pope Leo X, a title he continued to use even after he
had introduced a church with "himself as chief" and his own variety of reform. It remains
an official title of the English monarch.

Literature: King 2006; O'Donovan 1908.

3.5    Stephen Gardiner (c. 1495 – 1555). *De vera obediencia . . .
nowe translated into English and printed by Michal Wood.*
From Roane [London?]: [John Day], 26 October 1553.
*ESTC* S117128; *STC* 11586. Shelfmark: UIUC IUB00173.

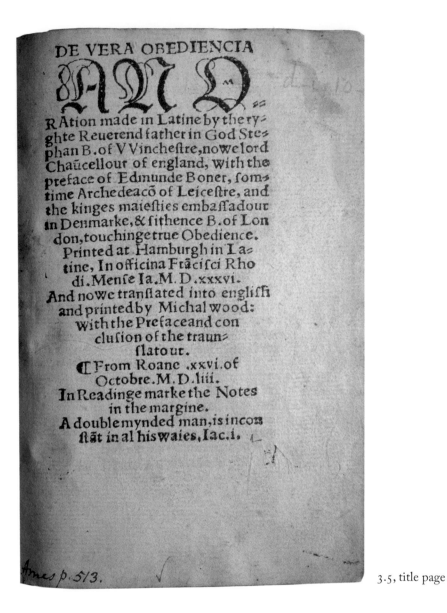

DE VERA OBEDIENCIA

ORAtion made in Latine by the ryghte Reuerend father in God Stephan B. of VVincheſtre, nowe lord Chaūcellour of england, with the preface of Edmunde Boner, ſomtime Archedeacō of Leiceſtre, and the kinges maieſties embaſſadour in Denmarke, & ſithence B. of London, touchinge true Obedience. Printed at Hamburgh in Latine, In officina Frãciſci Rhodi. Menſe Ia. M. D. xxxvi. And nowe tranſlated into engliſh and printed by Michal wood: with the Preface and concluſion of the traunſlatour. ¶ From Roane .xxvi. of Octobre. M. D. liii. In Readinge marke the Notes in the margine. A double mynded man, is incōſtāt in al his waies, Iac.i.

3.5, title page

3.6    William Allen (1532–94). *A trve sincere and modest defence of English Catholiqves that svffer for their faith both at home and abrode: against a false, seditious and slaunderous libel intituled; The execvtion of ivstice in England. VVherein is declared, hovv uniustlie the Protestants doe charge Catholiques vvith treason.* [Rouen: Fr. Parsons' Press, 1584.]

*ESTC* S100110; *STC* 373. Shelfmark: UIUC Baldwin 2831.

These two books, published under Queen Mary and Queen Elizabeth, respectively, illustrate the politically and religiously charged nature of printing and control of the press in Tudor England.

The first work conceals its origins under false names for the translator, printer, and place of publication. The men behind the book are John Bale and John Day. Bale was bishop of Ossory under Henry VIII and a Reformation polemicist and playwright whose biting satire got him into trouble. Day enjoyed great success as a printer of almanacs and primers until his star fell under Queen Mary because of his Protestant leanings. The object of this clever polemic is Stephen Gardiner (c. 1495–1555), Mary's bishop of Winchester in the year this book was published (1553), though formerly a defender of Henry VIII's supremacy. Seeking to discredit Gardiner as a hypocrite and to embarrass Mary, Bale translated Gardiner's 1535 *De vera obedientia*, in which he defends the Henrician settlement, validating both the divorce and the royal supremacy. Bale describes Gardiner and others like him as

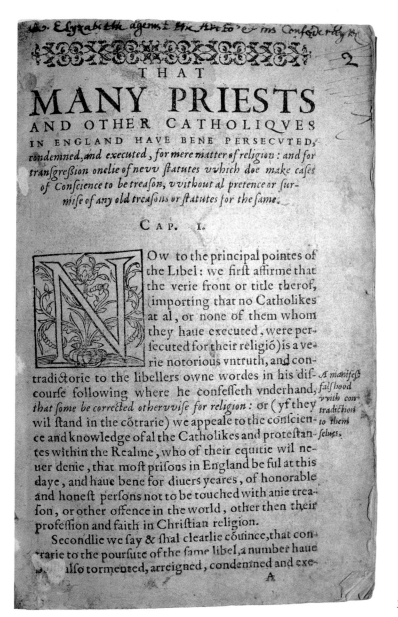

3.6, fol. A1ʳ

hypocrites, "like wethercockes, ersy vercy, as the wind bloweth," who have now "set vppe their father Antichriste of Romes Religion in this Realme agayne" (A3ᵛ). Obviously, such a work could not pass a censor, nor appear in the Stationers' Company registry; therefore it was printed surreptitiously and with a false place of publication.

The tables were turned with Queen Elizabeth, who repressed and exiled Catholics as eagerly as her half sister had persecuted Protestants. The book by William Allen was printed in France and smuggled back to English readers. Allen fled England in 1565 and later established the College of Douai, a school in Flanders for training English Catholics. Despite the sincere and modest tone of the book's title, Allen was a polemical apologist and a daring Catholic activist. He recruited young men for the priesthood and dangerous missions back to England ("storm troopers for counter-reformation," as Eamon Duffy has called them) and he attacked Elizabeth's government in his writings. He also oversaw Gregory Martin's translation of the Bible into English (item 4.16) as part of his evangelical efforts in England. In *A True, Sincere and Modest Defence,* Allen glorifies the martyrdom of Edmund Campion and his companions, killed, he says for their beliefs, not for treasonous activities as Elizabeth claimed. He argues that his priests have no political intentions and that the Catholics of England want only to be able to practice their faith in peace. His stance shifted (or his earlier disingenuousness became clear) four years later, when he rallied English Catholics to depose Elizabeth in his *Admonition to the Nobility and the People of England.*

Literature: *ODNB* ("Bale, John" by John N. King, and "Allen, William" by Eamon Duffy).

3·7    *Iniunctions giuen bye the Queene Maiestie. Anno Dom. 1559. The first yeere of the raigne of our soueraign Lady Queene Elizabeth.* [London: Printed by assignment of Robert Barker, 1600.]

*ESTC* S121266; *STC* 10110. Shelfmark: UIUC IUA02844.

Queen Elizabeth issued the first royal injunction to the Stationers' Company in 1559 "because there is grete abuse in the printers of bokes." According to this ruling, every book had to be reviewed and licensed by the archbishop of Canterbury, the archbishop of York, or the bishop of London. The injunction also gave the Stationers' Company the responsibility—and authority—to inspect and control all print shops. Throughout her reign (in 1566, 1569, 1570, 1571, 1573, 1586, 1588, and 1599, for example), Elizabeth found it necessary to reiterate rules of censorship and to impose restrictions on printers. Nonetheless, enforcement was uneven. Although there are records of printers being fined for printing without license, many books continued to be produced without them, registered at the Stationers' Company, but not licensed by one of the required authorities. In the year immediately following the Injunction of 1559, for example, only three of the ninety-one books in the Stationers' Register were authorized. When a book, printer, or author offended the Crown or annoyed others in power, however, these laws of censorship were enforced rigorously.

Literature: Clegg 1997b; Fox 1947, 100; Siebert 1952, 56–57.

## 22

## Iniunctions.

oz such like Song, to the pzaise of almightie God in the best sozt of melodie and Musicke that may bee conueniently deuised, hauing respect that the sentence of the Hinne may be vnderstanded and perceiued.

<sub>50</sub>
**Against slanderous and infamous wozdes.** Item, because in all alterations, and specially in Rites and Ceremonies, there happeneth discozdes among the people, and thereupon staunderous wozds and raylings, whereby charitie the knot of all Christian societie is losed: the Queens Maiestie being most desirous of all other earthly thinges, that her people shoulde liue in charitie both towards GOD and man, and therein abound in good wozkes, willeth, and straightlye commaundeth all maner her subiects, to fozbeare all vaine and contentious disputacions in matters of Religion, and not to vse in despight oz rebuke of any person, these conuitious wozds, Papist oz papisticall hererike, schismatike, oz sacramentary, oz any such like wozds of reproach. But if any maner of person shall deserue the accusation of any such, that first he be charitably admonished thereof, and if that shall not amende him, then to denounce the offender to the Ozdinarie, oz to some higher power, hauing authozitie to cozrect the same.

<sub>51</sub>
**Against heretical and seditious bookes.** Item, because there is a great abuse in the Printers of Bookes, which foz couetousnesse cheefly, regard not what they pzint, so they may haue gaine, whereby ariseth great disozder by publication of vnfruitfull, vaine, and infamous bookes,

## Iniunctions.

bookes and papers, the Queenes maiestie straitly chargeth and commaundeth, that no manner of person shal pzint any maner of booke oz paper, of what sozt, nature, oz in what language soeuer it bee, except the same bee first lycenced by her Maiestie, by expzesse woozdes in wziting, oz by six of her pziuie counsel: oz be perused and licenced by the Archbishops of Canterburie and Pozke, the Bishop of London, the Chauncellozs of both Vniuersities, the Bishop being Ozdinarie, and the Archdeacon also of the place where any such shalbe pzinted, oz by two of them, whereof the Ozdinary of the place to be alwaies one. And that the names of such as shall allow the same, to bee added in the end of euerie such woozke, foz a testimonie of the allowaunce thereof. And bycause many Pamphlets, Playes, and Ballads, be oftentimes Pzinted, wherein regarde woulde bee had, that nothing therein should be either hereticall, seditious, oz vnseemly foz Christian eares: Her Maiestie lykewise commaundeth, that no maner of person shall enterpzise to Pzint any such except the same bee to him licenced by such her Maiesties Commissioners, oz thzee of them, as be appointed in the Citie of London, to heare and determine diuers causes Ecclesiasticall, tending to the execution of certaine statutes, made the last Parliament, foz vnifozmitie of ozder in Religion. And if any shall sell oz vtter any maner of bookes oz papers, beeing not licenced as is abouesaide: that the same partie shall be punished by ozder of the said Commissioners, as to the qualitie of the

D fault

## 23

3.7, fol. C4ᵛ–D1ʳ

3.8  William Shakespeare (1564–1616). *The tragedie of King Richard the Second. As it hath been publikely acted by the Right Honourable the Lord Chamberlaine his seruants.* London: W. W. [William White] for Mathew Law, 1608.

*ESTC* S111139; Greg 142(d*); *STC* 22310. Shelfmark: Yale Elizabethan Club, EC 178.

This is the fourth quarto edition of *Richard II* but the first to contain the abdication scene (IV.i.154–318) shown here. Since the play deals with the deposition of a reigning English monarch, it was politically sensitive. Perhaps with this play in mind, Queen Elizabeth remarked to William Lambarde, historian and archivist of the Tower of London, "I am Richard II, know ye not that?"[4] Because of her uneasiness, the abdication scene was omitted in all the quarto editions published during her lifetime — the first quarto of 1597 and the second and third quartos of 1598. When the Earl of Essex led a rebellion against Elizabeth

God saue King *Harry*, vnkingd *Richard* sayes,
And send him many yeeres of Sun-shine dayes.
What more remaines?
  *North.* No more,but that you read
These accusations, and these greeuous crimes,
Committed by your person,and your followers,
Against the State and profit of this Land;
That by confessing them,the soules of men
May deeme that you are worthily depofde.
  *Rich.* Must I doe so? and must I rauell out
My weaud vp Folly,gentle *Northumberland*?
If thy offences were vpon record,
Would it not shame thee in so faire a troope,
To read a lecture of them,if thou wouldst,
There shouldst thou finde one haynous article,
Contayning the deposing of a King,
And cracking the strong warrant of an Oath,
Markt with a blot,damd in the booke of heauen:
Nay of you that stand and looke vpon,
Whilst that my wretchednesse doth bate my selfe;
Though some of you (with *Pilat*) wash your hands,
Shewing an outward pittie, yet you *Pilates*,
Haue heere deliuer me to my sowre Crosse,
And water can not wash away your sinne.
  *North.* My Lord dispatch,read ore these Articles.
  *Rich.* Mine eyes are full of teares,I cannot see;
And yet salt water blindes them not so much,
But they can see a sort of Traytors heere:
Nay, if I turne mine eyes vpon my selfe,
I find my selfe a Traytor with the rest;
For I haue giuen heere my soules consent
To vndecke the pompous body of a King;
Made Glory base,and Soueraigntie a slaue;
Proud Maiestie a subiect,State a peasant.
  *North.* My Lord.
  *Rich.* No Lord of thine,thou haught insulting man,
Nor no mans Lord; I haue no name,no title,

No

No not that name was giuen me at the Font,
But tis vsurpt; alacke the heauie day
That I haue worne so many Winters out,
And know not now,what name to call my selfe.
O that I were a mockerie King of Snow,
Standing before the sunne of *Bullingbrooke*,
To melt my selfe away in water drops.
Good King,great King; and yet not greatly good:
And if my name be starling, yet in England
Let it commaund a mirour hether strayte
That it may shew me what a face I haue,
Since it is banckrout of his Maiestie.
  *Bull.* Goe some of you and fetch a Looking-glasse.
  *North.* Read ore this paper while the Glasse doth come.
  *Rich.* Feind,thou torments me ere I come to Hell.
  *Bull.* Vrge it no more my Lord Northumberland.
  *North.* The Commons will not then be satisfied,
  *Rich.* They shall be satisfied,Ile read enough,
When I doe see the very Booke indeed,
Where all my sinnes are writ,and that's my selfe.
Giue me the Glasse : no deeper wrinckles yet?
Hath Sorrow stroke so many blowes vpon this
Face of mine,and made no deeper woundes?
Oh flattering Glasse, like to my followers in prosperitie!
Was this the face that euery day vnder his
Houshould roofe did keepe ten thousand men?
Was this the face that faast so many follies,
And was at last outfaast by *Bullingbrooke*?
A brittle Glorie shineth in this face,
As brittle as the Glorie is the face,
For there it is crackt in a hundred shiuers:
Marke silent King the morall of this sport,
How soone my sorrow hath destroyde my face.
  *Bull.* The shadow of your sorrow hath destroyd
The shadow of your face.
  *Rich.* Say that againe : the shadow of my sorrow;
Ha lets see : tis very true, my griefe

H 3.                                   Lies

3.8, fol. H2ᵛ–H3ʳ

in February 1601, his supporters paid the Lord Chamberlain's Men to perform the play during the afternoon preceding the rebellion (presumably to muster public support for the uprising). At Essex's subsequent trial, this performance of *Richard II* was cited as evidence for his guilt. When the play is reprinted in the First Folio of 1623, a somewhat improved version of the abdication scene appears.

A license to print the play—without the offending scene—appears in the Stationers' Register on 29 August 1597 under the name of the bookseller Andrew Wise. In 1603, Wise transferred copyright to Mathew Law, who apparently saw no need to seek another license when he had his assign William White print the fourth quarto in 1608 with the deposition scene restored. Law made no secret of the addition, however, using it as a selling point on some copies of the quarto, where the title page includes the advertisement: "With new additions of the Parliament Sceane, and the deposing of King Richard."

Literature: Arber [1875–94] 1950, 3:23; Bergeron 1974; Chambers 1930, 2:327; Clare 1990b; Clegg 1997a.

**3.9**  Thomas Nashe (1567–1601). *Nashes Lenten stuffe, containing, the description and first procreation and increase of the towne of Great Yarmouth in Norffolke: With a new play neuer played before, of the praise of the red herring.* London: [Thomas Judson and Valentine Simmes] for N. L. [Nicholas Ling] and C. B. [Cuthbert Burby], 1599.

*ESTC* S113098; *STC* 18370. Shelfmark: UIUC IUB00190.

"By my troth, thou sayst true; for since the little wit that fools have was silenced, the little foolery that wise men have makes a great show." In this quip from *As You Like It* (I.ii.84–86), Shakespeare may be referring to the recent "Bishops' Ban" (1 June 1599), an order that made it illegal to print any work containing satire: "That noe Satyres or Epigramms be printed hereafter. That noe English historyes bee printed excepte they bee allowed by somme of her maiesties privie Counsell. That noe playes bee printed excepte they bee allowed by such as have auctoritie. That all Nasshes bookes and Doctor Harveyes bookes be taken wheresouer they maye be found and that none of theire bookes bee euer printed hereafter."[5]

The ban singled out books by Thomas Nashe and Gabriel Harvey (items 5.4 and 1.8) as well as nine titles by other authors for burning. The order, issued by John Whitgift

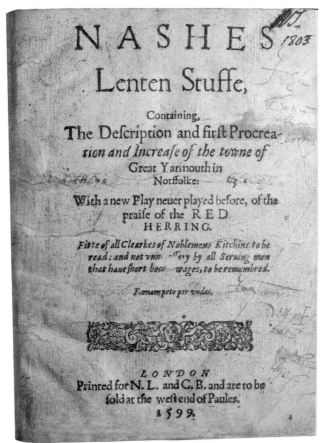

3.9,
title page

(1530 / 31 – 1604), archbishop of Canterbury, and Richard Bancroft (1544 – 1610), bishop of London, represents the last major attempt at censorship during Elizabeth's reign. Some have argued that the Bishops' Ban targeted sexually charged works and satires,[6] while others have seen it as a political move to remind the English that their government was monitoring popular literature.[7]

This work by Thomas Nashe, then, should have been turned over to the authorities and burned, but somehow this copy escaped. *Lenten Stuff* contains a tongue-in-cheek description of the town of Yarmouth with "The Praise of the Red Herring," the town's chief product. In it Nashe refers to another run-in with the censors, when the Privy Council condemned his *Isle of Dogs,* a satirical play he cowrote with Ben Jonson in 1597. Three of its actors (including Jonson) were imprisoned. "The straunge turning of the *Ile of Dogs* from a commedie to a tragedie two summers past . . . had well neere confounded mee," Nashe admits. Nashe apparently fled London but had a difficult time of it. Now, however, he plunges "aboue water once againe," and threatens the censors with further satire: "let them looke to it, for I will put them in bryne, or a piteous pickle euery one" (B1[r]). And in his *To his Readers, hee cares not what they be,* he promises, "I will make you laugh your hearts out," after excusing himself with a reference to his work with printers (he worked as a corrector), "I am cald away to correct the faults of the presse, that escaped in my absence from the Printing-house" (A4[v]).

Fools could not be silenced, nor satire contained, of course, and we find another work by Nashe published in late 1600 (item 5.4), just before his death. In an elegy, Ben Jonson feared that Nashe's death — not any governmental legislation — would bring about "a generall dearthe of witt throughout this land."[8]

---

Literature: Boose 1994; Clegg 1997b, 213 – 16; McCabe 1981; *ODNB* ("Nashe, Thomas" by Charles Nicholl); Patterson 1984.

### 3.10  George Chapman (1559? – 1634), Ben Jonson (1572 – 1637), and John Marston (c. 1576 – 1634). *Eastward Hoe. As it was playd in the Black-friers. By the Children of her Maiesties Reuels.* London: [George Eld] for William Aspley, 1605.

*ESTC* s108676; Greg 217(b); *STC* 4972. Shelfmark: UIUC IUA02701.

Under James I, censorship and press regulation continued, targeting both religious and political writings. Plays were more popular than ever, and also more at risk of censorship. George Chapman, Ben Jonson, and John Marston got off to a bad start with the new king in their play *Eastward Ho.* The play satirized James and his fellow Scots, raising an eyebrow at the large number of newly minted knights following in James's wake and even lampooning Scottish accents (I.ii.50, 98; II.iiii.83; III.iii.40 – 47; IV.i.179). After a complaint by Sir James Murray, who happened to be one of the new knights, Jonson and Chapman were imprisoned and threatened with having their ears and noses cut. Marston seems to have escaped imprisonment. Whether the performance or the publication of the play pre-

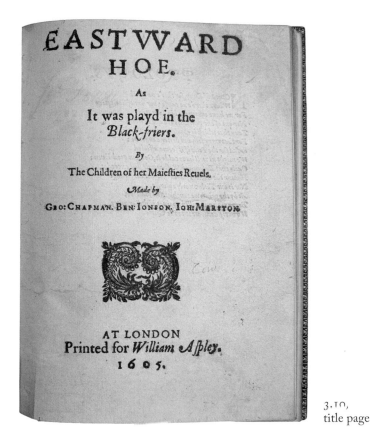

3.10,
title page

cipitated the arrests is a matter of scholarly debate,[9] but it is a fact that one passage about Scots printed in the first issue of the first quarto (III.iii.40–47) was deleted in subsequent printings. (Other Scottish jokes were left standing.) One wonders if there also might be a slight jab at a rival playwright in the naming of a lowly footman Hamlet (III.ii.5–10), especially since the play of that title was enjoying great success at the time (item 5.10).

There were three editions (four issues) in the first year, 1605, all printed by George Eld for William Aspley. The University of Illinois copy is the second edition.

Literature: Brettle 1928; Chambers [1923] 1974, 3:254–56; Greg 1928.

3.11    Thomas Middleton (d. 1627). *A game at chæss. As it was acted nine dayes to gether at the Globe on the Banks-side.* [London: s.n., 1625.]

*ESTC* S112572; Greg 412(a); *STC* 17882. Shelfmark: UIUC IUB00191.

The King's Men scored a great success with *A Game at Chess*, performed to record crowds for nine days in August 1624, before its notoriety resulted in the closing of the Globe. In this anti-Spanish play, the Spanish ambassador Gondomar, the archbishop of Spalato, and Prince Charles and James I are parodied under the clever conceit of a game of chess. The

3.11, engraved title page

White Knight (Charles) foils the plans of the Black House (Spain), but the White King (James) does not escape criticism for being too easily manipulated. The actors managed the impersonations so skillfully that the play became the talk of London. For precisely the same reason, the Spanish ambassador demanded that the players be punished. In order to avoid further scandal or political incident, James duly summoned the author and players before the Privy Council. Since the Master of the Revels had approved their playbook, they were not fined, but further performance of the play—or any play—was forbidden, and the Globe was shuttered until 27 August on the charge of portraying a living monarch on the stage. At the insistence of the Spanish ambassador, Don Carlos de Coloma,

3.11, seventeenth-century note on flyleaf

a warrant was issued for Middleton's arrest, and there is evidence that he may have been imprisoned briefly.[10]

The printing history of *A Game at Chess* is interesting. Prohibited from performing a play that people were still clamoring to see, Middleton produced several manuscripts of the play and negotiated with three different printers to issue the play to capitalize on its success. It was printed four times in 1625, all unlicensed and without imprint information, though we know the printers to have been Augustine Matthews, Edward Allde, and Nicholas Oakes.

The ambitious engraved title page of the first two quartos is as daring as the text itself, depicting scenes from the play with the characters carefully drawn to the likenesses of the political personages parodied.

The University of Illinois copy of the first quarto contains a contemporary note that provides evidence for the popularity of the play and corroborates the claim that Middleton spent time in prison. Moreover, the note, written in an early seventeenth-century hand on the flyleaf, offers new information about the profitability of the play, apparently gleaned from the actors themselves: "After nine dayes wherein I have heard some of the Actors say ye tooke fifteen hundred pounds: the Spanish faction being then prevalent got it suppressed [and] ye Author Maisster Thos. Middleton committed to prison where he lay for some time at last got out upon his petition to King James."[11]

Literature: Clare 1990a, 190–99; Clegg 2001, 187–89; Howard-Hill 1991, 109–10; J. Moore 1935, 761–62.

3.12    *A Decree of Starre-Chamber concerning printing. Made the eleuenth day of July last past. 1637.* London: Robert Barker, printer to the Kings most Excellent Maiestie, and by the assignes of John Bill, 1637.

*ESTC* S795; *STC* 7757.2. Shelfmark UIUC 343.420998 G798d.

fonment, and fuch other punifh-ment, as by this Court, or the faid high Commifsion Court refpectiuely, as the feuerall Caufes fhall require, fhall bee thought fit.

XIV. *Item*, That no Ioyner, or Carpenter, or other perfon, fhall make any printing-Preffe, no Smith fhall forge any Iron-worke for a printing-Preffe, and no Founder fhall caft any Let-ters for any perfon or perfons whatfoeuer, neither fhall any perfon or perfons bring, or caufe to be brought in from any parts beyond the Seas, any Letters Founded

Founded or Caft, nor buy any fuch Letters for Printing ; Vn-leffe he or they refpectiuely fhall firft acquaint the faid Mafter and VVardens, or fome of them, for whom the fame Preffe, Iron-works, or Letters, are to be made, forged, or caft, vpon paine of fuch fine and punifhment, as this Court, or the high Commifsi-on Court refpectiuely, as the fe-uerall caufes fhall require, fhall thinke fit.

XV. *Item*, The Court doth declare, that as formerly, fo now, there fhall be but Twentie Ma-fter Printers allowed to haue the
E 2 vfe

3.12, fol. E1$^v$–E3$^r$

3.13    *An order of the Lords and Commons assembled in Parliament. For the regulating of printing, and for suppressing the great late abuses and frequent disorders in printing many false, scanda-lous, seditious, libellous and unlicensed pamphlets, to the great defamation of religion and Government: Also, authorizing the masters and wardens of the Company of Stationers to make diligent search, seize and carry away all such books as they shall finde printed, or reprinted by any man having no lawfull interest in them, being entred into the hall book to any other man as his proper Copies.* London: Printed for I. Wright, 16 June 1643.

*ESTC* R2144; Wing E-1711. Shelfmark: UIUC 343.420998 En3420 1643.

Among scores of efforts to restrict the freedom of the press in Tudor and Stuart England, the Star Chamber decree of 1637 stands out as legislation with a particularly deleterious effect on freedom of the press in England. It required authors and printers to submit two copies of their manuscripts to ecclesiastical and secular licensing authorities for approval prior to publication and mandated that names of the author, printer, and licenser appear on every imprint. Prepublication censorship was nothing new in English politics, but other more stringent stipulations set this decree apart from earlier restrictive legislation. It required a reapplication for licensing for any subsequent editions, and, most drastically, it reduced the number of master printers to twenty, wreaking havoc in the Stationers' Company as its members jockeyed and petitioned for the coveted status of master printer. Moreover, a £300 deposit was required from every master printer "as a surety not to print or suffer to be printed anything not licensed."

The 1637 decree was short-lived, however, and when the Star Chamber disbanded in 1641, a brief period of relative freedom of the press ensued. Polemical authors found more outlets for their work, and unlicensed pamphlets and books rolled off the presses during the tumultuous early years of the English civil wars.

Freedom of the press was not necessarily the goal of the Stationers' Company, which had seen its influence (and patents) wane after 1641. In June 1643, its complaints about "rogue" printers to the Long Parliament finally resulted in the issuing of a declaration to

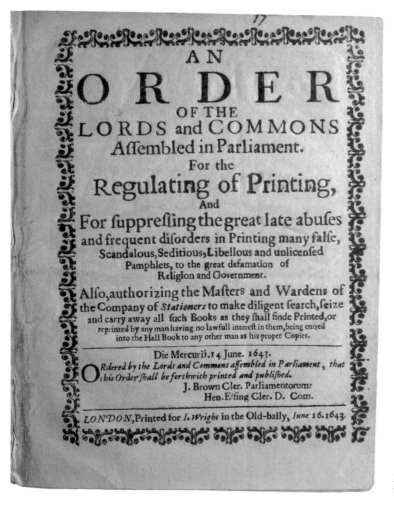

3.13, title page

suppress the "great late abuses and frequent disorders in printing." The order reinstates prepublication censorship and greatly magnifies the authority of the Stationers' Company, declaring that no "Book, Pamphlet, paper, nor part of any such Book, Pamphlet, or paper, shall from henceforth be printed, bound, stitched or put to sale by any person or persons whatsoever, unless the same be first approved of and licensed under the hands of such person or persons as both, or either of the said Houses shall appoint for the licensing of the same, and entred in the Register Book of the Company of Stationers, according to Ancient custom, and the Printer therof to put his name therto" (A3$^r$).

It was in protest against this Order of 1643 that John Milton wrote his *Areopagitica* in 1644.

Literature: Greg 1944; Siebert 1952, 156–78.

3.14    John Milton (1608–74). *Areopagitica, A speech of Mr. John Milton for the liberty of vnlicenc'd printing to the Parliament of England.* London: [s.n.], 1644. With manuscript warrant issued to John Milton on 25 June 1650.

*ESTC* R210022; Wing M-2092. Shelfmark: UIUC 821 M64 N6.

John Milton, arguably the most significant English poet of the seventeenth century, was also a republican politician, a religious renegade, and a vocal polemicist on the issues of his day. He flouted the Star Chamber decree of 1637 when he published his tracts on divorce without license. His *Areopagitica* also appeared without permit or notice of publisher as required by the law. It claims to be a "speech" before Parliament in reaction to the Order of 1643 (item 3.13), whereas, in fact, it was never delivered. The title refers to the highest judicial court of Athens, located on the Areopagus ("hill of Ares"). Milton is comparing his (supposed) parliamentary address to an ancient Athenian's oration before the court of Areopagus. However, it had no impact whatsoever on the control of the press during Milton's lifetime or for generations afterward. Eventually, Milton's *Areopagitica* found an audience, and its argument that without the liberty of the press there can be no freedom of thought has had an enormous impact on modern society. Considering the history of English censorship up through Milton's era, it is striking (or perhaps inevitable?) that so influential a text on free speech came from this corner of the world.

The *Areopagitica* presents the history of censorship from antiquity to Milton's day in an eloquent and compelling narrative. Freedom of speech and freedom of the press are presented as inalienable rights of humankind. Without free exchange of ideas, Milton claims that moral, intellectual, and societal development is impossible. From this book comes one of the most powerful statements on the freedom of the press ever written: "as good almost kill a Man as kill a good Book; who kills a Man kills a reasonable creature, God's Image; but hee who destroys a good Book, kills reason it selfe" (4). Ironically, six years later, in 1650, Milton was issued a warrant to search the rooms of William Prynne, the Puritan writer with whom he had often squabbled in print. The warrant authorizes Milton to seize "all writings by him written . . . of dangerous nature against the

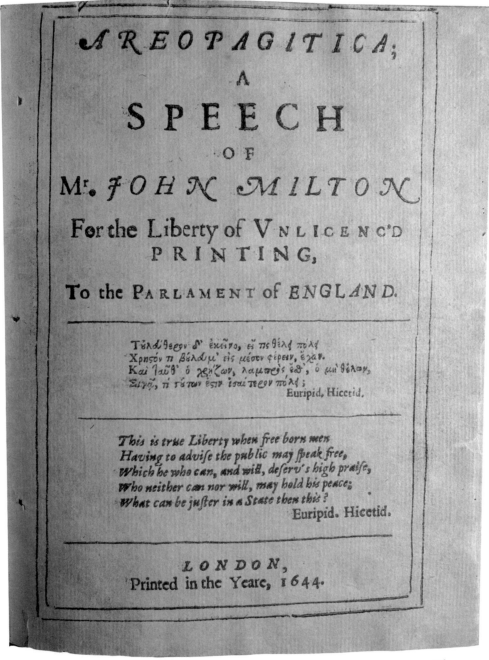

# AREOPAGITICA;

A

# SPEECH

OF

# Mr. JOHN MILTON

For the Liberty of VNLICENC'D
PRINTING,

To the PARLAMENT of ENGLAND.

Τὑλδ'θερον δ' ἐκεῖνο, εἴ τις θέλᾳ πόλᾳ
Χρησόν τι βέλδμ' εἰς μέσον φέρειν, ἔχᾱ.
Καὶ ταῦθ' ὁ χρήζων, λαμπρός ἐσθ', ὁ μὴ θέλων,
Σιγᾷ, τί τὐτων ἐσιν ἰσαίτερον πόλᾳ;

Euripid, Hicetid.

This is true Liberty when free born men
Having to advise the public may speak free,
Which he who can, and will, deserv's high praise,
Who neither can nor will, may hold his peace;
What can be juster in a State then this?

Euripid. Hicetid.

LONDON,
Printed in the Yeare, 1644.

3.14, title page

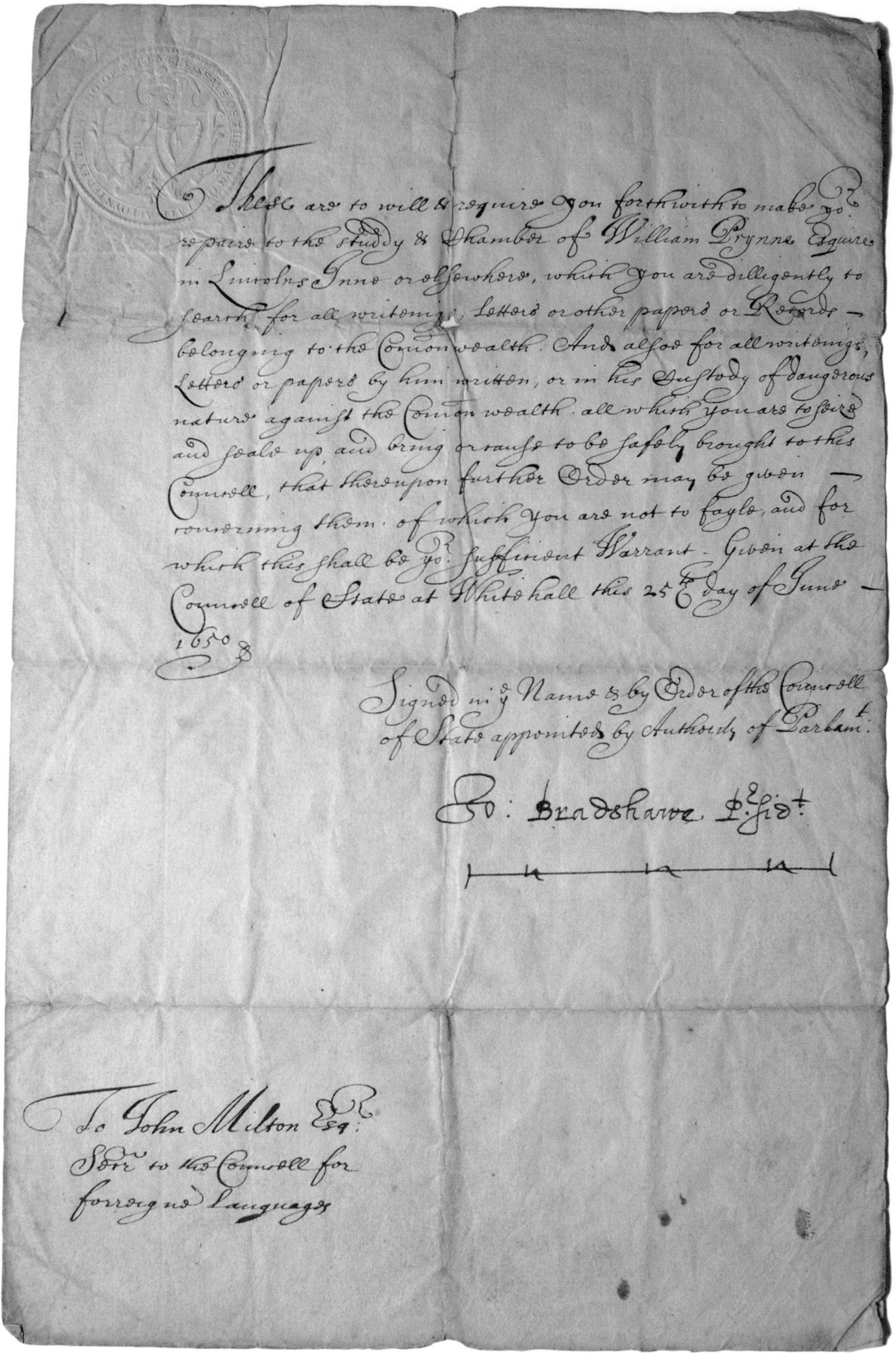

These are to will & require you forthwith to make yo^r
repaire to the studdy & Chamber of William Prynne Esquire
in Lincolns Inne or elsewhere, which you are dilligently to
search for all writeings, letters or other papers or Records —
belonging to the Comonwealth. And alsoe for all writeings,
letters or papers by him written, or in his Custody of dangerous
nature against the Comon wealth. all which you are to seize
and seale up, and bring or cause to be safely brought to this
Councell, that thereupon further Order may be given —
concerning them. of which you are not to fayle, and for
which this shall be yo^r sufficient Warrant — Given at the
Councell of State at Whitehall this 25^th day of June —
1650

Signed in y^e Name & by Order of the Councell
of State appointed by Authoritye of Parliam^t.

Jo: Bradshawe P^te^side^t.

To John Milton Esq^r:
Sec^r to the Councell for
forraigne Languages

Warrant issued to John Milton, 1650

Commonwealth," and Prynne was, in fact, arrested five days after this warrant was issued and sentenced to three years in prison for expressing views contrary to those held by Milton and the Commonwealth.

Literature: D. Loewenstein 1988; *ODNB* ("Milton, John" by Gordon Campbell); Osgood 1945.

3.15     *A Proclamation for calling in, and suppressing of two books written by John Milton; the one intituled . . . Angli pro populo Anglicano Defensio, contra Claudii Anonymi aliàs Salmasii, Defensionem Regiam; and the other in answer to a book intituled, The Pourtraicture of his Sacred Majesty in his Solitude and Sufferings.* London: John Bill and Christopher Barker, Printers to the King's most Excellent Majesty, 1660.

         *ESTC* R13189; Wing C-3322. Shelfmark: UIUC IUZ00005.

Milton was accustomed to both fame and notoriety. As early as 1644, his writings, specifically the divorce tracts, had been condemned. Nonetheless, it must have been difficult for Milton, who authored England's defense of regicide after the beheading of Charles I (*Angli pro populo Anglicano defensio,* 1651), to feel safe after the reinstitution of the monarchy, for he went into hiding in May 1660. This proclamation appeared in June, and copies of the books listed in it were rounded up and burned "by the common hangman" on 27 August 1660. Two days later, however, the Act of Free and General Pardon, Indemnity, and Oblivion made it safe for Milton to emerge from hiding. Despite the amnesty, Milton was arrested in early November 1660 and held until mid-December before being released without charge.

     The proclamation (shown opposite page 83) makes it clear that Milton's concept of freedom of the press was still far from becoming a reality in England.

Literature: Nelson and Daems 2006, 325–27; Nicholson 1912.

# THE
# ANCIENT, FAMOVS
## And Honourable History of
# Amadis de Gaule.

### DISCOVRSING THE ADVENTVRES,
Loues and Fortunes of many Princes, Knights and
Ladies, *as well of* Great Brittaine, *as of many*
other Kingdomes beside, &c.

Written in French by the Lord of *Essars*, *Nicholas de Herberay*,
Ordinarie Commissarie of the Kings Artillerie, and his
Lieutenant thereof, in the Countrie and gouernment
of *Picardie*, &c.

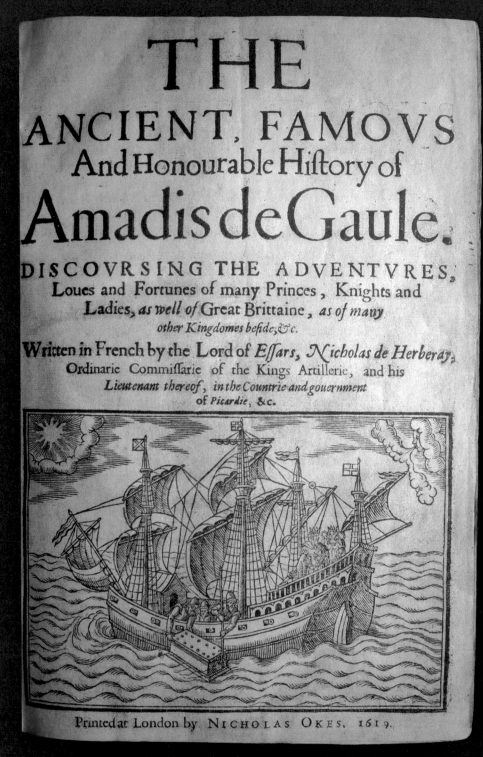

Printed at London by NICHOLAS OKES. 1619.

# 4

# THE PLACE OF
# TRANSLATION IN EARLY
# ENGLISH PRINTING

4.1    Gui de Roye (1345 – 1409). *Thus endeth the doctrinal
       of sapyence the whyche is ryght vtile and prouffytable to
       alle crysten men, whyche is translated out of Frenshe in
       to Englysshe by Wyllyam Caxton.* [Westminster:
       William Caxton, after 7 May 1489.]

       BMC xi, 169; *ESTC* S109174; Goff D-302; *GW* 8625; *ISTC* id00302000;
       *STC* 21431. Shelfmark: UIUC Incunabula Q. 230 R814d 1489.

William Caxton began his literary career not as a printer, but as a translator. In the epilogue to the first book printed in English, *The Recuyell of the Historyes of Troye* (1473 / 74),
he claims that requests for additional copies of his translation induced him to learn the
art of printing in the first place.

    Caxton is credited with over one hundred imprints.[1] About 60 percent of his books
were in English, and Caxton himself translated more than twenty of these.[2] The texts
he chose to translate range from romances to histories to practical treatises to religious
works.

    *The Doctrinal of Sapyence* is a translation of a late fourteenth-century handbook for
priests, the *Manipulus curatorum,* sometimes attributed to Gui de Roye, archbishop of
Sens, and sometimes to Jean Gerson (1363 – 1429), but probably by an anonymous monk
at Cluny. Caxton did not work from the Latin original, but rather from a French version
of the text, thus creating a translation of a translation, a common phenomenon in the
English Renaissance. Intended as a theological and practical guide for parish priests, the

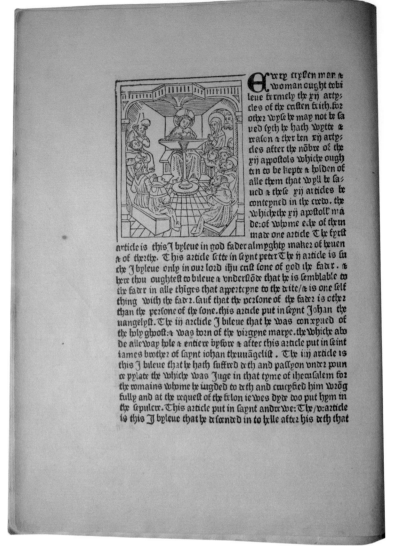

Euery crysten man & woman ought to bi leue fermely the xij artyc les of the crsten faith. for other wyse he may not be sa ued syth he hath wytte & rason & ther ten xij artyc les after the nōbre of the xij apostols whiche ough ten to be kepte & holden of alle them that woll be sa ued & these xij artycles be contepned in the crede. the whiche the xij apostoll ma de: of whome eche of them made one article The fyrst article is this J byleue in god fader almyghty maker of heuen & of therthe. This article sette in saynt peter The ij article is su the J byleue only in our lord ihu crist sone of god the fader. & here thou oughtest to bileue & vnderstōde that he is semblable to the fader in alle thinges that appertepne to the deite/& is one self thing with the fader. sauf that the persone of the fader is other than the persone of the sone. this article put in saynt Johan the euangelyst. The iij article J bileue that he was conceyued of the holy ghost:& was born of the virgyne marye. the whiche abo de alle way hole & entiere byfore & after this article put in seint iames brother of saynt iohan theuuāgelist. The iiij article is this J bileue that he hath suffred deth and passyon vnder poun ce pylate the whiche was Juge in that tyme of theru salem for the romains whome he iugded to deth and crucyfyed him wrōg fully and at the request of the felon iewes dyde doo put hym in the sepulcre. This article put in saynt andrewe: The v. article is this J byleue that he descended in to helle after his deth that

*Doctrinal* treats such topics as "sorceryes and devynacyons," "the synne of envye," and "how the dampned soules complaine in helle" (A2ʳ–A3ʳ). It also includes a syllabus of sorts for the theological education of the laity, beginning with an admonition that "Every crysten man and woman ought to bileve fermely the xii artycles of the cristen faith" (B2ᵛ), by which is meant the Apostles' Creed.

The French version of the *Doctrinal* circulated widely in manuscript and print before Caxton, with ten editions in print before 1487. For the most part, Caxton adheres closely to his source, sometimes even transferring French words directly into English. For example, the French *dommaige* becomes "dommage," for "injury" (C1ʳ).

A hallmark of Caxton's style as a translator is the tendency to offer two or even three synonyms to render one word from the original. In the *Doctrinal,* he uses this multiple translation technique some 328 times.[3] For example, in the first line of the prologue "en-seigner" becomes "lerne and teche" (A1ʳ). In a chapter entitled "How one ought to make amendes," "son dommaige" is not taken over from the French as it was in the passage quoted above, but in this context becomes "his scathe and hurte" (L2ʳ).

The *Doctrinal* is illustrated with two simple woodcuts, both reused from Caxton's 1486 edition of *Speculum vitae Christi*. Early English printers reused, copied, and shared woodcuts with each other. The woodcuts produced in England were often copied from continental images. The simplicity of English book illustration in this period has typically elicited scorn. Hodnett put it rather bluntly when he wrote, "England stumbles on to the book-illustration stage with some of the poorest cuts ever inserted between covers."[4] The image of Jesus among the doctors, with Mary and Joseph in the background (A3ᵛ), is somewhat worn (note the breaks in the border lines) but not unattractive, and it serves its purpose well.

Literature: Blake 1969, 140–42; Blake 1991, 70–73; Crotch [1928] 1971; France 2000, 44–45; Gallagher 1993, 7–46; Hellinga and Trapp 1999, 3:17; Hodnett [1935] 1973, 1–7; Needham 1986; Painter 1976, 170–72.

4.2     Pseudo-Jerome. *Vitas Patrum. The lyff of the holy faders.* [Translation from the French version of the *Vitae sanctorum patrum* by William Caxton.] Westminster: Wynkyn de Worde, 1495 [before 21 August].

BMC xi, 197; *ESTC* S109796; Goff H-213; *ISTC* ih00213000; *STC* 14507. Shelfmark: UIUC Incunabula Q. 922 V83:Ec.

According to the colophon by Wynkyn de Worde, Caxton completed this translation on the day he died: "Thus endyth the moost vertuouse hystorye of the deuoute [and] right renommed lyues of holy faders . . . translated out of Frensshe in to Englysshe by Wyllyam Caxton of Westmynstre late deed, and fynysshed it at the laste daye of his lyff."

When Caxton died in late 1491 or early 1492, Wynkyn de Worde became his successor. De Worde rented his shop; used his fonts, woodcuts, and presses; and even based his own printer's device on Caxton's. In the period between Caxton's death and the appearance of this volume, De Worde printed nine other books, three reprints of earlier works by Caxton, and six new titles, as he began to find his own way as a printer and businessman. The three-year delay in printing Caxton's last translation may have been caused by the preparation of new woodcuts for the work,[5] which were copied from Caxton's source for his translation, the 1487 Lyon edition by Nicholas Philippe and Jean du Pré. There are 8 full-page illustrations and 40 smaller woodcuts that are used repeatedly to create a total of 159 images throughout the book. The woodcuts are simple and of English workmanship; according to Hodnett, they are "second in clumsiness only to the jack-knife embellishments of [Caxton's] *Myrrour of the Worlde*" (item 6.10).[6] There is a certain charm, however, in the conceit of showing Jerome in his study, surrounded by the men and women whose stories he tells in his saints' lives.

The work was commonly called *Vitas patrum* in the Middle Ages and Renaissance—and this is the title given on Wynkyn de Worde's unusual title page, where VITAS

¶ Here foloweth the fyrste parte

4.2, fol. Aa8ᵛ

---

¶ Of the chylde Orphenyn the whyche was made ryche / And begynneth
in latyn   ¶ Audiens. & cetera
Capl'm    C.lxxviii.

SOmetyme in Alexandrye was
say Almoner.the whyche had o
ne only sone/ The fad seenge
his ende to drawe nygh.made his sone
to be called.& sayd unto hym / My chyl
de by cause that I shall dey.I woll ma
ke the well to haue knowlege of alle þ
I am worthe/ ¶ Wryte it for trouthe þ
of all goodes & ryches.I haue but.x.li.
of golde/And therfore chose whether þ
woll be myn heyre.or elles that the bles
sid moder of god be the same/The chil
de had leuer that the Tresoresse & mo
de of Orphanes sholde be his fads hey
re than he hymself.and suffred that al
sholde be yeue for goddis sake/¶The
fad soo decesed.the childe contynuelly

nyghte & daye kept hymself in the chyrche of the blessid moder of god.makyng
to her deuowte prayers & orysons/ Of
the whyche thynge.the holy patryarke
had knowlege /that neuertheles made
coūtenance as he had knowen no thyn
ge/ ¶ Wythin short tyme after he ma
de to be called a Notary.to whom he cō
maūded to take an olde skynne of par
chempn.chenly to wryte a Testament.
for.& in the name of one namyd The
ophente/ And þ he sholde affeme by þ
Testament.that the fad of þ sayd chil
de.& the sayd patryarke were bredery
germany/Chargynge moreouer the say
de Notary to shewe the chylde of the sa
me.shewynge to hym the sayd Testa
ment, for & to the entent he sholde gyue
hym courage & boldnesse to aske of the
sayde patryarke ayde & socours/ The
whiche thyng the sayd Notary dyde in
contynent. but neuertheless the chylde
durste not goo to hym. ¶ Soo sente he
twyes for hym/ And fynably came to
warde hym.toke & kyssed hym sayeng
Thou arte welcome my neuewe . And
made to be knowen that he was of his
kyn/ And whan he was grete he ga
ue hym an hous. and alle thynges þ to
hym were nedefull/And maryed hym
honestly/ ¶ Wherby it apperyth þ god
leuyth neuer those that haue theyr ho
pe in hym/

¶ Of a begyler that borowed thyrty
pounde of golde of the holy patryarke
And begynneth in latyn ¶ Impreten-
mille/Capl'm    C.lxxix.
    v ii

4.2, fol. 151ʳ

PATRUM appears in white on a black ground.[7] Attributed to St. Jerome, the collection of saints' lives was popular in Latin and vernacular translations throughout Europe with fifty-six editions and translations printed before 1501.

The year before his death, Caxton claimed that he had adapted a new technique for translation. In the prologue to *The Book of Eneydos* (printed after 22 June 1490), he explains that some had criticized him for using "over-curyous termes whiche coude not be understande of comyn peple."[8] This probably refers to his tendency to transfer French words basically untranslated into his earlier works. He also notes that his task is made more difficult by the fact that there is no standard form of English and that the language varies from shire to shire.[9] To strike a balance, he says he will "reduce and translate" in a style "not overrude ne [nor] curyous," but "in a meane bytwene bothe." A passage from "Of the Chylde Orphenym" in the *Lives of the Fathers* seems to confirm this method:

> "My chylde by cause that I shall dey, I woll make the[e] well to haue knowlege of alle that I am worthe. Wyte it for trouthe that of all goodes and ryches, I haue but x.li [41 pieces?] of golde. / And therfore chose whether ye woll be myn heyre, or elles, that the blessid moder of god be the same." / The childe had leuer that the Tresoresse and moder of Orphanes shold be his faders heyre than he hymself and suffred that al sholde be geve for goddis sake. The fader soo deceased, the childe contynuelly nyghte and daye kept hymself in the chyrche of the blessid moder of god, makyng to her dovowte prayers and orysons. (151ʳ)

The English style, which reads more like a fairy tale than a saint's life, is rich in words with Old English or Germanic roots ("worthe," "trouthe," "goodes," "wyte," "lever" [liefer]), though French/Latinate words such as "tresoress" and "orysons" create a balance — as Caxton said — "between rude and curious." Although his word choices may have shifted somewhat, he nonetheless retains his word-for-word approach to translating.

The University of Illinois copy is noteworthy for its height, 290 mm (11.5 inches), making it one of the tallest recorded copies. Also curious are the pinholes one finds in the margins of some pages, perhaps indicative of printers' practice of holding the page in place with pins while lowering it onto the type.

---

Literature: Blake 1971; Blake 1973a, 79–80; Hodnett [1935] 1973, 9–10; Painter 1976, 87; Rosenthal 1936, 11.

4.3  Ovid. *Metamorphoses.* Venice: Aldus Manutius, 1502.

Shelfmark: UIUC 871 O8m.a.

4.4  Ovid. *The .xv. Bookes of P. Ouidius Naso, entytuled Metamorphosis, translated oute of Latin into English meeter, by Arthur Golding gentleman, a worke very pleasaunt and delectable.* London: William Seres, [1567].

*ESTC* S110249; *STC* 18956. Shelfmark: UIUC IUB00176.

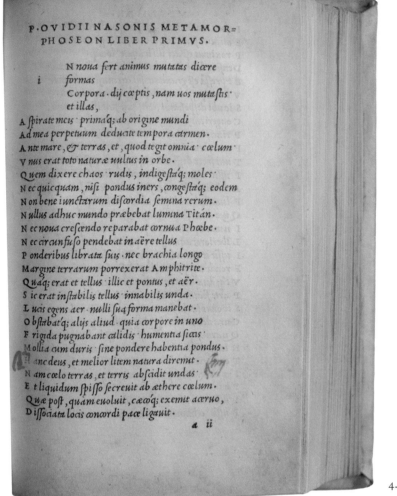

4.3, fol. A2ʳ

Aldus Manutius, one of the most learned and elegant printers of the Renaissance, produced his edition of Ovid's *Metamorphoses* in Venice with his new italic typeface (first used the year before in 1501). If we compare an Aldine imprint with English printing of the same period, the technical and aesthetic disparities are remarkable. By the date of the first English Ovid (1567), however, English printing had advanced considerably, and William Seres, the printer of Golding's Ovid, could produce a respectable page. He used a black-letter typeface for English and roman for classical place names and characters.

Ovid was much admired in medieval and Renaissance schools on the Continent and in England. His *Metamorphoses* plays a significant role in early English literature, attracting such translators and imitators as Geoffrey Chaucer, John Gower, and William Caxton before 1500.[10] The metrical version of 1567 by Arthur Golding (1535 / 36–1606) is the first complete English translation of Ovid's *Metamorphoses*. Ezra Pound dubbed it "the most beautiful book in the English language,"[11] though others disagree, including a University of Illinois Elizabethan scholar and collector, T. W. Baldwin, who forty years ago called it merely "a necessary evil in the background of Shakspere" [*sic*].[12]

Arthur Golding had translated several prose works, including the first complete English version of Caesar's *Gallic Wars*, before he turned to Ovid. He was also a translator of Calvin and other Reformation writers. But it is his Ovid that has earned him a place in literary history. Golding renders Ovid's dactylic hexameter into fourteeners (that is, a line in tetrameter followed by a trimeter for a total of fourteen syllables), giving his version a somewhat lighter touch than the original. Golding emphasizes the poetic nature of his translation in his preface to the reader, saying of Ovid: "And now I haue him made so well acquainted with our toong / As that he may in English verse as in his owne bee soong" (A3$^r$).

Shakespeare's use of Ovid is often noted. He borrowed stories and phrases and even placed Ovid's works in the libraries of his characters, as in *Titus Andronicus*, IV.i. 41–43, where a copy of the *Metamorphoses* plays a dramatic role, or the embedded play of Pyramus and Thisbe in *A Midsummer Night's Dream.* Shakespeare's contemporaries, such as Christopher Marlowe (1564–93), Thomas Heywood (c. 1573–1641), and Ben Jonson, were also well versed in Ovid. It is clear from their "borrowings" that many of them knew

4.4, fol. B1$^r$

*The Metamorphoses* in both the original Latin and in Arthur Golding's metrical translation. We know, for example, that Shakespeare used works by Ovid that had not been translated into English, such as the *Fasti,* which was a major source for *The Rape of Lucrece.* A copy of the Aldine Ovid in the British Library inscribed "William Shakespear" was once thought to offer additional proof of the playwright's use of Ovid in Latin, but the signature is no longer considered authentic.

The Aldine and Golding *Metamorphoses* are open to an oft-quoted passage obviously used by Shakespeare as the source for Prospero's "farewell speech" in act V, scene i, of *The Tempest.*[13]

Ovid: auraeque et venti montesque amnesque lacusque / dique omnes nemorum, dique omnes noctis adeste. [Literal translation: O breezes and winds and mountains and rivers and lakes, come all you gods of the woods and of the night.] [*Metamorphoses* vii, 197–98]

Golding's Ovid: Ye Ayres and windes: ye Elves of Hilles, of Brookes, of Woods alone, / Of standing Lakes, and of the Night, approche ye everychone. [fol. 83$^v$]

Shakespeare's Prospero: Ye elves of hills, brooks, standing lakes and groves / And ye that on the sands with printless foot / Do chase the ebbing Neptune.

Literature: Braden 1978, 35–55; Lathrop 1967, 126–29; Lyne 2001; Nims 2000; *ODNB* ("Golding, Arthur" by John Considine).

4.5    Euclid. *The Elements of Geometrie of the most auncient philosopher Euclide of Megara* [sic]. *Faithfully (now first) translated into the Englishe toung by H. Billingsley . . . Whereunto are annexed certaine scholies, annotations, and inventions of the best mathematiciens . . . With a very fruitfull praeface made by M. I. Dee . . .* London: John Day, [1570].

ESTC S106699; STC 10560. Shelfmark: UIUC 516.2 Eu:E 1570.

Like so many classical texts, Euclid's *Elements of Geometry* would have been imported to England in continental imprints. From its first edition in 1482 (in Latin), the production of this monument of mathematics has required substantial skill because of its numerous illustrative figures. It was not attempted in England until 1570. The English printer with the ability to undertake such a project was John Day. Day had printed with William Seres before setting up his own shop, where he published Protestant tracts and translations. Though he was arrested under Queen Mary and seems to have printed with false continental imprints during her reign, his fortunes rose under Elizabeth. He received lucrative patents, including the monopoly for printing the psalter of Sternhold and Hopkins. He was also the publisher of Foxe's richly illustrated *Acts and Monuments,* or *The Book of Martyrs* (item 3.4). By 1570, he oversaw a large operation that could hire printers and journeymen trained on the Continent. Thus, he was able to produce this beautiful and elaborate folio, ward narower and narower, at length ende their angles (at the heigth or toppe therof) in one point. So all their angles there ioyned together, make a folide angle. And for the better fight thereof, I haue fet here a figure wherby ye fhall more eafily conceiue it, the bafe of the figure is a triangle, namely, A B C, if on euery fide of the triangle A B C, ye rayfe vp a triangle, as vpon the fide A B, ye raife vp the triangle A F B, and vpon the fide A C the triangle A F C, and vpon the fide B C, the triangle B F C, and fo bowing the triangles raifed vp, that their toppes, namely, the pointes F meete and ioyne together in one point, ye fhal eafily and plainly fee how thefe three fuperficiall angles A F B, B F C, C F A, ioyne and clofe together, touching the one the other in the point F, and fo make a folide angle.

10    *A Pyramis is a folide figure contained vnder many playne fuperficieces fet vpon one playne fuperficies, and gathered together to one point.*

Tenth diffinition.

Two fuperficieces rayfed vpon any ground can not make a Pyramis, forthat two fuperficiall angles ioyned together in the toppe, cannot (as before is fayd) make a folide angle. Wherfore whē thre, foure, fiue, or moe (how many foeuer) fuperficieces are raifed vp frō one fuperficies being the ground, or bafe, and euer afcending diminifh their breadth, till at the lēgth all their angles cōcurre in one point, making there a folide angle: the folide inclofed, bounded, and terminated by thefe fuperficieces is called a Pyramis, as ye fee in a taper of foure fides, and in a fpire of a towre which containeth many fides, either of which is a Pyramis.

And becaufe that all the fuperficieces of euery Pyramis afcend from one playne fuperficies as from the bafe, and tende to one poynt, it muft of neceffitie come to paffe, that all the fuperficieces of a Pyramis are trianguler, except the bafe, which may be of any forme or figure except a circle. For if the bafe be a circle, then it afcendeth not with fides, or diuers fuperficieces, but with one round fuperficies, and hath not the name of a Pyramis, but is called (as hereafter fhall appeare) a Cone.

Of Pyramids there are diuers kindes. For according to the varietie of the bafe is brought forth the varietie and diuerfitie of kindes of Pyramids. If the bafe of a Pyramis be a triangle, then is it called a triangled Pyramis. If the bafe be a figure of fower angles, it is called a quadrangled Pyramis. If the bafe be a Pentagon, then is it a Pentagonall or fiueangled Pyramis. And fo forth according to the increafe of the angles of the bafe infinitely. Although the figure of a Pyramis can not be well expreffed in a playne fuperficies, yet may ye fufficiently conceaue of it both by the figure before fet in the definition of a folide angle, and by the figure here fet, if ye imagine the point A together with the fines A B, A C, and A D, to be eleuared on high. And yet that the reader may more clerely fee the forme of a Pyramis, I haue here fet two fundry Pyramids which will appeare bodilike, if ye erecte the papers wherin are drawen the triangular fides of eche Pyramis, in fuch fort that the pointes of the angles F of ech triangle may in euery Pyramis concurre in one point, and make a folide angle: one of which hath to his bafe a fower fided figure, and the other a fiue fided figure. The forme of a triangled Pyramis ye may before beholde in the example of a folide angle. And by thefe may ye conceaue of all other kindes of Pyramids.

one of the first books to include "pop-ups." Perhaps as a sign of pride of accomplishment, the colophon includes a woodcut portrait of Day.

Henry Billingsley (d. 1606) is responsible for this first English translation of Euclid's *Elements*. Billingsley was not only an accomplished mathematician and Greek scholar, but also a political figure, later serving as Lord Mayor of London (1596). His translation was made from the original Greek, reflecting the strides in humanist education in England in the sixteenth century. In his "Translator to the Reader," Billingsely claims that "without diligent studie of Euclides *Elementes*, it is impossible to attaine unto the perfecte knowledge of Geometrie, and consequently of any of the other Mathematicall sciences." He undertook the task, he writes, because of "the want and lacke of such good authors hitherto in our Englishe touengue" (\*2ᵛ).

The mathematician John Dee (1527–1609) wrote the preface, an interesting survey of contemporary mathematics that may surprise modern readers by linking science with magic, though it probably did not faze readers of the Renaissance. Interestingly, Dee himself had a reputation as a conjuror, a charge he denies in a section of the preface entitled "A Digression Apologetical." He may not have been a magician, but Dee did, in fact, blur the lines between mathematics and magic. He not only supplied Queen Elizabeth and others with astrological charts, but also dabbled in alchemical studies, and devoted several years to communicating with spirits through a medium. Some even claim that Shakespeare based his Prospero on Dee.[14]

The Illinois copy includes six pages of manuscript notes and figures dated 1588 and apparently by a student of Dee.

---

Literature: French 1972; Lathrop 1967, 216–16; *ODNB* ("Day, John" by Andrew Pettegree, "Billingsley, Henry" by Anita McConnell, and "Dee, John" by R. Julian Roberts); Sherman 1995, 95–96; Woolley 2001, 4–19; Zetterberg 1980.


4.6     Plutarch. *The lives of the noble Grecians and Romanes. . . . Translated out of Greeke into French by James Amyot, Abbot of Bellozane, Bishop of Auxerre, one of the Kings privy counsel, and great Amner of Fraunce, and out of French into Englishe, by Thomas North.* London: Thomas Vautroullier, 1579.

*ESTC* S121873; *STC* 20065. Shelfmark: UIUC IUQ03510.

Sir Thomas North (1535–1603?) humbly dedicated his translation of Plutarch to Queen Elizabeth, "though this booke be no booke for your Maiesties selfe, who are meeter to be the cheife storie, than a student therein, and can better vnderstand it in Greeke, than any man can make it Englishe." North claims, however, that the queen may benefit from his work when her subjects read these examples of "honor, loue, obedience, reuerence, zeale, and deuocion to Princes" and are "animated to the better seruice of your Maiestie" (\*2ʳ).

As it turned out, he was quite right; her more literary subjects were inspired by the examples they found in North's English Plutarch. Despite the fact that North translated

A faire corps as could be. *Alexander* left *Roxane* great with childe, for the which the MACEDO-
NIANS did her great honor: but she did malice *Statira* extreamely, & did finely deceiue her by
a counterfeat letter she sent, as if it had comen from *Alexander*, willing her to come vnto him.
But when she was come, *Roxane* killed her and her sister, and then threw their bodies into a
well, and filled it vp with earth, by *Perdiccas* helpe and consent. *Perdiccas* came to be king, im-
mediatly after *Alexanders* death, by meanes of *Arideus*, whom he kept about him for his gard,
and safety. This *Arideus*, beeing borne of a common strumpet and common woman, called
*Philinna*, was halfe lunaticke, not by nature nor by chaunce: but, as it is reported, put out of his
wits when he was a young towardly boy, by drinkes, which *Olympias* caused to be geuen him,
and thereby continued franticke.

*Statira slaine by Roxane.*
*Arideus, Alexanders bastard brother.*

*The end of Alexanders life.*

# THE LIFE OF
## *Iulius Cæsar.*

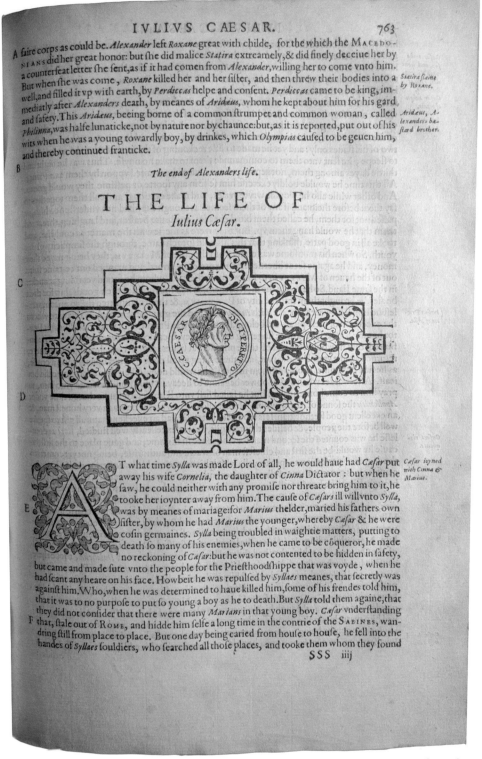

AT what time *Sylla* was made Lord of all, he would haue had *Cæsar* put
away his wife *Cornelia*, the daughter of *Cinna* Dictator: but when he
saw, he could neither with any promise nor threate bring him to it, he
tooke her ioynter away from him. The cause of *Cæsars* ill will vnto *Sylla*,
was by meanes of mariage: for *Marius* thelder, maried his fathers own
sister, by whom he had *Marius* the younger, whereby *Cæsar* & he were
cosin germaines. *Sylla* being troubled in waightie matters, putting to
death so many of his enemies, when he came to be cōqueror, he made
no reckoning of *Cæsar*: but he was not contented to be hidden in safety,
but came and made sute vnto the people for the Priesthoodshippe that was voyde, when he
had scant any heare on his face. Howbeit he was repulsed by *Syllaes* meanes, that secretly was
against him. Who, when he was determined to haue killed him, some of his frendes told him,
that it was to no purpose to put so young a boy as he to death. But *Sylla* told them againe, that
they did not consider that there were many *Marians* in that young boy. *Cæsar* vnderstanding
that, stale out of ROME, and hidde him selfe a long time in the contrie of the SABINES, wan-
dring still from place to place. But one day being caried from house to house, he fell into the
handes of *Syllaes* souldiers, who searched all those places, and tooke them whom they found

*Cæsar ioyned with Cinna & Marius.*

SSS iiij

Plutarch's *Parallel Lives* not from the original Greek but from Jacques Amyot's (1513–93) French version, he was able to capture the vigor and energy of Plutarch's characters in a way that captivated English readers of the day. The stories found their way into Shakespeare's *Coriolanus, Julius Caesar, Antony and Cleopatra,* and *Timon of Athens;* George Chapman's *Caesar and Pompey;* and Ben Jonson's *Cataline,* to name only a handful of Renaissance dramatists indebted to his work. It was also a source for John Milton and John Donne. As Charles Whibley put it, "Plutarch's *Lives of the Noble Grecians and Romans* fell happily into the hands of Sir Thomas North, whose skill gave [it] a second and larger immortality."[15]

The printer, Thomas Vautroullier, was a Huguenot refugee from France who printed a great deal of Protestant literature, including the first English translation of Calvin's *Institutes* in 1578. His Calvinist leanings later led him to Scotland, where he printed King James's first book, *Essays of a Prentise* (1585). In general, his work is noteworthy for its high quality, and this production of North's Plutarch is rather lavish, with a medallion portrait of the subject preceding each biography.

Literature: Bennett 1965, 95–103; Clair 1965; Lathrop 1967, 183–87; *ODNB* ("North, Thomas" by Tom Lockwood); Spencer 1964.

## 4.7 Homer. *Homer, prince of poets. Translated according to the Greeke in twelve bookes of his Iliads, by George Chapman.* London: [Humphrey Lownes] for Samuel Macham, [1609?].

*ESTC* S104163; *STC* 13633. Shelfmark: UIUC IUB00177.

"For every one who has read Chapman's *Homer* there have been hundreds who have only heard of it through the remarks of Pope, Lamb, Coleridge, Matthew Arnold, or Swinburne, or perhaps only through the inspired testimony of Keats' great sonnet."[16] Thus begins a review of a modern edition of George Chapman, and it is true even among English scholars that his translations are more often praised than read. The situation may have arisen from the relative dearth of editions of Chapman's *Iliad;* only three editions were published between 1609 and 1800 and the first modern, readable edition did not appear until 1956.[17] Whether unread, overrated, or underappreciated, Chapman nonetheless has pride of place as the first to translate the entire *Iliad* into English.

George Chapman was a playwright as well as a translator. He served as chief dramatist for the Admiral's Men in the 1590s and also composed for the Rose Theatre and the Children of the Queen's Revels at Blackfriars, among others. His plays and masques were satirical, sentimental, farcical, and sometimes dangerously political. Indeed, the 1605 play *Eastward Ho,* which he wrote with Ben Jonson and John Marston (item 3.10), resulted in the imprisonment of Chapman and Jonson for their presumed critique of James I and Scotland. Often in debt and eventually dying in poverty, Chapman supplemented his work as a playwright by seeking patronage from noblemen to whom he dedicated poems and translations.

Little is known of Chapman's education. He says he taught himself Greek and he was obviously well versed in the classics, drawing upon Virgil, Juvenal, Ovid, Seneca, Homer,

4.7, title page

Hesiod, and other Latin and Greek writers in his poems and plays. Chapman's interest in Homer is evident as early as 1598, when he published seven books of the *Iliad* (books 1–2 and 7–11). These were substantially revised in the *Twelve Books of the Iliad* that appeared in 1609, preceding *The Complete Iliads* in 1611. Chapman translated Homer into fourteeners, a meter that fell from favor even within the Elizabethan period. He changed to pentameter couplets for his translation of the *Odyssey*, which appeared with the *Iliad* in *The Whole Works of Homer* in 1616.

In his preface to the 1609 *Iliad*, Chapman criticizes other translators for their word-for-word approach, likening their efforts to making "Fish with foule, or Camels with vvhales engender" (A4ʳ). He instead aspires "to reach the spirit that was spent" by his poet, often paraphrasing rather than translating. Chapman praises English as a poetic language equal to Homeric Greek. Its short and strong words, he says, are especially well suited for rendering Homer:

> For verse, and that sweet Musique to the eare
> Strooke out of rime, so naturally as this;
> Our Monosyllables, so kindly fall
> And meete, opposed in rime, as they did kisse.

(A5ʳ)

Chapman states that his goal is to write as Homer would have written in English (A4ʳ). Some critics have considered this a fault, as when Samuel Coleridge opines that Chapman wrote "Greekified English," but he had to admit that "detached passages could not be improved; they were Homer writing English."[18] The beauty of Chapman's verse has had its admirers through the centuries, most famously John Keats, whose sonnet "On First Looking into Chapman's Homer" (1816) describes his experience: "Yet did I never breathe its pure serene / Till I heard Chapman speak out loud and bold."

---

Literature: Braden 1978, 115–19; Collier 1856; Lord 1958; Nicoll 1956, xvi–vii; *ODNB* ("Chapman, George" by Mark Thornton Burnett); Spivack 1967.

4.8    Fabian Johnson (fl. 1591). *Trve intelligence sent from a gentleman of account: concerning, the estate of the English forces now in Fraunce, under the conduct of the Right Honorable the Earle of Essex. Particularly expressing what hath beene doone since his departure from England, untill the second of September last, 1591.* [London: J. Wolfe] for Thomas Nelson, 1591.

*ESTC* S113329; *STC* 14657.5. Shelfmark: UIUC B.E78j.

4.9    *Trve nevves from one of Sir Fraunces Veres companie. Concerning Delftes-Isle, and sundry other townes in the Lowe Countries, yeelded to the generall since May last. Of the great armie, nowe comminge out of Germanie for the aide of the French King, and their hope for the speedye winninge of Antwerpe. With the bloody persecution and marterdome which sundry cheefe persons of account did lately suffer in*

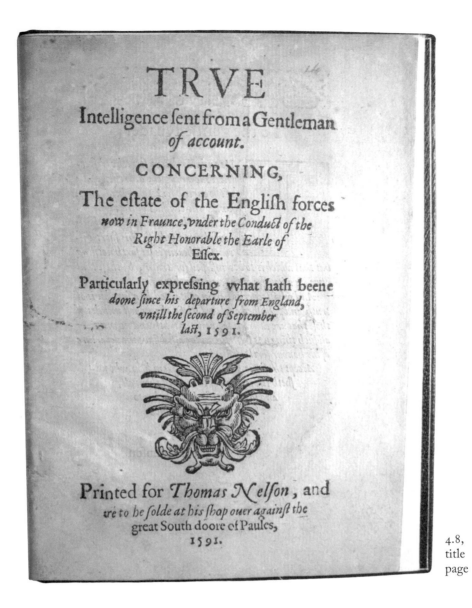

TRVE
Intelligence sent from a Gentleman
of account.

CONCERNING,

The estate of the English forces
now in Fraunce, vnder the Conduct of the
Right Honorable the Earle of
Essex.

Particularly expressing vvhat hath beene
doone since his departure from England,
vntill the second of September
last, 1591.

Printed for *Thomas Nelson*, and
are to be solde at his shop ouer against the
great South doore of Paules,
1591.

4.8,
title
page

*Spaine for the profession of Christ Iesus. Translated out
of Dutch. Seene and allowed.* London: [Edward Allde]
for Thomas Nelson, 1591.

*ESTC* S119062; *STC* 24652. Shelfmark: UIUC 949.203 T766.

English translations of the classics are a hallmark of Tudor scholarship, but more contemporary matters from the Continent also needed "translation" to the shores of England. Although the first regularly issued newspapers did not appear in England until 1622, translations of foreign news reports and news-filled letters from other lands (especially the Netherlands, Germany, France, and Spain) began to find their way into print in the 1590s.

The format for English news was often the broadside or single sheet, whereas small booklets were the norm for translated news or reports from Englishmen abroad. All news was quickly and cheaply printed, meant for immediate consumption, not posterity. Hence, early English news booklets are fairly rare. The report by Fabian Johnson, though only four pages in length, contains a preface "To the gentle Reader" in which Johnson vouches for the truth of his account and criticizes "unjust rumors, secretlie dispersed, concerning the distressed estate of the English forces now in France" under the leadership of the Earl of Essex (A1ᵛ). The other pamphlet is a translation from a Dutch news source concerning battles in the Lowlands and reports of religious persecution in Spain. Both accounts are couched in the form of letters, the first to "my good cussen," the other "to a Ladie in England," but they are obviously intended for broader circulation.

Literature: Shaaber 1966, 1–12 and 168–203.

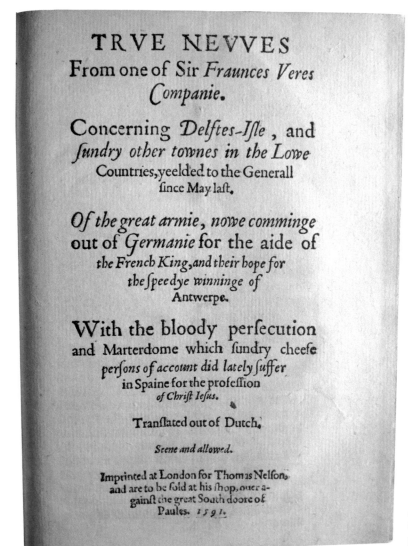

4.9, title page

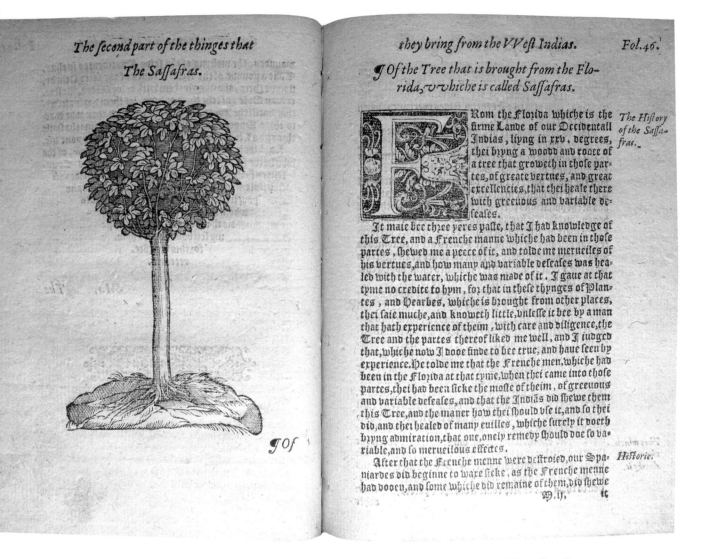

The second part of the thinges that
The Saſſafras.

they bring from the VVeſt Indias. Fol.46.

¶ Of the Tree that is brought from the Florida, vvhiche is called Saſſafras.

Rom the Florida whiche is the firme Lande of our Occidentall Indias, liyng in xxv. degrees, thei bryng a woodd and roote of a tree that groweth in those partes, of greate vertues, and great excellencies, that thei heale there with greeuous and variable deseales.

It maie bee three yeres paste, that I had knowledge of this Tree, and a Frenche manne whiche had been in those partes, shewed me a peece of it, and tolde me merueiles of his vertues, and how many and variable deseases was healed with the water, whiche was made of it. I gaue at that tyme no credite to hym, for that in these thynges of Plantes, and Hearbes, whiche is brought from other places, thei saie muche, and knoweth little, vnlesse it bee by a man that hath experience of theim, with care and diligence, the Tree and the partes thereof liked me well, and I iudged that, whiche now I dooe finde to bee true, and haue seen by experience. He tolde me that the Frenche men, whiche had been in the Florida at that tyme, when thei came into those partes, thei had been sicke the moste of theim, of greeuous and variable deseases, and that the Indias did shewe them this Tree, and the maner how thei should vse it, and so thei did, and thei healed of many euilles, whiche surely it dooeth bryng admiration, that one, onely remedy should doe so variable, and so merueilous effectes.

After that the Frenche menne were destroied, our Spaniardes did beginne to waxe sieke, as the Frenche menne had dooen, and some whiche did remaine of them, did shewe

M.ij.

4.10, fol. 45ᵛ–46ʳ

4.10    Nicolás Monardes (c. 1512–88). *Ioyfvll nevves out of the newe founde worlde, wherein is declared the rare and singuler vertues of diuerse and sundrie hearbes, trees, oyles, plantes, and stones, with their aplications, as well for phisicke as chirurgerie . . . : Also the portrature of the saied hearbes, very aptly discribed. Englished by John Frampton, marchaunt.* London: William Norton, 1577.

streames of pleasant fire; which serpents will much occupie these about the place to defend themselves in their upper parts, when they will no lesse be busied by the balles of fire, which seemes to annoy their feete.

### Of Balles of fire.

THese are very various according to a mans fancie some of which are made with very small *Rockets*, the head of one tyed to the neck of another: the ball being made may be covered over with pitch except the hole to give fire to it; this *Ball* will make fine sport amongst the standers by, which will take all a fire, and rowle sometimes this way, sometimes that way, betweene the legs of those that are standers by, if they take not heede, for the motion will be very irregular, and in the motion will cast forth severall fires with reports. In the second kind there may be a chanell of *Iron* placed in divers places in spirall manner, against which may be placed as many small petards of paper as possible may be, the Channell must be full of slow composition and may be covered as the former, and made fit with his *Rockets* in the middle: this *Ball* may bee shot out

out of a morter *Peece* or charged on the top of a *Rocket* : for in its motion it will fly here and there, and give many reports in the Ayre: because of the discharge of the petards.

### Of fire upon the Water.

PLaces which are situated upon *Rivers* or great *Ponds*, are proper to make *Recreative* fires on : and if it be required to make some of consequence, such may conveniently bee made upon two *Boats*, upon which may be built two *Beasts*, *Turrets*, *Pagents*, *Castles*, or such like, to

ceive or hold the diversity of *Fire workes* that may be made within it, in which may play divers fires, *Petards*, &c. and cast out many ample *Grenades*, *Balls* of fire to burne in the water

4.11, pp. 258–59

4.11    Jean Leurechon (1591–1670), under pseudonym Hendrick van Etten. *Mathematicall recreations. Or a collection of sundrie problemes, extracted out of the ancient and moderne philosophers, as secrets in nature, and experiments in arithmeticke, geometrie, cosmographie, horolographie, astronomie, navigation, musicke, opticks, architecture, staticke, machanicks, chimestrie, waterworkes, fireworks, &c.* London: T. Cotes for Richard Hawkins, 1633.

*ESTC* S108485; *STC* 10558.5. Shelfmark: UIUC 793.74 L57r:E 1633.

Works on practical matters of interest to English readers form another body of English translations in the sixteenth and seventeenth centuries. The English desire to keep abreast of the latest discoveries and to consult European authorities kept many a translator and printer in bread and butter. French, Italian, German, Spanish, and Dutch books on everything from gardening and cooking to surgical procedures and scientific observations made their way into English.

The medical tract entitled *Joyfull Newes* is a translation from the Spanish *Historia medicinal de las cosas que se traen de nuestras Indias Occidentales que sirven en medicina* by John Frampton, who identifies himself as a "merchant." In 1577, interest in the New World ran high, and the Spanish—as the first colonizers—were considered authorities. The *Joyful Newes* offers "cures" supposedly from the ancient wisdom of Native Americans, including the miraculous effects of ginger, rhubarb, and coca, as well as one section on the great virtues of tobacco, which "hath particular vertue to heale griefes of the head," "griefes . . . in them that are shorte breathed," "greife of the stomacke," and, for women, "the evill of the Mother" (i.e., uterus) ($35^r$–$35^v$). Another chapter deals with preventatives against the plague, providing hope from the New World for the distinctly Old World scourge.

The *Mathematicall Recreations* concerns matters less practical, but perhaps more scientific. The work was extremely popular in France, going through thirty editions between 1624 and 1700. Leurechon, a Jesuit priest and professor of mathematics, takes a pleasant approach to a variety of scientific challenges posed by Latin, Greek, French, Italian, and German scholars and proposes solutions meant to entertain as well as enlighten. The first English version appeared in 1633 by an unnamed translator; it has been attributed variously to Francis Malthus (fl. 1629) or, in later editions, to William Oughtred (1575–1660). The rather crudely printed book includes simple engravings to illustrate Leurechon's solutions and recreations, including images of fireworks. It covers many diverse and diverting topics, such as: "How to make the string of a Viole sencibly shake, without any one touching it" (126), "Many Dice being cast, how artificially to discover the number of points that may arise" (60), and how to make "balles of fire" (258) and "fire upon the water" (259ff). This wide-ranging and fascinating work of the early Enlightenment also includes the earliest known description of an ear trumpet.

Literature: Romano 1999, 589–90.

4.12    Baldassare Castiglione (1478–1529). *The Courtyer, of Count Baldessar Castilio diuided into foure bookes; Very necessary and profitatable for yonge gentilmen and gentilwomen abiding in court, palaice or place; done into Englyshe by Thomas Hoby.* London: William Seres, 1561.

*ESTC* S122029; *STC* 4778. Shelfmark: UIUC IUA02503.

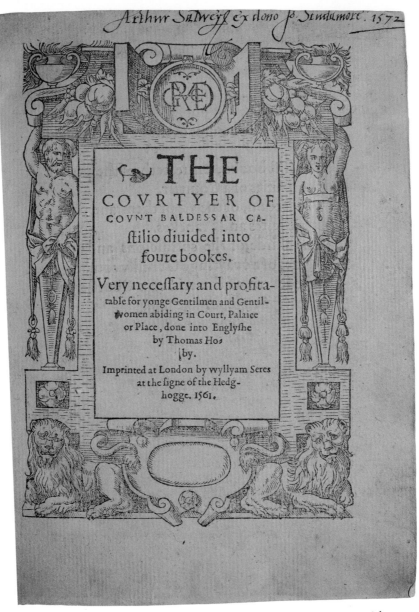

4.12, title page

Castiglione's work on courtly manners influenced most of Renaissance Europe and had a significant impact on the development of modern manners and customs. Written in dialogue form and obviously influenced by Plato's *Symposium, The Courtier* defines proper training and behavior for men and women of the upper classes. It was first published in 1528 and soon translated into nearly every European language. The humanist Roger Ascham (1514 / 15 – 1568), advised young gentlemen to read Hoby's Castiglione, saying it would do them more good than "three yeares travel abrode spent in Italie."[19] Even as late as 1773, Samuel Johnson (1709 – 84) contended that *The Courtier* remained "the best book that ever was written upon good breeding."[20]

Like Castiglione, his first English translator, Sir Thomas Hoby, was a diplomat whose success depended on proper decorum. According to the printer's note to the reader, the English version of Castiglione circulated first in manuscript, apparently taking longer than a decade to come to press.[21] Indeed, Hoby's dedication to Lord Henry Hastings, Earl of Huntington, is dated five years before the imprint date, also attesting to the delay in printing. In that dedication, Hoby claims that through his translation Castiglione "is beecome an Englishman" (A3ʳ). He further recommends to the earl that he embrace the English Castiglione, for then "other yonge and Courtly Gentlemen will not shonn hys company: and so both he shall gete him the reputation now here in Englande which he hath had a good while since beyonde the sea, in Italy, Spaine and Fraunce" (A3ᵛ).

Hoby comments at length on English translation in general, criticizing "our learned menne" who believe that having the sciences "in the mother tunge, hurteth memorie and hindreth lerning" (A4ᵛ). Hoby argues to the contrary that "the translation of Latin or Greeke authours, doeth not onely not hinder learning, but it furthereth it, yea it is learning it self, and a great staye to youth, and the noble ende to the whiche they oughte to applie their wittes" (A4ᵛ). Further, when translating into English, neologisms and loanwords should be avoided: "our own tung shold be written cleane and pure, vnmixt and vnmangeled with borowing of other tunges" (zz5ʳ).

Literature: Molinaro 1959; *ODNB* ("Hoby, Thomas" by L. G. Kelly); Woodhouse 1978, 1–3.

## 4.13   *The ancient, famovs and honourable history of Amadis de Gaule. Translated by Anthony Munday.* London: Nicholas Okes, 1619.

*ESTC* S106806; *STC* 544. Shelfmark: UIUC IUA00243.

Courtly manners may have crossed the channel in the form of Thomas Hoby's English Castiglione, but chivalric epics and courtly romances had been a staple of aristocratic entertainment long before the printing press came to England. The first book printed in English, *The Recuyell of the Historyes of Troye,* after all, recounts the story of Troy as a tale of noble knights and ladies. Malory and Chaucer, both printed in the incunabular period, are native sources of romance, but translations, especially of French courtly literature, also found their way to England. *Amadis de Gaul,* translated from a French version of the fifteenth-century anonymous Spanish original, was another natural choice for translation since it concerns English nobles. The translator, Anthony Munday (1560–1633), was a printer, actor, playwright, and historian, as well as a translator. His *Amadis de Gaul* appeared in parts, at various printers, beginning as early as 1590. The second book was edited by Munday but translated by one Lazarus Pyott (a pseudonym for Munday?). This copy (shown opposite page 107), actually two imprints of 1618 and 1619 that were issued together, was printed by Nicholas Okes, who also printed (and pirated) works by Shakespeare. Munday's translation influenced both Sidney's *Arcadia* and Spenser's *Faerie Queene.*

Literature: H. Moore 2004; O'Connor 1970; *ODNB* ("Munday, Anthony" by David M. Bergeron).

4.14    *The Byble, which is all the holy scripture: In whych are contayned the Olde and Newe Testament truly and purely translated into Englysh.* [Antwerp: Matthew Crom for Richard Grafton and Edward Whitchurch, 1537.]

DMH 34; *ESTC* S121981; *STC* 2066. Shelfmark: UIUC IUQ00026.

The history of the Bible in English is one of censorship, intrigue, violence, and, ultimately, glory.[22] First translated into Middle English in the late fourteenth century by followers of John Wyclif (d. 1384), the vernacular text was tainted by its association with the Lollard movement and therefore outlawed. In almost every other country in Europe, the Bible circulated openly in the vernacular throughout the Middle Ages (there are, for example, nineteen printed German translations of the Bible before Luther's), but in England, because of its connection to a heretical sect, the Bible in translation was illegal from 1408 until 1535.

In the 1520s, inspired by Martin Luther's return to the Hebrew and Greek sources for his Bible translation, William Tyndale translated the Bible into English, beginning with the New Testament. Because of the ban on English translations, however, Tyndale had to work in exile on the Continent. The first printing of the New Testament (Cologne, 1525) was stopped in press and destroyed; the second (Worms, 1526) was confiscated and burned, surviving in only three copies (one of which is a fragment). Sir Thomas More and others in England tried to stop Tyndale's work because they feared the influence of Luther, whose own vernacular Bible had done so much to foster the continental Reformation. Thomas Elyot, the lexicographer (see item 2.6), was even sent to the Lowlands as a spy to entrap Tyndale. Eventually, Tyndale was betrayed and burned at the stake for the crime of translating the Bible into English. He left behind not only the New Testament in English, but also the Pentateuch and, it seems likely, the historical books from Joshua to 2 Chronicles. The year after his death, Tyndale's friend John Rogers published a complete Bible in English, using Tyndale's translations and, for the parts not finished by Tyndale, the translation by Miles Coverdale from Luther's German. Perhaps still a bit skittish about the political fate of the English Bible even three years after Henry's break with Rome, Rogers published the work under the pseudonym Thomas Matthew and had it printed on the Continent, not in London. It is known as the Matthew Bible.

The influence of William Tyndale's translation on the English Bible is immense and his impact on the English language, therefore, is significant. The words and phrases of Tyndale appear in nearly every subsequent English Bible translation, including the King James Version.

---

Literature: Bruce 1978, 24–53, 64–66; Daniell 1994, 333–57; Pelikan 1996, 142–43; Price and Ryrie 2004, 49–51, 64–67.

4.15    *The. Holie. Bible.* London: Richard Jugge, printer to the Queenes Maiestie, 1572.

DMH 132; *ESTC* S121300; *STC* 2107. Shelfmark: UIUC IUQ00047.

## ¶ The Gospell of Sayncte John.

¶ The euerlastyng byrth of Christ/and how he became man. The testimony of Jhon. The callynge of Andrew. Peter. ꝛc.

¶ The fyrst Chapter. ✠

IN the begynnynge was the worde/& the worde was with God: and the worde was God. The same was in the begynnynge wyth God. All thynges were made by it/and wythout it/was made nothynge that was made. In it was lyfe/& the lyfe was the lyght of men/&

a * The lyght shyneth in ẏ darcknes darcknes ꝛc. but the darcknes comprehended it not.

By the light is vnderstonde Christ: by the darcknes vngodly: vnbeleuynge mē/amōg whome Christ came & they receaued him not as Ephe.iiꞇ.d b * The worlde knewe him not The worlde here taken for: the people of the worlde/as after in the vii.a and Mat.xvi.c.

There was a man sent from God/whose name was John. The same cam as a witnes to beare wytnes of the lyght/that all men through him myght beleue. He was not that lyght: but to beare witnes of the lyght. That was a true lyght whych lyghteth all mē that come into the worlde. He was in the worlde and the worlde was made by hym: and yet b * the worlde knewe hym not.

He cam amonge hys awne/and hys awne receaued hym not. But as many as receaued hym/to them he gaue power to be the sonnes of God in that they beleued on hys name: whych were borne/not of bloude nor of the wyll of the flesche/nor yet of the will of man: but of God.

And the worde was made flesche and dwelt amonge vs/and we sawe the glory of it/as the glory of the only begotten sonne of the father/whych worde was full of grace and verite. ✠

✠ John bare wytnes of hym and cryed sayinge: Thys was he of whome I spake/he that cometh after me/was before me/because he was yer then I. And of hys fulnes haue al we receaued/euen ᵉ*(grace)for grace. For the lawe was geuen by Moses: but grace and truthe came by Jesus Chryst.

b * No man hath sene God at eny tyme. The only begotten sonne/which is in the bosome of the father/he hath declared him. ✠

✠ And this is the recorde of John: when the Jewes sent Prestes and Leuites frō Jerusalem/to aske hym/what arte thou? And he confessed and denyed not & sayde playnly: I am not Christ. And they asked hym: what then? arte thou Helyas? And he sayde: I am not. Arte thou ẏ Prophete? And he answered no. Then sayd they vnto him: what arte thou that we maye geue an answer to them that sent vs: What sayest thou of thy selfe? He sayde: I am ẏ ᵉ*voyce of a cryar in ẏ wildernes/make strayght the waye of the Lorde/as sayde the Prophete Esaias.

And they whych were sent/were of the Pharyses. And they asked hym/and sayde vnto him: why baptisest thou then yf thou be not Christ/nor Helyas/nether a Prophete? John answered the sayinge: I baptyse wyth water: but one is come amonge you/whom ye knowe not/he it is that cometh after me/whiche was before me/whose sho latchet I am not worthy to vnlose. These thynges were done in Bethabara beyonde Jordā where John dyd baptise. ✠

✠ The nexte daye John sawe Jesus commynge vnto him/and sayde: beholde ẏ lambe of God/which taketh awaye the synne of the worlde. This is he of whom I sayd. After me cometh a man/whych was before me/for he was yer then I/and I knew him not: but that he shuld be declared to Israel/therfore am I come baptysinge wyth water.

And John bare recorde sayinge: I sawe ẏ sprete descende from heuen/lyke vnto a doue and abyde vpon him/and I knewe hym not. But he that sent me to baptise in water/the same sayde vnto me:*vpon whom thou shalt se the sprete descende and tary styll on hym/the same is he which baptiseth with the holy goost. And I sawe and bare recorde that this is the sonne of God. ✠

Math.iii.d
Mark.i.b
Luke.iij.d

The nexte daye after/John stode agayne/and two of hys disciples. And he behelde Jesus as he walked by/and sayde: beholde the lambe of God. And the two dysciples hearde hym speake and folowed Jesus. And Jesus turned about/and sawe them folowe/& sayd vnto thē: what seke ye? They sayd vnto him: Rabbi (which is to saye by interpretacyon/Master) where dwellest thou? He sayde vnto them: come and se. They came & sawe where he dwelt: and abode with him that daye. For it was about the tenth houre.

One of

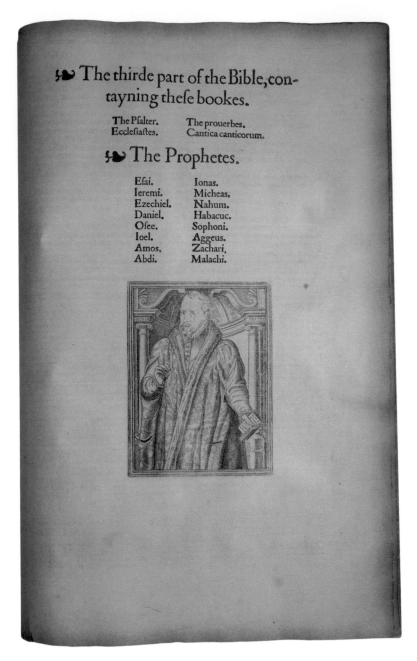

The thirde part of the Bible, contayning thefe bookes.

The Pfalter.      The prouerbes.
Ecclefiaftes.     Cantica canticorum.

The Prophetes.

Efai.          Ionas.
Ieremi.        Micheas.
Ezechiel.      Nahum.
Daniel.        Habacuc.
Ofee.          Sophoni.
Ioel.          Aggeus.
Amos.          Zachari.
Abdi.          Malachi.

4.15,
fol. L17ʳ

The King James Version of the Bible is rightly famous, but Queen Elizabeth also sponsored
a Bible translation. Her goal was to improve upon the authorized translation produced
under Henry VIII, the Great Bible (item 3.1). Matthew Parker, Elizabeth's archbishop
of Canterbury, encouraged her to support a project to produce a more scholarly translation, one based on the original languages and on the best biblical scholarship of the day.
He also may have wanted an alternative to the popular—and Calvinist—Geneva Bible
(item 6.4), the English version produced by English exiles in Switzerland during Queen
Mary's reign.

4.15,
fol. Bbb1<sup>r</sup>

Working with a team of bishops, some fifteen in all, Parker doled out portions of the Great Bible and asked his colleagues to correct it "where it varieth manifestly from the Hebrew or Greek original." He also asked them to mark passages that were "not edifying" and to rephrase any offensive or obscene passages.[23] As editor of the whole, Parker did not manage to smooth out the disparate styles of the contributions or to correct their varying degrees of competency. Parts of the Bishops' Bible, as it is called, live on in the King James Version, particularly the New Testament, but other parts had no lasting impact. The Psalms, for example, failed miserably in the Bishops' Bible translations. Archbishop Parker himself may have had his doubts about the felicity of the Psalms, for in the preface he asks the reader to excuse the fact that they may not "sounde agreeably to his eares in his wonted woords and phrases, as he is accustomed with" (Aaa1ᵛ). So disagreeable was the sound, indeed, that the second edition of 1572 conceded defeat by printing the Psalms in the version of the Book of Common Prayer (largely Coverdale's translation taken over from the Great Bible) side by side with the Bishops' Bible version. In the example shown here, the Bible is open to Psalm 23, which shows the two texts with the older, beloved version in black letter and the new translation in roman typeface. An interesting engraving with a political rather than pious purpose formed the "B" in "Blessed is the man" in the 1568 edition; it is a portrait of William Cecil, Lord Burghley (1520 / 21 – 1598), the queen's chief advisor. In the 1572 edition, the same portrait appears on the title page of the "thirde part of the Bible."

Literature: Pelikan 1996, 145; Pollard 1911, 297 – 98; Price and Ryrie 2004, 93 – 104.

4.16    *The Nevv Testament of Iesvs Christ, translated faithfvlly into English, out of the authentical Latin, according to the best corrected copies of the same, diligently conferred vvith the Greeke and other editions in diuers languages.* Rheims: John Fogny, 1582.

DMH 177; *ESTC* S102491; *STC* 2884. Shelfmark: UIUC IUA01454.

The Rheims New Testament, the first Catholic Bible in English, came into being as a part of the effort to keep a persecuted faith alive during the reign of Elizabeth I. It stands, therefore, as the final monument in the long and distinguished history of creating illegal Bibles in the English vernacular.

The name of the first Catholic translation — the Douai-Rheims — indicates its origin as the work of English exiles on the Continent. Upon the accession of Elizabeth, William Allen fled England and founded a seminary in Douai (Flanders) for the education of priests who would undertake perilous missions back to England. The seminary was temporarily in Rheims when the New Testament appeared in print in 1582; by 1609 – 10, when the Old Testament finally appeared, the seminary had returned to Douai.

Gregory Martin, professor of Greek and Hebrew at the seminary, translated the entire Bible, apparently single-handedly. It is one of the most independent renderings of scripture from the English Renaissance. In sharp departure from the practices of Protestant translators, the Latin Vulgate served as the base text for the translation. This is a direct consequence of the decree in Session 4 of the Council of Trent (1546) that the "Latin Vulgate edition . . . should be kept as the authentic text . . . and no one is to dare or presume on any pretext to reject it."[24] Nonetheless, while Martin followed the Vulgate text scrupulously, his notes offered numerous comparisons to readings and variants in the Hebrew and Greek versions.

In the preface to the New Testament, Martin explains that his English usage "at the first may seeme strange" (c3ʳ) because he has chosen to adhere to the syntax and the vocabulary of the Latin as closely as possible. Citing Jerome's own assertions, he argues that the Vulgate is itself a word-for-word rendering of the Hebrew and Greek originals; thus, according to Martin, a literal rendering of the Vulgate should yield a close translation of the original-language versions. The resulting translation, however, proves him wrong. Moreover, Martin's approach is at odds with the stylistic history of the English Bible ever since the creation of the second Wycliffite version. Martin acknowledges this, but compensates for it with an attack against the literary aesthetics of Protestant translations.

Martin felt the need to include a glossary of fifty-eight unusual terms. Some of the new words never made it into English, such as "Dominical day" (for "dies dominica," i.e., the sabbath) or "repropitiate" (for "repropitiare," i.e., to propitiate). Nonetheless, a few of his neologisms have become accepted English words, such as "acquisition," "advent," "cooperate," and "holocaust."[25] A good example of the Latinate style of the Rheims New Testament is the translation of the Lord's Prayer: "Ovr Father which art in heauen, sanctified be thy name. Let thy Kingdom come. Thy wil be done, as in heauen, in earth also. Give vs today our supersubstantial bread. And forgiue us our dettes, as we also forgiue our detters. And leade vs not into tentation. But deliver vs from euil. Amen" (B4ʳ).[26]

The Old Testament appeared posthumously (Martin died in 1582). Martin's colleagues at Douai edited the text lightly to make it conform to the new standard Latin text, sponsored by the papacy, the Sixto-Clementine Vulgate of 1592.

Literature: Pope 1952, 249–307; Pelikan and Hotchkiss 2003, 2:823; Price and Ryrie 2004, 105–14.

## 4.17 *The Holy Bible, conteyning the Old Testament, and the New: Newly translated out of the originall tongues: & with former translations diligently compared and reuised by his Maiesties speciall commandement.* London: Robert Barker, 1611.

DMH 309; *ESTC* S124527; *STC* 2216. Shelfmark: UIUC Q. 220.52 B47 1611.

After suppressing the Bible in their vernacular for more than 130 years, the English made up for lost time by creating no fewer than fifteen different translations of the Bible between 1535 to 1600 in a variety of forms and formats — 248 editions in all. The idea of producing yet another English translation had not entered the mind of the new king, James I, when he met with religious leaders at Hampton Court in January 1604. But when a Puritan activist, John Reynolds (1549–1607), president of Corpus Christi College, asked that the king "direct that the Bible be now translated, such versions as are extant not answering to the original," James seized upon the idea and the great translation project got underway. James may have agreed that advances in biblical and philological scholarship warranted such an undertaking, but he could also see the political benefit of supplanting the popular Geneva translation (item 6.4).

King James wanted a Bible free from religious partisanship. The guidelines for the fifty-four translators, divided into six translation committees, were drafted by the project coordinator, Archbishop Richard Bancroft, and James himself. No marginal notes were to be included, unless for the explanation of Hebrew or Greek words; old ecclesiastical words were to be retained (i.e., "church," not "congregation"); and a careful system of checking and conferring with one another was put into place. Translators were instructed to work from the original Hebrew and Greek and to consult the Bishops' Bible, the Great Bible, the Matthew Bible, the Geneva version, Tyndale, and Coverdale. Remarkably, out of this cumbersome and archly academic structure rose a cultural monument. Drawing on the best biblical scholarship, as well as previous English translations, the committees refined the language where necessary, producing not only an accurate English translation, but also a great work of English literature. An example from Psalm 23 illustrates the subtle yet masterly changes that one finds throughout the King James Version:

Geneva Version (1560): Douetles kindenes, and mercie shal follow me all the dayes of my life, and I shal remaine a long season in the house of the Lord. (Oo4ʳ)

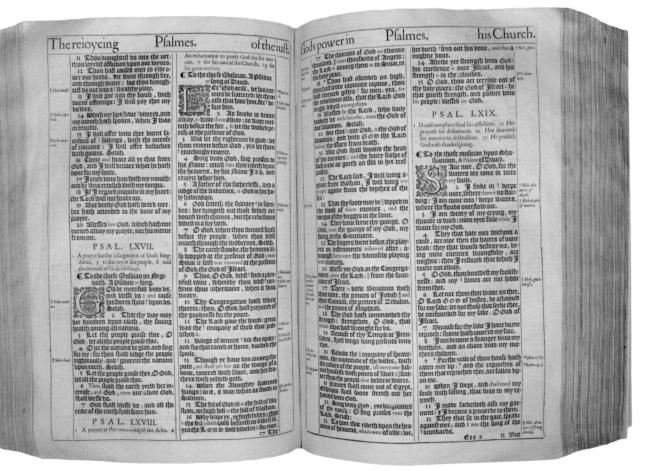

4.17, fol. Eee1ᵛ–Eee2ʳ

King James Version (1611): Surely goodnes and mercie shall followe me all the daies of my life: and I will dwell in the house of the Lord foreuer. (ccc3ʳ)

The King's Printer, Robert Barker, acquired the rights to print the new Bible. The first edition, a handsome folio, appeared in 1611. The 1611 edition exists in two states, or "issues," with over two hundred minor variations in the texts of the two caused by the fact that it was probably printed at more than one press. Hence, we have the famous "He" and "She" Bibles, a designation based on the way Ruth 3:15 was printed. The copy shown here is a "He Bible," generally considered the earlier of the two issues.

Although it is riddled with typographic errors (Genesis 32:15 reads "ashes" where it ought to read "asses," for example), the King James Bible is nonetheless a masterpiece of book design. Moreover, in its page layout, it quietly incorporates a sophisticated scholarly apparatus through the use of different fonts: the translated text is set in black letter, like most English Bibles of the time; words added for syntactical sense or words of questionable status in the original are set in roman typeface; and the few notes required in the margins are in italics.

Literature: Pelikan 1996, 149; Price and Ryrie 2004, 115–43.

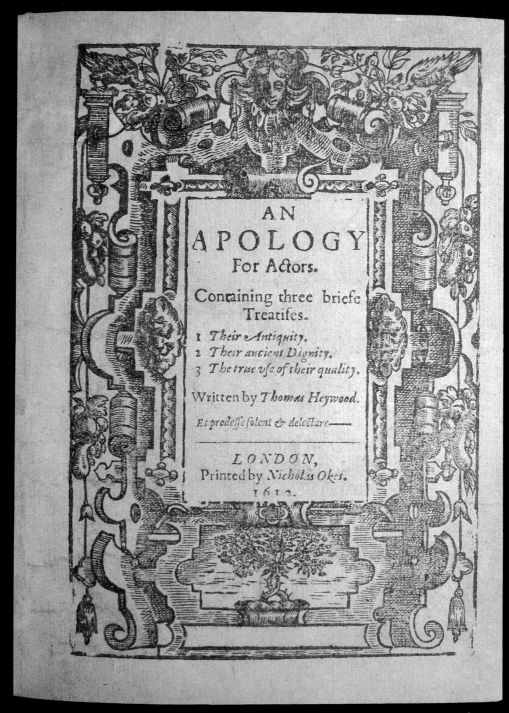

AN
APOLOGY
For Actors.

Containing three briefe
Treatifes.

1 *Their Antiquity.*
2 *Their ancient Dignity.*
3 *The true vfe of their quality.*

Written by *Thomas Heywood.*

*Et prodeffe folent & deleCtare*————

*LONDON,*
Printed by *Nicholas Okes.*
1612.

5.28, title page

# 5
## FROM THE STAGE
## TO THE PAGE

5.1      John Bale (1495–1563). *A nevve comedy or enterlude concernyng thre lawes, of nature, Moises, and Christe, corrupted by the sodomytes, Pharysies, and papistes: compyled by Iohn Bale: and nowe newly imprynted.* London: Thomas Colwell, 1562.

ESTC S104458; Greg 24(b); STC 1288. Shelfmark: UIUC IUA00768.

5.2      W. S. (fl. 1595). *The lamentable tragedie of Locrine, the eldest sonne of King Brutus, discoursing the warres of the Britaines, and Hunnes, with their discomfiture: the Britaines victorie with their accidents, and the death of Albanact. No lesse pleasant then profitable. Newly set foorth, ouerseene and corrected, by VV.S.* London: Thomas Creede, 1595.

ESTC S106301; Greg 136(a); STC 21528. Shelfmark: UIUC IUB00197.

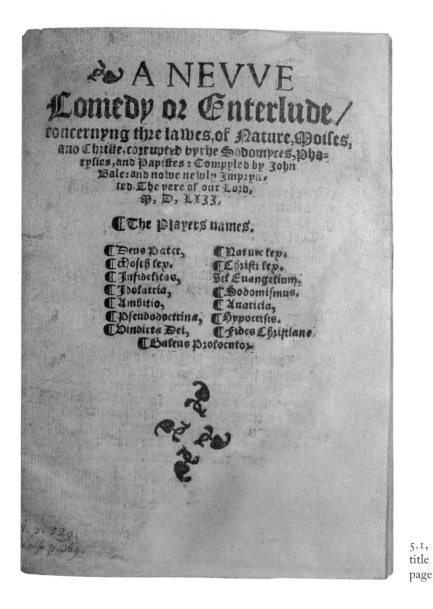

5.1,
title
page

5.3     *The returne from Pernassus: or The scourge of simony.*
*Publiquely acted by the students in Saint Iohns Colledge*
*in Cambridge.* London: G. Eld for John Wright, 1606.

ESTC S114071; Greg 225(b); STC 19310. Shelfmark: Elizabethan Club
159 (UIUC IUA10546).

No monopolies or general patents were issued for the printing of plays, masques, or interludes. This may reflect a certain disregard for such works as literature, at least in the Elizabethan period. Whatever the reason, the lack of royal patents for the genre meant that any
member of the Stationers' Company could register and print a work for the stage. Such a
situation engendered a degree of disorder. Printers frequently obtained texts in unorthodox
ways, infringing on the rights of acting troupes, playwrights, and other printers. In addition,

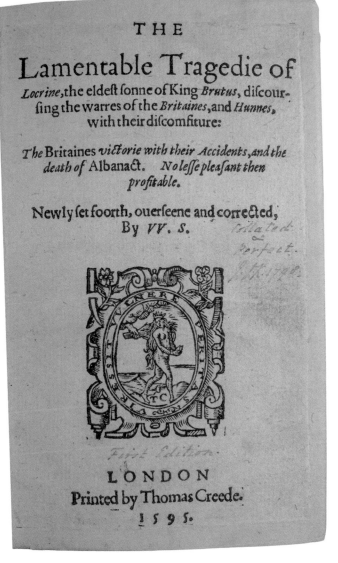

THE

Lamentable Tragedie of

Locrine, the eldeſt ſonne of King Brutus, diſcour-
ſing the warres of the Britaines, and Hunnes,
with their diſcomfiture:

The Britaines victorie with their Accidents, and the
death of Albanact. No leſſe pleaſant then
profitable.

Newly ſet foorth, ouerſeene and corrected,
By VV. S.

LONDON
Printed by Thomas Creede.
1 5 9 5.

5.2,
title
page

plays were not well printed as a rule; quick and shoddy in workmanship, they have more in common with ephemera and broadside printing than with other literary imprints.

The printers represented here exemplify the irregular world of early play printers in England. None of them was particularly egregious for their times, yet all ran afoul of the law: Thomas Colwell (d. c. 1575) was fined twice for printing works registered to others; Thomas Creede (c. 1554–1616) pirated at least one book; and John Danter's (d. 1599) press was raided by the Stationers' Company in 1597 for secretly printing patented works.[1]

Thomas Colwell registered and issued more plays than any other printer in the decade between 1562 and 1572, some fourteen in all. John Bale's *Comedy Concernyng Thre Lawes* is the first play Colwell published. Bale (see item 3.5), who had recently died, certainly had nothing to do with the printing. But even living playwrights in this period often had little or no participation in the printing of their plays. Typically, an author sold a play to an acting troupe, thereby surrendering all rights to the work. The acting troupe, in turn,

A Churchyard and a graue to bury all.

Inge. *Thomas Naſhdo.*

I, here is a fellow *Iudicio* that carried the deadly ſtocke in his pen,whoſe muſe was armed with a gag tooth,and his pen po-ſſeſt with *Hercules* furyes.

Iudg. Let all his faults ſleepe with his mournefull cheſt, And then for euer with his aſhes reſt, His ſtile was witty,though he had ſome gall, Something he might haue mended,ſo may all. Yet this I ſay,that for a mother wit, Few men haue euer ſeene the like of it.

Ing. *Reades the reſt.*

Iud. As for theſe,they haue ſome of them bin the old hedg-ſtakes of the preſſe, and ſome of them are at this inſtant the bots and glanders of the printing houſe. *Fellowes* that ſtande only vpon tearmes to ſerue the turne,with their blotted pa-pers,write as men go to ſtoole,for needes,& when they write, they write as a Beare piſſes,now and then drop a phamphlet.

Ing. *Durum telum neceſſitas*, Good ſayth they do as I do,ex-change words for money,I haue ſome trafficke this day with *Danter*,about a little booke which I haue made,the name of it is a Catalogue of *Chambridge* Cuckolds, but this Beluedere, this methodicall aſſe,hath made me almoſt forget my time:Ile now to Pauls Churchyard,meete me an houre hence, at the ſigne of the Pegaſus in cheap-ſide, and ile moyſt thy temples with a cup of Claret,as hard as the world goes. *Exit. Iudicio.*

### Act. 1.Scen. 3.

#### *Enter Danter the Printer.*

Ing. *Danter* thou art deceiued , wit is dearer then thou takeſt it to bee,I tell thee this libell of Cambridge has much fat and pepper in the noſe: it will ſell ſheerely vnderhand,when all theſe bookes of Exhortations and Catechiſmes, lie moulding on thy ſhopboard.

Dan. It's true, but good faith M. *Ingenioſo*, I loſt by your laſt booke: and you knowe there is many one that paies mee largely for the printing of their inuentions, but for all this you

B 3                                                      ſhall

5·3,
fol. B3[r]

might sell the text to a printer (usually after the show had run its course), or printers might acquire the text in less legitimate ways in order to capitalize on a play's popularity while it was still on the boards. By reviving Bale's play, which was first published in 1548 (under a false imprint during Mary's reign), Colwell probably hoped to find a new audience for it, banking on a reserve of admiration (safely expressed under Elizabeth) for the reforming zeal of the late Bale.

Thomas Creede was a prolific printer of plays, issuing some forty-two between 1591 and 1616.[2] He is best known as the printer of the first quarto editions of Shakespeare's *2 Henry VI* (1594) and *Henry V* (1600). Creede assigns *Locrine,* a play about early British history, to "W. S.," apparently indicating William Shakespeare was the author. And, indeed, the play would appear in the third folio of 1664 among the additional plays attributed to Shakespeare (item 5.31) though it is now consigned to the status of "apocrypha." Other printers issued quartos with title page attributions to W. S. (*Thomas Lord Cromwell,* 1602, and *The Puritan,* 1607, for example), and Creede put William Shakespeare's name on the title page of *The London Prodigal* (1605). It is unclear whether such attributions occurred because of genuine confusion about authorship or in the hope of increasing sales by attaching the well-known playwright's name to an imprint.

George Eld, printer of Jonson's quartos and Shakespeare's *Sonnets,* produced the third item in this group, *The Return from Parnassus* (*Pernassus* on the title page), an anonymous academic satire played at St. John's College in Cambridge. According to the imprint, Eld printed it "for" John Wright, giving us some insight into the world of "jobbing," in which printers worked for stationers, booksellers, and even other printers. Of interest to Shakespeare scholars for its allusions to his poetry and for the inclusion of Richard Burbage and William Kempe as characters, the play also offers an amusing view of the relation between authors and printers. An actual printer named John Danter appears in the play, negotiating over a manuscript with a fictional poet named Ingenioso. In real life, Danter was the publisher of what may be the first play by Shakespeare to appear in print, *Titus Andronicus* (1594), as well as the so-called "bad" quarto of *Romeo and Juliet* (1597). In the play, he represents the worst type of mercenary hack printer and pirate. When Ingenioso attempts to sell a new work, Danter, complaining, "I lost by your last booke," offers a mere forty shillings and a bottle of wine. The author declines, claiming that his work—ribald stuff he calls "a chronicle of Cambridge cuckolds"—deserves better. At the mention of bawdy content, Danter becomes enthusiastic and says, "Oh this will sell gallantly: ile haue it whatsoever the cost" (B3$^r$–$^v$).

Literature: Arber [1875–94] 1950, 1:239, 315, 421; Chambers [1923] 1974, 3:157–200; Hale 1964; McKerrow 1910; Pinciss 1970; Plomer 1906; Yamada 1994.

5.4    Thomas Nashe (1567–1601). *A pleasant comedie, called summers last will and testament.* London: Simon Stafford for Walter Burre, 1600.

    *ESTC* S110081; Greg 173; *STC* 18376. Shelfmark: UIUC IUB00198.

5.5    Ben Jonson (1572–1637). *Every man ovt of his hvmor.* London: Printed for Nicholas Linge, 1600.

    *ESTC* S109227; Greg 163(c); *STC* 14769. Shelfmark: UIUC IUB00180 (Elizabethan Club 105).

My father I will quickly freeze to death,
And then ſole Monarch will I ſit and thinke,
How I may baniſh thee, as thou dooſt me.
    *Winter.* I ſee my downefall written in his browes:
Conuay him hence, to his aſſigned hell.
Fathers are giuen to loue their ſonnes too well.
    *Wil Summer.* No by my troth, nor mothers neither, I am ſure
I could neuer finde it. This *Back-winter* playes a rayling part to
no purpoſe, my ſmall learning findes no reaſon for it, except as
a *Back-winter* or an after winter is more raging tempeſtuous,
and violent then the beginning of Winter, ſo he brings him in
ſtamping and raging as if he were madde, when his father is a
iolly milde quiet olde man, and ſtands ſtill and does nothing.
The court accepts of your meaning; you might haue writ in
the margent of your play-booke, Let there be a fewe ruſhes
laide in the place where *Back-winter* ſhall tumble, for feare of
raying his cloathes: or ſet downe, Enter *Back-winter*, with his
boy, bringing a bruſh after him, to take off the duſt if need require. But you will ne're haue any ward-robe wit while you
liue. I pray you holde the booke well, we be not *nonplus* in the
latter end of the play.
    *Summer.* This is the laſt ſtroke, my toungs clock muſt ſtrike,
My laſt will, which I will that you performe:
My crowne I haue diſpoſde already of.
Item, I giue my withered flowers, and herbes,
Vnto dead corſes, for to decke them with,
My ſhady walkes to great mens ſeruitors,
Who in their maſters ſhadowes walke ſecure,
My pleaſant open ayre, and fragrant ſmels,
To Croyden and the grounds abutting round,
My heate and warmth to toyling labourers,
My long dayes to bondmen, and priſoners,
My ſhort nights to young married ſoules,
My drought and thirſt, to drunkards quenchleſſe throates,
My fruites to *Autumne* my adopted heire,
My murmuring ſprings, muſicians of ſweete ſleepe,
To murmuring male-contents, with their well tun'de cares,
                                                    Channeld

5.4,
fol. H4[v]

5.6     *Everie vvoman in her humor.* London: E. A.
        [Edward Allde] for Thomas Archer, 1609.

*ESTC* S120276; Greg 283(a); *STC* 25948. Shelfmark: UIUC IUA04707
(Elizabethan Club 67).

Walter Burre, Nicholas Ling, and Thomas Archer were stationers who acted as publishers
and booksellers, rather than printers. In the world of playbook publishing, it is not uncommon to find trade printers jobbing for a publisher. The onus of registering the text and
facing the censors fell to the publisher (as did the lion's share of the profits, however). In
the case of plays, a license for printing had to be granted by the same person who approved
the staging of the play, the reigning monarch's Master of the Revels.

How the publisher got the text he entrusted to the trade printer is a matter of conjecture in most cases. We have the fictional account of John Danter haggling with an author over a manuscript (see item 5.3), but we have little real knowledge of how a play moved from the stage to the page. Theories that plays were stolen from the stage via shorthand or passed to printers in deals with dishonest brokers have been questioned in modern scholarship, though contemporary complaints of such practices are not uncommon (see items 5.8 and 5.29).[3]

Walter Burre was taking something of a risk in publishing a play by Thomas Nashe in 1600, since only a year earlier, the Bishops' Ban had explicitly forbidden any further printing of Nashe's works (item 3.9). *Summers Last Will and Testament,* a play about the seasons, has little controversial material in it, but it is interesting in the history of playwriting because characters within the play speak of the need for stage directions. Wishing Winter were less annoyed with him, Will Summer says, "you might have writ in the margent of your play-booke, Let there be a fewe rushes laide in the place where *Back-winter* shall tumble,

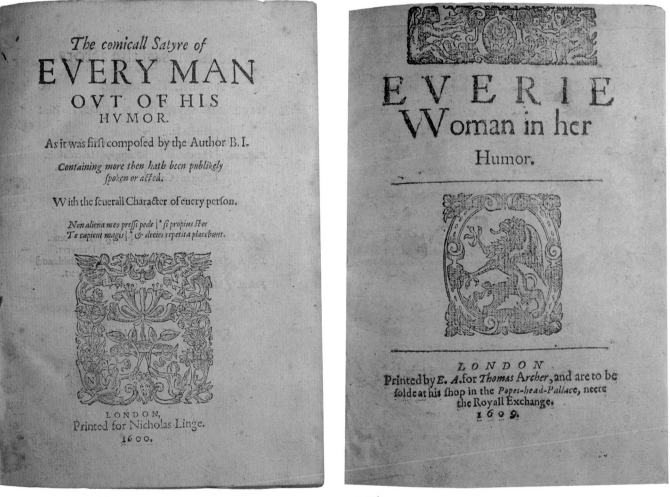

5.5, title page

5.6, title page

for feare of raying his cloathes: or set downe, 'Enter *Back-winter,* with his boy, bringing a brush after him, to take off the dust if need require'" (H4ᵛ).

Another publisher, William Holme, issued Ben Jonson's *Every Man out of His Humor* twice in 1600. Seeing its marketability, Nicholas Ling pirated the Jonson imprint and issued a third printing in the same year. There is no indication that Ling had permission to reprint the edition, nor any record of his having been penalized for doing so. The title page—taken over directly from the first issue—tells us that the printed form of a play could include more than the acted version: "Containing more then hath been publikely spoken or acted."

The anonymous author of the third play has built upon the success of Jonson's *Every Man out of His Humor* and its sequel, *Every Man in His Humor.* This sort of wordplay, parodying titles of other plays, is common in Elizabethan and Jacobean drama. *Every Woman in Her Humor* was not entered in the Stationers' Register or licensed, a potential risk that was frequently taken in this era (although neither registration nor licensing could guarantee ownership). Indeed, seven years earlier, the trade printer of this play, Edward Allde, had been fined 6s. 8d. "for printinge a booke without entrance Contrary to thorders."[4] Its publisher, Thomas Archer, had several run-ins with the authorities and was finally imprisoned in 1621 for printing a newsbook with a false imprint.[5]

Literature: Hanson 1938; Lesser 2004, 115–56; McKerrow 1929.

## 5·7     *"Loves Labor Won."* Fragments of a Stationer's Account Book, 9–17 August 1603.

Shelfmark: UIUC Pre-1650 MS 153.

This fragment from the account book of a stationer in southern England provides evidence of a bookseller's stock in the early seventeenth century, with a tally of items sold over the course of a few days in August 1603. What makes it truly remarkable, however, is the inclusion of the following list of plays for sale under the heading "[inter]ludes & tragedyes":

> marchant of vennis
> taming of a shrew
> knack to know a knave
> knak to know an honest man
> loves labor lost
> loves labor won

The final title provides contemporary evidence that a play by Shakespeare entitled *Love's Labour's Won* existed in print form in 1603. The possibility is corroborated by a 1598 publication by Francis Meres (1565/66–1647) that praises Shakespeare's comedies and mentions "his *Gentlemen of Verona,* his *Errors,* his *Love labors lost,* his *Love labours wonne,* his *Midsummers night dreame,* & his *Merchant of Venice.*"[6]

As Wells and Taylor make clear in their edition of Shakespeare, the existence of lost plays by Shakespeare is entirely plausible. "We know of at least one other lost play attributed

5.7, fragment from a stationer's account book, 1603

to Shakespeare [*Cardenio*], and of many lost works by contemporary playwrights. No copy of *Titus Andronicus* was known until 1904 … and we now know that *Troilus and Cressida* was almost omitted from the 1623 Folio … despite its authenticity."[7]

This fragment at the University of Illinois was discovered in 1953 in the binding of a collection of sermons by Thomas Gataker (1637).[8]

---

Literature: Bald 1958; Baldwin 1957; Wells and Taylor 1986, 349.

5.8    Thomas Heywood (d. 1641). *Pleasant dialogves and dramma's.* London: R. O. [Oulton] for R. H. [Hearne] and are to be sold by Thomas Slater, 1637.

*ESTC* S104070; *STC* 13358. Shelfmark: UIUC 821 H492p (Elizabethan Club 98).

248    *Prologues and Epilogues.*

You cannot in this letter read me plaine,
Hee'l next appeare, in texted hand againe.
*The Epilogue.*
Great I confesse your patience hath now beene,
To see a little *Richard* : who can win,
Or praise, or credit ? eye, or thinke to excell,
By doing after what was done so well ?
It was not my ambition to compare,
No envie, or detraction : such things are
In men of more growne livers, greater spleene,
But in such lads as I am, seldome seene.
I doe, but like a child, who sees one swim,
And (glad to learne) will venter after him,
Though he be soundly duckt for't, or to tell
My mind more plainely, one that faine would spell,
In hope to read more perfect : all the gaines
I expect for these unprofitable paines,
Is, that you would at parting from this place
Doe but unto my littlenesse that grace
To spie my worth, as I have seene dimme eyes
To looke through spectacles, or perspectives,
  That in your gracious view I may appeare,
  Of small, more great ; of coming far off, neare.

*A Prologue to the Play of Queene* Elizabeth *as it was last revived at the* Cock-pit, *in which the author taxeth the most corrupted copy now im-printed, which was published without his consent.*
*Prologue.*
Playes have a fate in their conception lent,
Some so short liv'd, no sooner shew'd, than spent ;
But borne to day, to morrow buried, and
Though taught to speake, neither to goe nor stand.
This : (by what fate I know not) sure no merit,
That it disclaimes, may for the age inherit.

Writing

*Prologues and Epilogues.*    249

Writing 'bove one and twenty; but ill nurst,
And yet receiv'd, as well perform'd at first,
Grac't and frequented, for the cradle age,
Did throng the Seates, the Boxes, and the Stage
So much ; that some by Stenography drew
The plot : put it in print: (scarce one word trew :)
And in that lamenesse it hath limp't so long,
The Author now to vindicate that wrong
Hath tooke the paines, upright upon its feete
To teach it walke, so please you sit, and see't.
*Epilogue.*
The Princesse young *Elizabeth* y'have seene
In her minority, and since a Queene.
A Subject, and a Soveraigne : in th' one
A pittied Lady : in the royall Throne
A potent Queene. It now in you doth rest
To know, in which she hath demeand her best,

*Upon his Majesties last birth-night, he being then thirty five yeares of age, and the Queene great with child.*
A Star appearing of bright constellation,
More luminous than those of the same station,
The powers Cœlestiall much amaz'd thereat
To know the cause thereof, in Councell sate,
And summond *Mercury* the winged god
To search and find what wonder it might bode,
Who brought them word that *Lachesis* then drew
A thread from *Clothoes* distaffe, which to 'his view
Was of such splendor, and withall so fine,
(The substance gold) and of so close a twine,
No edge could sunder, and that Star (so bright)
Rose five and thirty yeares since, as this night.
You are (if time we may compute) by story
In the meridian of your age and glory.
Your *Cynthia* too that shines by you so neare,
And now with such rare splendor fills her sphere,

Whose

5.8, pp. 248–49

5.9, fol. 3ʳ

## 5·9
*New Testament in Shorthand.*
Manuscript, England, c. 1650.

Shelfmark: UIUC Post 1650 MS 68.

Thomas Heywood was a prolific playwright and actor, having written or collaborated on more than two hundred plays, or as he put it "two hundred and twenty, in which I haue had either an entire hand, or at the least a maine finger."[9] Only twenty-four of these plays are now extant. Heywood himself explains the reasons: "one reason is, That many of them by shifting and change of Companies, haue beene negligently lost. Others of them are still retained in the hands of some Actors, who thinke it against their peculiar profit to haue them come in Print. And a third, that it neuer was any great ambition in me, to bee in this kind Volumniously read."[10] In this valuable passage, Heywood gives us a sense of the hectic world of playwriting and the unpredictable fortunes of play scripts.

In the modest collection of *Pleasant Dialogves and Drammas* that Heywood assembled near the end of his life, he included a new prologue to his play *If you know not me, You know no bodie; or, The troubles of Queene Elizabeth* that offers further information about the fate of plays. He complains about an earlier printed version of the play, a "most corrupted copy now imprinted, which was published without his [the author's] consent" (248). Though the pirated edition was printed some thirty-two years earlier, the theft of his text still rankled the playwright. He blames an unscrupulous printer (most likely Thomas Purfoot for Nathaniel Butter) for using the relatively new art of stenography to steal the text during the stage performance:

> Some by Stenography drew
> The plot: put it in print: (scarce one word trew:)
> And in that lamenesse it hath limp't so long,
> The Author novv to vindicate that wrong
> Hath tooke the paines, upright upon its feete
> To teach it vvalke, so please you sit, and see't.
>
> (249)

Heywood also alluded to the practice of unauthorized aural transcription in the 1608 quarto of his *Lucrece,* noting that some of his plays had been "coppied onely by the eare."[11]

Heywood's statement has been cited as an explanation for the inferior texts of many quartos of early English drama and the variants among different editions of the same play. Scholars have debated the significance of shorthand, and there were certainly other ways of obtaining texts (such as stolen scripts or actors' accounts).[12] We have a wealth of evidence, however, that the new shorthand techniques were used in this period to capture sermons and lectures that were then printed. Moreover, several of the men behind those imprints also published playbooks.[13] George Buc, who served as Master of the Revels from 1610 to 1622, mentions the advantages of shorthand for recording the spoken word in *The Third University* (1615), where he specifically refers to plays, claiming, "they which know it can reasonably take a Sermon, Oration, Play, or any long speech, as they are spoken, dictated, acted, and uttered in the instant."[14]

Timothy Bright devised the first English system of shorthand in 1588 and was quickly followed by Peter Bales's *Brachygraphy* (1590) and John Willis's *Stenographie* (1602). The Willis system was revised by Jeremiah Rich in 1646. The manuscript of the New Testament in shorthand exhibited here is written using Rich's system and it dates from about that time. Rich's shorthand technique also migrated to colonial America, where it was popular. At the Salem witch trials, it was used to record depositions.

---

Literature: Davidson 1992 and 1996; Duthie 1949; Kawanami 1996; Matthews 1932, 1933.

5.10    William Shakespeare. *The tragicall historie of Hamlet, Prince of Denmarke. Newly imprinted and enlarged to almost as much againe as it was, according to the true and perfect coppie.* London: J. R. [James Roberts] for N. L. [Nicholas Ling], 1604.

ESTC S111107; Greg 197(b); STC 22276. Shelfmark: Elizabethan Club 168.

5.10,
title
page

The second edition of *Hamlet* is generally regarded as the most authoritative text of the play. It may have been rushed to print after the first appearance of the play (1603), a pirated imprint with many lines badly garbled and half the text missing. The publisher's note on the title page of the second edition says it is "enlarged to almost as much againe as it was" in the first edition. The "true and perfect coppie" from which the second edition was made could have been Shakespeare's autograph manuscript or a fair copy of it. The second edition was reprinted in 1611. The edition in the First Folio of 1623 (item 5.29) presents yet another variant apparently made from a prompt copy of *Hamlet* with non-Shakespearean additions and alterations.

The publishing history of *Hamlet* illustrates the mutability of Elizabethan plays. A playwright's original script might be edited for acting, changed for different audiences, or partially censored by the Master of the Revels, so that different performances were, in fact, different versions. It is no wonder, then, that printed playbooks might reflect different versions, depending on the text in hand and whether it was derived from the author's manuscript, a fair copy, an acting version, players' memories, shorthand dictation, or some other source. In the case of *Hamlet*, we have a vivid representation within the text itself of how variants might come to be. Hamlet, serving as Master of the Revels, informs the actors that he will add a "speech of some dozen or sixteen lines" to their play, *The Murder of Gonzago*, to "catch the conscience of the King" (II.2.88–90).

This copy of the 1604 quarto is one of three surviving exemplars of this edition and the only perfect one. It is, then, the only surviving (complete) copy of the most authentic text of *Hamlet*.

---

Literature: Parrot and Craig 1938; Thomas 1976.

5.11     *The whole contention betvveene the tvvo famous houses, Lancaster and Yorke. With the tragicall ends of the good Duke Humfrey, Richard Duke of Yorke, and King Henrie the sixt. Diuided into two parts: and newly corrected and enlarged.* London: [William Jaggard] for T. P. [Thomas Pavier], [1619].

With: *The late, and much admired play, called Pericles, Prince of Tyre.* London: [William Jaggard] for T. P. [Thomas Pavier], [1619].

*ESTC* S111147; Greg 119(c), 284(d); *STC* 26101. Shelfmarks: UIUC 822.33 W5 1619 and UIUC 822.33 U1 1619 (Elizabethan Club 207 and 189).

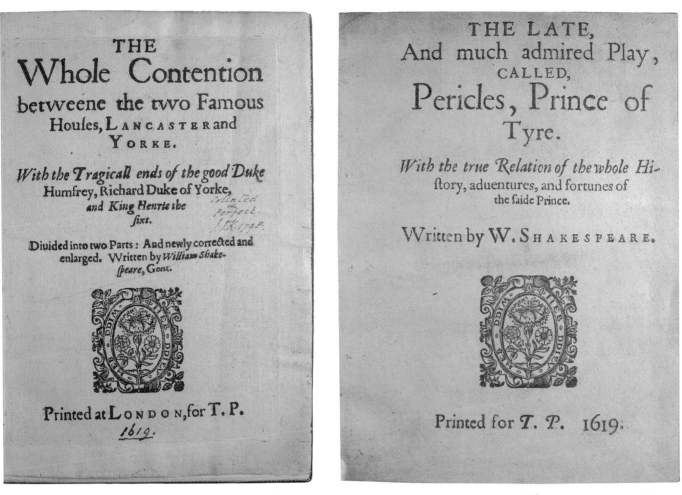

THE
# Whole Contention
betweene the two Famous
Houſes, L A N C A S T E R and
Y O R K E.

*With the Tragicall ends of the good Duke*
*Humfrey, Richard Duke of Yorke,*
*and King Henrie the*
*ſixt.*

Diuided into two Parts : And newly correcɫed and
enlarged. Written by *William Shake-*
*ſpeare, Gent.*

Printed at L O N D O N, for T. P.
*1619.*

THE LATE,
And much admired Play,
CALLED,
Pericles, Prince of
Tyre.

*With the true Relation of the whole Hi-*
*ſtory, aduentures, and fortunes of*
*the ſaide Prince.*

Written by W. S H A K E S P E A R E.

Printed for *T. P.* 1619.

5.11, title page · · · · · · · · · · · · 5.11, title page

5.12     *The excellent history of the merchant of Venice.* [London]:
           J. Roberts [i.e., William Jaggard for Thomas Pavier],
           1600 [i.e., 1619].

           *ESTC* S111195; Greg 172(b); *STC* 22297. Shelfmark: UIUC 822.33 P3 1619
           (Elizabethan Club 181).

5.13     *A most pleasant and excellent conceited comedy, of Sir Iohn*
           *Falstaffe, and the merry vviues of VVindsor.* [London]:
           [William Jaggard] for Arthur Johnson [i.e., Thomas
           Pavier], 1619.

           *ESTC* S111206; Greg 187(b); *STC* 22300. Shelfmark: UIUC 822.33 P5 1619
           (Elizabethan Club 182).

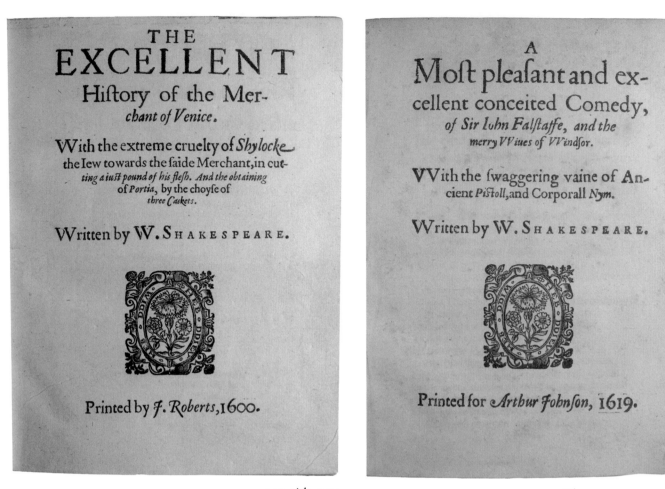

THE
EXCELLENT
Hiſtory of the Mer-
chant of Venice.

With the extreme cruelty of Shylocke
the Iew towards the ſaide Merchant, in cut-
ting a iuſt pound of his fleſh. And the obtaining
of Portia, by the choyſe of
three Caskets.

Written by W. SHAKESPEARE.

Printed by J. Roberts, 1600.

A
Moſt pleaſant and ex-
cellent conceited Comedy,
of Sir Iohn Falſtaffe, and the
merry VViues of VVindſor.

VVith the ſwaggering vaine of Ancient Piſtoll, and Corporall Nym.

Written by W. SHAKESPEARE.

Printed for Arthur Johnson, 1619.

5.12, title page                    5.13, title page

5.14    *M. William Shake-speare, his true chronicle history of*
        *the life and death of King Lear, and his three daughters.*
        [London]: [William Jaggard] for Nathaniel Butter,
        1608 [i.e., 1619].

        ESTC S111098; Greg 265(b); STC 22293. Shelfmark: UIUC 822.33 T3
        1619 (Elizabethan Club 177).

5.15    *The chronicle history of Henry the fift.* [London]:
        [William Jaggard] for T. P. [Thomas Pavier],
        1608 [i.e., 1619].

        ESTC S111119; Greg 165(c); STC 22291. Shelfmark: UIUC 822.33 W3 1619
        (Elizabethan Club 176).

5.16    *A midsommer nights dreame.* [London]: Printed
by James Roberts [i.e., William Jaggard for
Thomas Pavier], 1600 [i.e., 1619].

*ESTC* S111174; Greg 170(b); *STC* 22203. Shelfmark:
UIUC 822.33 P7 1619 (Elizabethan Club 184).

In 1619, three years after Shakespeare's death, the publisher Thomas Pavier (c. 1570–1625)
decided to issue several of Shakespeare's plays (and plays attributed to Shakespeare). Ten
quartos, known as the Pavier Quartos, appeared, eight of which are shown here. The first
three quartos (*IIenry VI*, parts 2 and 3, and *Pericles*) were issued with continuous signatures,
a fact that has led many scholars to conclude that Pavier envisioned the project as a collection.[15] And, indeed, the ten are found bound together in at least two early bindings.[16]
The Pavier texts, which contain many variants and often abbreviate parts of the plays, have
been dubbed "bad" quartos. There is some mystery surrounding Pavier's actions, but the
traditional image of him as a scoundrel who obtained his copy from unscrupulous actors
may not be entirely justified. After all, Pavier held the copyright for four of the ten works

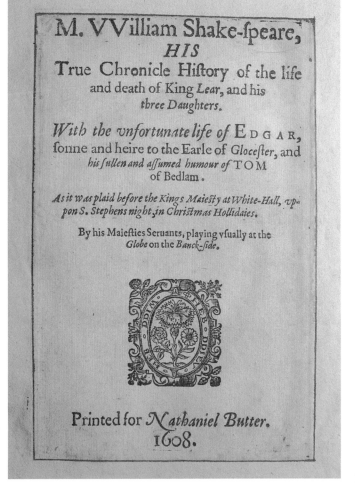

5.14,
title
page

and perhaps negotiated rights with holders of the others. Nonetheless, it is true that the texts differ from those of the First Folio (item 5.29), and it appears that Pavier may have intentionally disguised the productions of 1619 with false imprint dates, perhaps in order to sell them as old stock.

Shakespeare's acting troupe, the King's Men, may have caused Pavier to change his plans in midstream when its patron William Herbert, Earl of Pembroke (1580–1630), officially informed the Stationers' Company that none of the plays acted by the King's Players could be printed without the consent of members of the troupe.[17]

The printer, William Jaggard, would later be involved in the production of the First Folio. His workmanship in the Pavier Quartos is undistinguished, as is common for play-books of the time.[18] The First Folio did not include texts of three of the plays issued by Pavier (*Pericles, A Yorkshire Tragedy, Sir John Oldcastle*), but those plays, in different versions, were added to the second issue of the third folio (1664). Of these, only *Pericles* is now included among Shakespeare's works.

---

Literature: Berger and Lander 1999, 403–5; G. Johnson 1992; Neidig 1910; Plomer 1906; Thomas 1976; Willoughby 1934.

5.15, fol. E1ᵛ–E2ʳ

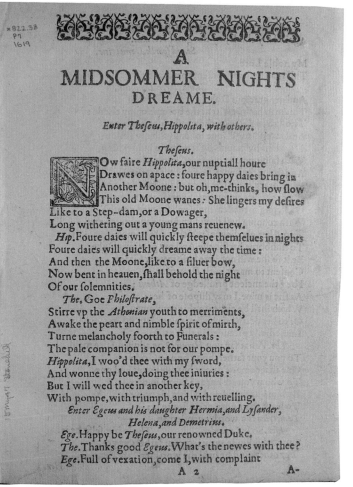

×822.33
P9
1619

A

MIDSOMMER NIGHTS
DREAME.

*Enter Theseus, Hippolita, with others.*

*Theseus.*

Ow faire *Hippolita*, our nuptiall houre
Drawes on apace : foure happy daies bring in
Another Moone : but oh, me-thinks, how flow
This old Moone wanes : She lingers my defires
Like to a Step-dam, or a Dowager,
Long withering out a young mans reuenew.
*Hip.* Foure daies will quickly fteepe themfelues in nights
Foure daies will quickly dreame away the time :
And then the Moone, like to a filuer bow,
Now bent in heauen, fhall behold the night
Of our folemnities.
    *The.* Goe *Philoftrate*,
Stirre vp the *Athenian* youth to merriments,
Awake the peart and nimble fpirit of mirth,
Turne melancholy foorth to Funerals :
The pale companion is not for our pompe.
*Hippolita*, I woo'd thee with my fword,
And wonne thy loue, doing thee iniuries :
But I will wed thee in another key,
With pompe, with triumph, and with reuelling.
        *Enter Egeus and his daughter Hermia, and Lysander,*
            *Helena, and Demetrius.*
    *Ege.* Happy be *Theseus*, our renowned Duke.
    *The.* Thanks good *Egeus*. What's the newes with thee ?
    *Ege.* Full of vexation, come I, with complaint
                    A 2                    A-

5.16,
fol. A2$^r$

5.17    William Shakespeare. *The most excellent and lamentable*
        *tragedie, of Romeo and Iuliet.* London: Thomas Creede
        for Cuthbert Burby, 1599.

        *ESTC* S111179; Greg 143(b); *STC* 22323. Shelfmark: Elizabethan Club 191.

5.18    William Shakespeare. *The historie of Henry the Fourth.*
        London: John Norton for Hugh Perry, 1639.

        *ESTC* S111125; Greg 145(k); *STC* 22287. Shelfmark: UIUC 822.33 W1 1639.

These two playbooks demonstrate that the flow of information was not always from the
stage to the page, for the printed play could also come back to the stage in the form of a
promptbook or actor's script.

The *most lamentable Tragedie*

That lets it hop a litle from his hand,
Like a poore prisoner in his twisted giues,
And with a silken threed, plucks it backe againe,
So louing Iealous of his libertie.
   *Ro.* I would I were thy bird.
   *Iu.* Sweete so would I,
Yet I should kill thee with much cherishing:
Good night, good night.
Parting is such sweete sorrow,
That I shall say good night, till it be morrow.
   *Iu.* Sleep dwel vpon thine eyes, peace in thy breast.
   *Ro.* Would I were sleepe and peace so sweet to rest
The grey eyde morne smiles on the frowning night,
Checking the Easterne Clouds with streaks of light,
And darknesse fleckted like a drunkard reeles,
From forth daies pathway, made by *Titans* wheeles.
Hence will I to my ghostly Friers close cell,
His helpe to craue, and my deare hap to tell.
                 *Exit.*

   *Enter Frier alone with a basket.*
   *Fri.* The grey-eyed morne smiles on the frowning
Checking the Easterne clowdes with streaks of light:
And fleckeld darknesse like a drunkard reeles,
From forth daies path, and *Titans* burning wheeles:
Now ere the sun aduance his burning eie,
The day to cheere, and nights dancke dewe to drie,
I must vpfill this osier cage of ours,
With balefull weedes, and precious iuyced flowers,
The earth that's natures mother is her tombe,
What is her burying graue, that is her wombe:
And from her wombe children of diuers kinde,
We sucking on her naturall bosome finde:
Many for many, vertues excellent:
None but for some, and yet all different.
O mickle is the powerfull grace that lies
In Plants, hearbes, stones, and their true quallities :
                     For

5.17,
fol. D4[v]

This copy of the second edition of *Romeo and Juliet* contains 775 more lines than the first edition of the 1597 "bad" quarto, hence the phrase, "Newly corrected, augmented, and amended" on the title page. Despite some typographical errors, the second edition is the most authoritative text of the play, which went through five quarto editions.

Notations in a seventeenth-century hand here and there in the text show a director's instructions for a performance of the play. These give us a precious glimpse of how a play went from page to stage in this early period. On the page displayed here Juliet's "Parting is such sweete sorrow . . ." is reassigned to Romeo and four lines are cut from Romeo's next speech; there is also an indication that Act II ends here, with directions for music to be played at this point. In modern texts, Act II ends three scenes later. Note that acts and scenes are not marked in the quarto edition.

Shakespeare is not named as the author in either this or the first edition, but he is so named in subsequent editions.

The 1639 edition of *1 Henry IV* was apparently used by a seventeenth-century actor who played Falstaff, for handwritten annotations affect only that character's lines. The changes and deletions all aim to mollify exclamations and potentially bawdy comments by Falstaff. "Zounds," "damnable," and "God" have been struck, for example, and the latter two words replaced by "base" and "heaven" (A4ᵛ). *Henry IV* was first published in 1600 (STC 22289), before James I forbade swearing in plays (1606), but by 1639, it is more likely that Puritan sensibilities (and complaints) caused the actor to tone down some of Falstaff's "earthier" lines.

---

Literature: Erne 2006; Levenson 1999.

5.18, fol. A4ᵛ–B1ʳ

5.19 William Shakespeare. *The tragoedy of Othello, the Moore of Venice. As it hath beene diuerse times acted at the Globe, and at the Black-Friers, by his Maiesties Seruants.* London: N. O. [Nicholas Okes] for Thomas Walkley, 1622.

*ESTC* S111186; Greg 379(a); *STC* 22305. Shelfmark: Elizabethan Club, 186.

*Othello* was performed on 1 November 1604 at the court of King James I and was probably written earlier that year (or possibly in 1603, the year of Elizabeth's death). As the title page of the 1622 quarto affirms, it was subsequently performed repeatedly at the Globe Theatre and the Blackfriars. This first edition of the play was printed after Shakespeare's death in 1616 and is, unlike earlier quarto editions of his plays, divided into acts and scenes, as is the text in the First Folio of 1623 (item 5.29).

If one compares the opening lines of this quarto edition with the opening lines of the First Folio, one sees that the oaths "Tush" and "'Sblood" (i.e., by God's blood) have been deleted in the 1623 printing. This is because of the 1606 Act to Restrain Abuses of Players, which made it illegal for actors to utter blasphemous oaths on the public stage on pain of a heavy fine (ten pounds) for each offense. The quarto was probably printed from a manuscript that antedated the law of 1606, while the First Folio was printed from a later manuscript with all the oaths deleted or softened. The mild interjection "Tush" is actually not blasphemous, but playwrights and printers tended to avoid using any and all interjections for fear of falling afoul of the restraining act of 1606.

Literature: Greg and Hinman 1975.

5.20 George Chapman (1559 / 60–1634) and Inigo Jones (1573–1652). *The memorable maske of the two honorable houses or inns of court; the Middle Temple, and Lyncolns Inne. As it was performd before the King, at White-Hall on Shroue Munday at night; being the 15. of February. 1613. At the princely celebration of the most royall nuptialls of the Palsgraue, and his thrice gratious Princesse Elizabeth. &c.* London: G. Eld, for George Norton, [1613].

*ESTC* S107695; Greg 310(a); *STC* 4981. Shelfmark: UIUC IUA02707.

5.21 Inigo Jones (1573–1652) and William D'Avenant (1606–68). *The Temple of Love. A Masque. Presented by the Qveenes Majesty and her ladies at White-hall on Shrove-Tuesday, 1634.* London: Printed for Thomas Walkley, 1634 [i.e., 1635].

*ESTC* S107859; Greg 497; *STC* 14719 Shelfmark: UIUC IUA07274.

## The Tragedy of Othello *the Moore* of Venice.

Enter *Iago* and *Roderigo*.
*Roderigo.*
TVsh, neuer tell me, I take it much vnkindly
That you *Iago*, who has had my purse,
As if the strings were thine, should'st know of this.
*Iag.* S'blood, but you will not heare me,
If euer I did dreame of such a matter, abhorre me.
*Rod.* Thou toldst me, thou didst hold him in thy hate.
*Iag.* Despise me if I doe not : three great ones of the Citty
In personall suite to make me his Lieutenant,
Oft capt to him, and by the faith of man,
I know my price, I am worth no worse a place.
But he, as louing his owne pride and purposes,
Euades them, with a bumbast circumstance,
Horribly stuft with Epithites of warre :
And in conclusion,
Non-suits my mediators : for certes, sayes he,
I haue already chosen my officer, and what was he?
Forsooth, a great Arithmetition,
One *Michael Cassio*, a Florentine,
A fellow almost dambd in a faire wife,
That neuer set a squadron in the field,
Nor the deuision of a Battell knowes,

B                                                        More

### THE MEMORABLE MASKE

of the two Honorable Houses or Inns of
Court ; *the Middle Temple, and*
Lyncolns Inne.

*As it was performd before the* King, *at*
White-Hall on Shroue Munday at night;
being the 15. of February. 1613.

*At the Princely celebration of the most* Royall
*Nuptialls of the* Palsgraue, *and his thrice gratious*
*Princesse* Elizabeth. &c.

*With a description of their whole show ; in the manner*
of their march on horse-backe to the Court from
the Maister of the Rolls his house : with all
*their right Noble consorts, and most*
*showfull attendants.*

Inuented, and fashioned, with the ground , and
speciall structure of the whole worke,

By our Kingdomes most Artfull and Ingenious
*Architect* INNIGO IONES.

*Supplied, Aplied, Digested, and written,*
*By* GEO: CHAPMAN.

AT LONDON,
Printed by *G. Eld* , for *George Norton* and are to be
sould at his shoppe neere Temple-bar.

5.19, fol. B1ʳ                    5.20, title page

5.22    John Milton (1608–74). [*Comus.*] *A maske presented*
*at Ludlow Castle, 1634: on Michaelmasse night, before*
*the Right Honorable, John Earle of Bridgewater, Vicount*
*Brackly, Lord Præsident of Wales, and one of His Maiesties*
*most honorable Privie Counsell.* London: [Augustine
Mathewes] for Humphrey Robinson, 1637.

*ESTC* S121854; Greg 524(a); *STC* 17937. Shelfmark: UIUC 821
M64 LI5 1637 (Elizabethan Club 135).

The masque, a ceremonial genre specifically designed for court performance, does not
share the same place in printing history with the play. Indeed, the masque was well suited
to printing since publication amplified the commemorative force of the performance at
court. Published masques combine description of the courtly activities with the text of the
performances. The goal is not to capture the voices of actors and the action of the stage in
print, but rather to glorify a royal festivity in verse, song, and pageant. Masques became
popular under James I largely because his wife, Anne of Denmark, and his son, Prince Henry,

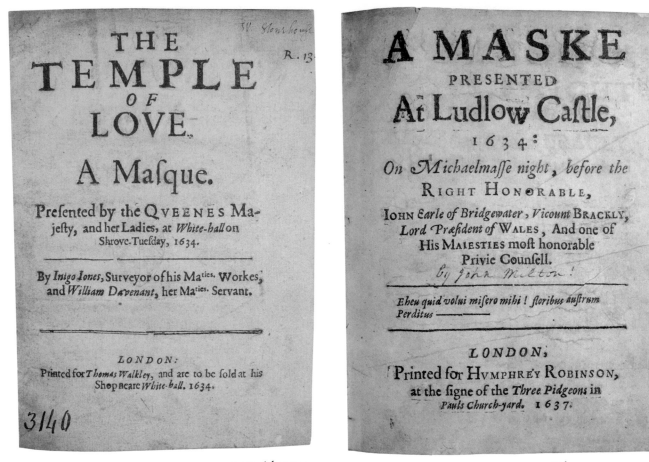

5.21, title page                            5.22, title page

enjoyed them. Ben Jonson, Thomas Campion, Francis Beaumont, and George Chapman were among the most popular writers of masques. Anne even commissioned masques so that she and her ladies could perform in them (often scandalizing the audience).[19]

The Memorable Maske by George Chapman was presented in honor of the marriage of James's daughter Elizabeth to Frederick, Count Palatine. The wedding celebrations also included performances of works by Francis Beaumont, John Fletcher, John Donne, Thomas Campion, and Shakespeare. Because lavish scenery and costumes were essential to masques, playwrights often collaborated with musicians, set designers, and even pyrotechnicians. The architect Inigo Jones himself worked with several playwrights on extravaganzas for the Jacobean court. His contributions to the Memorable Maske included designing elaborate arches, chariots bearing allegorical characters, costumes for Virginian gentlemen, and a parade of torch-bearing Indians in full regalia.

Charles I's queen, Henrietta Maria, also took part in masques, much to the dismay and disapprobation of Puritan factions. In The Temple of Love, the queen took on the role of Inamora, the queen of Narsinga, a representative of Platonic love, while various nobleman performed a dance dressed as "noble Persian youths." The aristocratic players are listed at the end of the published masque. Though William d'Avenant composed the text for the masque, it is Inigo Jones, the designer of the production, who gets first billing on the title page.

In 1634 Milton wrote a masque for performance at Ludlow Castle in honor of the inauguration of John Egerton, Earl of Bridgewater, President of Wales. Three of the earl's children took central roles, and some scholars have speculated that the young Milton played the role of the god Comus, who attempts to seduce a maiden in the woods. The music was composed by Henry Lawes (1546–1662), who may also have acted in the masque and who was certainly responsible for the publication. Milton is not given credit as the author in this first edition of 1637, but he later included it in his *Poems* of 1645.

Literature: Britland 2006; Daye 1998, 255–56; Kernan 1995; Sage 1971; Shohet 2006; Veevers 1989.

5.23    John Marston (1576–1634). *The malcontent. Augmented by Marston. With the additions played by the Kings Maiesties servants. Written by Jhon Webster.* London: V. S. [Valentine Simmes] for William Aspley, [1604].

*ESTC* S112291; Greg 203(c); *STC* 17481. Shelfmark: UIUC IUB00195.

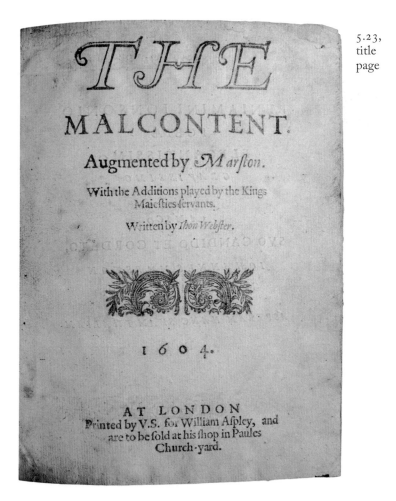

5.23, title page

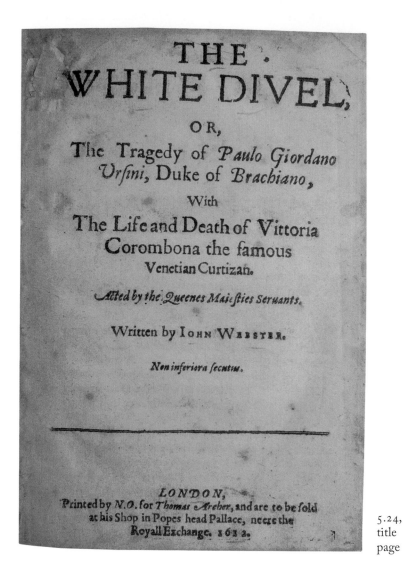

5.24,
title
page

5.24     John Webster (1578 / 80–1638?). *The White Divel.*
         London: N. O. [Nicholas Okes] for Thomas Archer,
         1612.

         ESTC S111501; Greg 306(a); STC 25178. Shelfmark: UIUC
         IUB00193.

5.25     Elizabeth Cary (1585–1639). *The Tragedie of Mariam,
         The faire Queene of Jewry.* London: Thomas Creede, for
         Richard Hawkins, 1613.

         ESTC S107482; Greg 308; STC 4613. Shelfmark: UIUC IUA04777
         (Elizabethan Club 28).

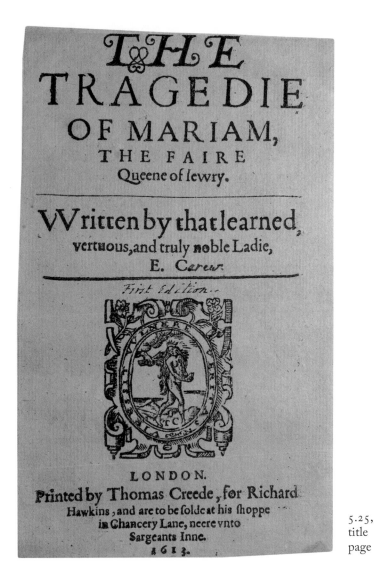

5.25,
title
page

The first edition of John Marston's *The Malcontent* (1604) (which Marston may have "augmented" for the printed version) contains additions made by John Webster when the play was performed by the King's Men. (Marston originally wrote the play for the Children of the Queen's Revels at Blackfriars.) Among Webster's additions is a brief exchange among the actors about how the script came to their acting troupe from another.[20] In his preface "To the Reader," Marston claims that any playbook is a poor attempt to recreate the action of the stage. Nonetheless, he feels he must do it to keep the text from being mangled if printed without his oversight. His discomfort with plays in print is evident:

> I would faine leaue the paper; only one thing afflicts me, to thinke that Scænes inuented, meerely to be spoken, should be inforciuely published to be read, and that the least hurt I can receive, is to do my selfe the wrong. But since others otherwise would doe me more, the least inconvenience is to be accepted. I have my selfe therefore set forth this Comedie; but so, that my inforced absence must much relye vpon the Printers

discretion: but I shall intreate, slight errors in orthographie may bee as slightly over passed; and that the vnhansome shape which this trifle in reading presents, may be pardoned, for the pleasure it once afforded you, when it was presented with the soule of lively action. (A2$^r$)

In the first edition of his tragedy *The White Devil*, John Webster provides a different reason for printing a play. Unlike Thomas Middleton, who rushed his popular *Game at Chess* to press in order to capitalize on its success (item 3.11), Webster says he hopes to find a readership for a play that did not enjoy much of an audience on the stage, "since it was acted, in so dull a time of Winter" (A2$^r$). He goes on to admit, rather churlishly, that he thinks the play can have a second life as a book, since "I haue noted, most of the people that come to that Play-house, resemble those ignorant asses (who visiting Stationers shoppes their vse is not to inquire for good bookes, but new bookes). I present it to the generall view with this confidence" (A2$^r$).

Finally, in Lady Elizabeth Cary's *The Tragedie of Mariam* we find a play written not for performance at all, but solely for private reading. This is the first play by a woman published in England. Her gender and social class as Viscountess of Falkland put her far outside the realm of the playhouse, but the fact that noble ladies were interested in reading plays attests to the ability of the genre to move from the stage to the page.

Literature: Cathcart 2006; Rasmussen 1997, 449; Webster 1996; Weller and Ferguson 1994.

5.26     Ben Jonson. *The workes of Beniamin Jonson.*
London: W. Stansby, for Rich. Meighen, 1616.

*ESTC* S112455; Greg, 1070–3; *STC* 14751. Shelfmark: Elizabethan Club, +13 (UIUC Q. 822 J73 1616; later state, same edition).

In 1616, Ben Jonson published this collection of his *Workes* in a grand folio format. The book—which includes a selection of nine of his plays (with revisions), his *Epigrammes* ("the ripest of my studies") and other poems, entertainments that he wrote for English royalty, and masques—has been called "a major event in the history of . . . the bibliographic ego."[21] He was ridiculed by his contemporaries for including plays among his "Works." Writings for the theater were thought by many to be ephemeral entertainment, not serious literature. But Jonson disagreed. His Latin presentation inscription to Francis Young on the page with the table of contents says, "To the dearest and, next to me, most learned . . . Francis Young. By the gift of his own D.D.L. Author Ben Jonson." Jonson's pride in his learning finds expression elsewhere as well, as when he says to William Drummond of Hawthornden (1585–1649) in the course of their private conversations that he was "better versed, and knew more in Greek and Latin than all the poets in England, and quintessenceth their brains."[22] More modest is his quotation from Catullus's "Dedication to Cornelius" handwritten below the words "The Catalogue": "Because you are accustomed to think my trifles to be something."

Literature: J. Loewenstein 1985; *ODNB* ("Jonson, Ben" by Ian Donaldson).

## The Catalogue.

| | |
|---|---|
| Euery Man in his Humor, | To M̃. CAMBDEN. |
| Euery Man out of his Humor, | To the INNES of COVRT. |
| Cynthias Reuells, | To the COVRT. |
| Poëtaster, | To M̃. RICH. MARTIN. |
| Seianus, | To ESME Lo. Aubigny. |
| The Foxe, | To the VNIVERSITIES. |
| The silent Woman, | To Sir FRAN. STVART. |
| The Alchemist, | To the Lady WROTH. |
| Catiline, | To the Earle of PEMBROK. |
| Epigrammes, | To the same. |
| The Forrest, | |
| Entertaynments, | |
| Panegyre, | |
| Masques, | |
| Barriers. | |

¶ 3

5.26,
fol. ¶3ʳ

5.27    Thomas Heywood (c. 1573–1641). *The fair maid of the vvest. Or, a girle worth gold.* London: [Miles Flesher] for Richard Royston, 1631.

*ESTC* S104035; Greg 445; *STC* 13320. Shelfmark: UIUC IUB00194.

To the READER.

Vrteous Reader, my Plaies have not beene expofed to the publike view of the world in numerous fheets, and a large volume; but fingly (as thou feeft) with great modefty, and fmall noife. Thefe Comedies, bearing the title of, The fair Maid of the Weft: if they prove but as gratious in thy private reading, as they were plaufible in the publick acting, I fhall not much doubt of their fucceffe. Nor neede they (I hope) much fear a rugged and cenforious brow from thee, on whom the greateft and beft in the kingdome, have vouchfafed to fmile. I hold it no neceffity to trouble thee with the Argument of the ftory, the matter it felf lying fo plainly before thee in Acts and Scenes, without any deviations, or winding indents.
Perufe it through, and thou maift finde in it,
Some mirth, fome matter, &, perhaps, fome wit.

He that would ftudie thy
content,

T. H.

5.27,
fol. A4r

5.28    Thomas Heywood. *An apology for actors.*
London: Nicholas Okes, 1612.

ESTC S106113; STC 13309. Shelfmark: Elizabethan Club 92
(UIUC 792 H516a).

In the quarto edition of Heywood's *The Fair Maid of the West*, the playwright casts aspersions on the practice of gathering plays into grand folios: "Curteous Reader, my Plaies have not beene exposed to the publicke view of the world in numerous sheets, and a large volume; but singly (as thou seest) with great modesty, and small noise" (A4r). Eventually, however, Heywood did assemble many of his writings in one volume, albeit in a diminutive octavo-sized volume (item 5.8), in order to correct the many errors he saw in quartos that had appeared without his oversight or permission.

Educated at Cambridge University and a gifted writer, Heywood claimed to have authored or contributed to two hundred twenty plays. Like Shakespeare, Heywood was both an actor and a playwright. He wrote nondramatic works as well, especially during enforced closings of theaters due to the plague. In response to a spate of denunciations of drama and the English theater by the Puritans Stephen Gosson, Anthony Munday, Philip Stubbes, and William Vaughan over the years 1577 to 1608, Heywood published *An Apology for Actors* (shown opposite page 137), the best of several defenses of the theater against Puritan attacks.

In a prefatory poem "To my good friend and fellow, Thomas Heywood," Christopher Beeston sums up Heywood's argument:

> Of all the modest pastimes I can finde,
> To content me, of playes I make best vse,
> As most agreeing with a generous minde.
> There see I vertues crowne, and sinnes abuse.
> Two houres well spent, and all their pastimes done,
> Whats good I follow, and whats bad I shun.
>
> (A3ʳ)

In a section on "actors and the true use of their quality," Heywood claims that plays, besides attracting people away from activities like drinking and gambling, provide inspiring models for good behavior, and display in satires the ugliness of vices, Heywood shrewdly adds that "Playes are writ with this ayme, and carryed with this methode, to teach the subiects obedience to their King, to shew the people the vntimely ends of such as haue moued tumults, commotions, and insurrections, . . . exhorting them to allegeance, dehorting them from all trayterous and fellonious strategems" (F3ᵛ).

Almost as an afterthought, Heywood notes that the English stage has also improved the English language:

> our English tongue, which hath ben the most harsh, vneven, and broken language
> of the world, part Dutch, part Irish, Saxon, Scotch, Welsh, and indeed a gallimaffry
> of many, but perfect in none, is now by this secondary meanes of playing, continu-
> ally refined, euery writer striuing in himselfe to adde a new florish vnto it; so that in
> processe, from the most rude and vnpolisht tongue, it is growne to a most perfect and
> composed language, and many excellent workes, and elaborate Poems writ in the same,
> that many Nations grow inamored of our tongue (before despised). (F3ʳ)

The book concludes with a note to the printer Nicholas Okes, whom Heywood praises for his careful and serious work, contrasting him to another printer, Jaggard, who once refused to print an errata sheet for him: "hee would not publish his owne disworke-manship, but rather let his owne fault lye vpon the necke of the Author" (G4ʳ).

A heated response to Heywood's treatises by one "I. G." entitled *A Refutation of the Apology for Actors* (1615) was undistinguished and had little effect.

---

Literature: Chambers [1923] 1974, 3:338–48; *ODNB* ("Heywood, Thomas" by David Kathman).

5.29    *Mr. William Shakespeares comedies, histories, & tragedies. Published according to the true originall copies.* London: Isaac Jaggard and Ed. Blount [for W. Jaggard, Ed. Blount, J. Smethwick, and W. Aspley], 1623.

*ESTC* S111228; *STC* 22273. Shelfmark: UIUC IUQ00001 (Elizabethan Club +28).

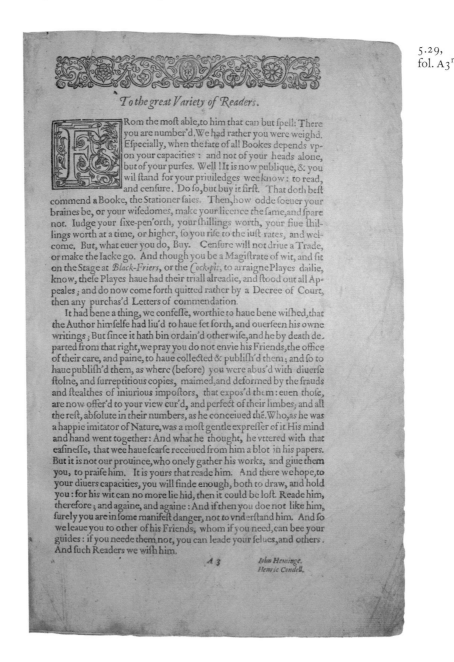

5.29,
fol. A3ʳ

## To the Reader

This Figure, that thou here seest put,
It was for gentle Shakeſpeare cut;
Wherein the Graver had a ſtrife
VVith Nature, to out-doo the life :
O, could he but have drawne his VVit
As well in Braſſe, as he hath hit
His Face; the Print vvould then ſurpaſſe
All, that was ever vvrit in Braſſe.
But, ſince he cannot, Reader, looke
Not on his Picture, but his Booke.

B. I.

M^R. WILLIAM
# SHAKESPEARES
COMEDIES,
HISTORIES, and
TRAGEDIES.
Publiſhed according to the true Originall Copies.
*The ſecond Impreſsion.*

LONDON,
Printed by *Tho. Cotes*, for *Robert Allot*, and are to be ſold at the ſigne
of the Blacke Beare in Pauls Church-yard. 1 6 3 2.

5.30, title page

5.30    *Mr. William Shakespeares comedies, histories,
and tragedies. Published according to the true
originall copies.* London: Tho[mas] Cotes for
Robert Allot, [John Smethwick, William
Aspley, Richard Hawkins, and Richard
Meighen], 1632.

*ESTC* S111235; *STC* 22274a. Shelfmark: UIUC IUQ00002
(Elizabethan Club +29).

Vpon the Effigies of my vvorthy
Friend, the Author Mafter VVilliam
Shakefpeare, and his VVorkes,

*Pectator, this Lifes Shaddow is ; To fee*
*The truer image and a livelier he*
*Turne Reader. But, obferve his Comicke vaine,*
*Laugh, and proceed next to a Tragicke ftraine,*
*Then weepe; So when thou find'ft two contraries,*
*Two different paffions from thy rapt foule rife,*
*Say, ( who alone effect fuch wonders could)*
*Rare Shake-fpeare to the life thou doft behold.*

An Epitaph on the admirable Dramaticke
Poet, VV. SHAKESPEARE.

*Hat neede my Shakefpeare for his honour'd bones,*
*The labour of an Age, in piled ftones*
*Or that his hallow'd Reliques fhould be hid*
*Vnder a ftarre-ypointing Pyramid ?*
*Deare Sonne of Memory, great Heire of Fame,*
*What needft thou fuch dull witneffe of thy Name ?*
*Thou in our wonder and aftonifhment*
*Haft built thy felfe a lafting Monument :*
*For whil'ft to th'fhame of flow-ende vouring Art*
*Thy eafie numbers flow, and that each part,*
*Hath from the leaves of thy unvalued Booke,*
*Thofe Delphicke Lines with deepe Impreffion tooke*
*Then thou our fancy of her felfe bereaving,*
*Doft make us Marble with too much conceiving,*
*And fo Sepulcher'd in fuch pompe doft lie*
*That Kings for fuch a Tombe would wifh to die.*

5.30,
fol. A5^r

5.31   *Mr. William Shakespear's comedies, histories, and tragedies.*
*Published according to the true original copies. The third*
*impression. And unto this impression is added seven playes,*
*never before printed in folio. viz. Pericles Prince of Tyre.*
*The London prodigall. The history of Thomas Ld. Cromwell.*
*Sir John Oldcastle Lord Cobham. The Puritan widow.*
*A York-shire tragedy. The tragedy of Locrine.* London:
[Roger Daniel, Alice Warren, and another] for P. C.
[Philip Chetwinde], 1664.

*ESTC* R30560; Wing S-2914. Shelfmark: UIUC IUQ00007 (Elizabethan
Club +31).

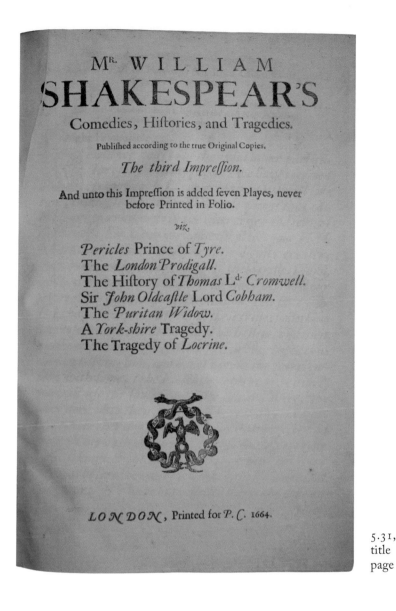

Mr William
SHAKESPEAR'S
Comedies, Histories, and Tragedies.

Published according to the true Original Copies.

The third Impression.

And unto this Impression is added seven Playes, never
before Printed in Folio.

viz.

Pericles Prince of Tyre.
The London Prodigall.
The History of Thomas Ld Cromwell.
Sir John Oldcastle Lord Cobham.
The Puritan Widow.
A York-shire Tragedy.
The Tragedy of Locrine.

LONDON, Printed for P. C. 1664.

5.31,
title
page

5.32    *Mr. William Shakespear's comedies, histories, and tragedies.*
*Published according to the true original copies. Unto which is*
*added, seven plays.* London: Printed for H. Herringman,
E. Brewster, and R. Bentley, 1685.

*ESTC* R25621; Wing S-2915. Shelfmark: UIUC IUQ00008
(Elizabethan Club +32).

As far as we know, Shakespeare never saw a play to press. Perhaps he agreed with his colleague John Marston (item 5.23), who felt a play's "life rests much in the Actors voice," and that "scænes invented, meerely to be spoken," should not be "inforcively published to be read."[23]

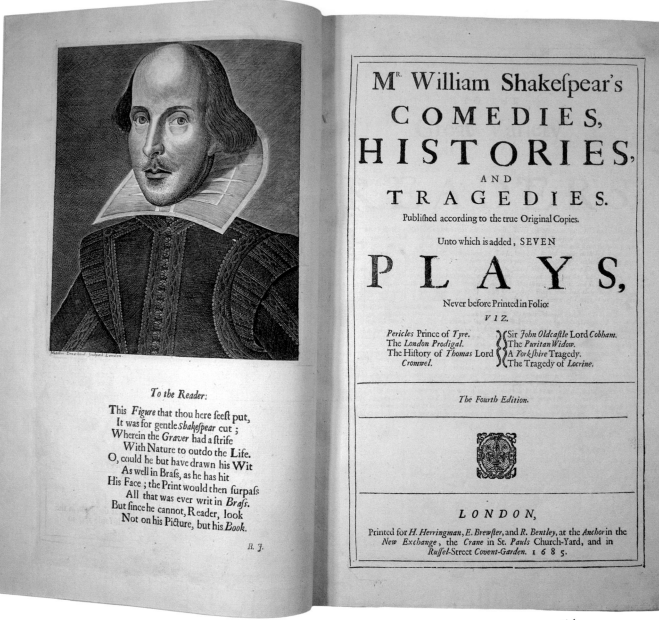

To the Reader:

This *Figure* that thou here feeft put,
It was for gentle *Shakefpear* cut ;
Wherein the *Graver* had a ftrife
With Nature to outdo the Life.
O, could he but have drawn his Wit
As well in *Brafs*, as he has hit
His Face ; the Print would then furpafs
All that was ever writ in *Brafs*.
But fince he cannot, Reader, look
Not on his Picture, but his *Book*.

B. J.

Mʀ William Shakefpear's
COMEDIES,
HISTORIES,
AND
TRAGEDIES.
Publifhed according to the true Original Copies.

Unto which is added, SEVEN
PLAYS,
Never before Printed in Folio:
V I Z.

*Pericles* Prince of *Tyre.*          ⎧Sir *John Oldcaftle* Lord *Cobham.*
The *London Prodigal.*          ⎪The *Puritan Widow.*
The Hiftory of *Thomas* Lord ⎨A *Yorkfhire* Tragedy.
*Cromwel.*                                  ⎩The Tragedy of *Locrine.*

The Fourth Edition.

LONDON,
Printed for *H. Herringman, E. Brewfter,* and *R. Bentley,* at the *Anchor* in the
*New Exchange,* the *Crane* in St. *Pauls* Church-Yard, and in
*Ruffel*-Street *Covent-Garden.* 1 6 8 5.

5.32, title page

Some seven years after the playwright's death, perhaps spurred on by Pavier "bad" quartos (items 5.11–16), or emboldened by Jonson's folio production (item 5.26), William Shakespeare's colleagues took it upon themselves to collect and have published in folio all of his plays. The First Folio appeared in 1623 and includes the texts of thirty-six plays, eighteen of which had never before been published, as well as variant texts for several previously published works. The chief compilers, Shakespeare's fellow actors John Heminge and Henry Condell, claim to have made use of "the true original copies" as their source texts. In their preface "To the Great Variety of Readers" (item 5.29) the compilers allude to pirated and stolen texts—"diverse stolne and surreptitious copies, maimed and deformed by the frauds and stealths of iniurious impostors"—that had been published before. They assure the reader that the plays in this folio are "now offer'd to your view cur'd, and perfect of their limbes, and all the rest, absolute in their numbers, as he conceiued them" (A3ʳ).

Ben Jonson's famous "To the Reader" poem that accompanies the engraving of Shakespeare advises readers to look not to portraiture for Shakespeare's character, but to his words. Another commendatory poem in that volume, by James Mabbe (1571 / 72 – 1642), equates printing with revival, in both a theatrical and a metaphysical sense:

> Wee wondred (Shake-speare) that thou went'st so soone
> From the Worlds-Stage, to the Graues-Tyring-roome.
> We thought thee dead, but this thy printed worth
> Tels thy Spectators, that thou went'st but forth
> To enter with applause. An Actors Art
> Can dye, and liue, to acte a second Part.
> That's but an Exit of Mortalitie;
> This, a Re-entrance to a Plaudite.
>
> (A6ʳ)

Originally priced between 15 shillings and £1, the last copy on the market sold for £2.8 million in July 2006.

The Second Folio, which appeared in 1632, is essentially a reprint of the First Folio, although it contains over sixteen hundred anonymous typographical and editorial corrections that have provided fodder (and headaches) for subsequent editors.[24] The Second Folio was issued with six variant title pages, one for each of the publishers involved in the project. Otherwise, a new text appears on the leaf conjugate to the imprint page, "An Epitaph on the admirable Dramaticke Poet, VV. Shakespeare," unsigned, but known to be by John Milton (item 5.30, A5ʳ). It is, in fact, the first published poem by Milton, who includes it in his 1645 edition of *Poems,* and dates it to 1630.

The Third Folio was issued twice, once in 1663 and again in 1664. The second issue, shown here, augmented the Shakespearean corpus with seven additional plays. Of the seven, only *Pericles* has stood the test of time and been accepted as authentic by modern scholarship. *Pericles* had appeared earlier in quarto, twice in 1609, in 1611, and in the 1619 aborted printing project of Thomas Pavier (items 5.11 – 16).

By the time the Fourth Folio came out in 1684, Shakespeare had been canonized in both senses of the word. Of the four folios, the Fourth has been called "the most readable text and the most workmanlike piece of printing."[25] The typography has been standardized, with stage directions consistently in italics, and punctuation has been improved. Nonetheless, it is the First Folio that continues to capture the imagination of book collectors and lovers of Shakespeare's plays.

---

Literature: Black 1936; Black and Shaaber 1937; Blayney 1991.

6.17, binding by Samuel Mearne, c. 1673

# 6

## MAKING
## ENGLISH BOOKS

6.1 William Shakespeare. *The tragedy of King Richard the third. . . . As it hath beene lately acted by the right honourable the Lord Chamberlaine his seruants.* London: Valentine Sims [and Peter Short], for Andrew Wise, 1597.

*ESTC* S111093; Greg 142(a); *STC* 22314. Shelfmark: Elizabethan Club +33.

This remarkable fragment of a Shakespeare quarto illustrates a sixteenth-century English book in the making. Normally, a quarto is printed as four pages on each side of a sheet and then folded twice to produce four leaves or eight pages of a book. In England, however, it was not uncommon for early printers to use half sheets, like the one shown here, presumably as oddments to add pages, to facilitate work on a smaller platen, or when type was in short supply. Indeed, many Elizabethan plays were printed in quarto on half sheets.[1] Unfolded sheets could serve as proof copy for the corrector in a print shop. Printers also delivered their books to stationers either in sheets or folded gatherings, where they were sold unbound. Customers might have the signatures stab-stitched (see item 6.13) or they might have them professionally bound, either alone or grouped with other books of similar genre or size.

The first quarto of *Richard III* was published in 1597, but stylistic features have persuaded most scholars that it was written several years earlier. Based upon Holinshed's *Chronicle,* the play was performed often and printed in quarto editions in 1597, 1598, 1602, 1605, 1612, 1622, 1629, and 1634.

6.1, *Richard III* half sheet, 1597

This item and other printer's sheets were acquired by the Elizabethan Club through an exchange in 1911 with the British Museum—hence the British Museum's duplicate stamp on each of the sheets.

Literature: Blayney 1997; BMC xi, 23–24; Bowers 1948; Maguire 1999; Mulryne 1975.

6.2     John Gower (c. 1325–1408). *Confessio amantis.*
         London: Thomas Berthelet, 1532.

         ESTC S106702; STC 12143. Shelfmark: UIUC IUQ03504.

6.3     *Ælfric, Abbot of Eynsham (d. 1005). A testimonie of antiqvitie, shewing the auncient fayth in the Church of*

6.4  *The Bible and Holy Scriptvres conteyned in the Olde and Newe Testament. Translated according to the Ebrue and Greke, and conferred with the best translations in diuers langages. With moste profitable annotations vpon all the hard places, and other things of great importance as may appeare in the Epistle to the Reader.* Geneva: Rouland Hall, 1560.

DMH 107; ESTC S101758; STC 2093. Shelfmark: UIUC IUA01212.

6.2, fol. 79ᵛ–80ʳ

6.3, fol. L7ᵛ and colophon

6.5     *Biblia sacra polyglotta.* Edited by Brian Walton. London: Thomas Roycroft, [1654–57].

ESTC R36567; Wing B-2797. Shelfmark: UIUC F. 220.56 P76 1655.

From Caxton's books at the end of the fifteenth century (items 1.3, 4.1, and 6.10) to the 1660 broadside condemning Milton's books (item 3.15), this exhibition includes numerous examples of typefaces generally known as "black letter." The term (also sometimes called "Gothic" or simply "English") is applied to a variety of fonts used in early printing in England and in contrast to the roman typeface that supplanted black letter in English and most other Western languages.[2] The black-letter fonts were imported to England first from France, but also from Germany and the Low Countries. Within the general category called black letter there are several different forms, most important, rotunda, textura, bastarda, and secretary. Caxton, for example, used eight different types. Although more common for vernacular texts, black letter existed side by side with roman and italic typefaces in England as of the early sixteenth century, often used together as typographic indications of textual nuances.

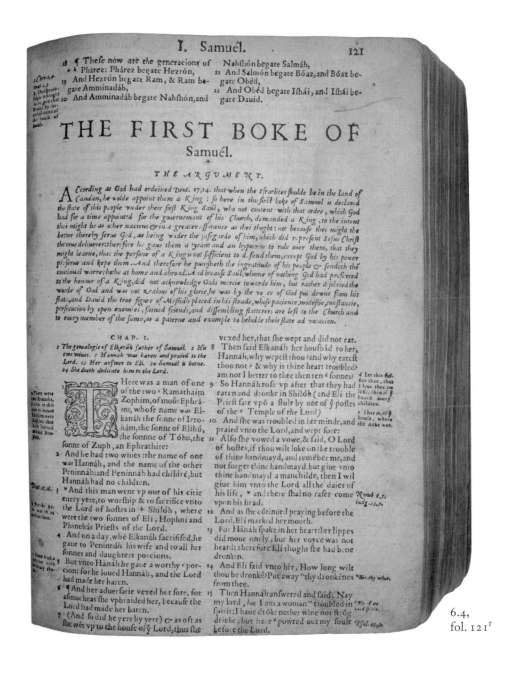

6.4,
fol. 121ʳ

In the *Confessio Amantis* of John Gower (the second edition after Caxton's 1483 imprint), Thomas Berthelet uses three typefaces, bastarda, rotunda, and roman, to distinguish between introductory material, English verse, and Latin text. Berthelet introduced several roman and italic fonts to England, apparently acquired from a foundry in Cologne. Similar mixtures of typeface occur in many other books in England, as is evident in a few examples from this exhibition: Chapman's *Homer* sets classical names in roman (item 4.7); the King James Bible distinguishes notes and conjectures from literally translated text through the use of typography (item 4.17), while the 1572 edition of the Bishops' Bible (item 4.15) used roman and black letter for its side by side renditions of the Psalms; and many grammars

*6.5, vol. 1, Prolegomena,* 11–12

and dictionaries use different fonts to distinguish between languages (items 2.6, 2.7, and 2.8, for example).

Early letter founding in England was, it seems, in the hands of French and Dutch punchcutters and founders, who either exported their wares to England or were at work in London.[3] The printer John Day is an important figure in early English letter founding. The typographic excellence of Day's work (see item 4.5) won him lucrative patents under Queen Elizabeth, but his most significant patron was Matthew Parker, the archbishop of Canterbury. It was for Parker that he produced (or had produced) the first truly "English" font made in England, Anglo-Saxon characters that first appeared in Parker's edition of Ælfric's *A testimonie of antiqvitie* in about 1566. The renowned French typographer François Guyot lived for a time in Day's house and may have contributed to his typographic interest and skill. In *A testimonie of antiqvitie*, Day included a type specimen (L7ᵛ) showing the twenty-four sorts used in his Anglo-Saxon font.

From the first edition of the complete English Bible in 1535 to the King James Bible of 1611, black letter was the preferred font for the sacred word in English. In 1560, however, a complete English Bible printed in a roman typeface appeared for the first time. The translators of the Geneva Bible, Protestant reformers who fled Queen Mary's England, produced a foreign-looking but fresh translation of the English Bible from the original languages. Its smaller format (quarto), roman type, and reform-oriented marginal notes, however, did nothing to dampen its popularity in England in the years after Mary's death. Quite the contrary; this new translation, also the first English Bible to be divided into verses, became the most popular Bible translation in Elizabethan England. It was largely to counter the popularity of the Geneva version—with its Calvinist notes—that King James agreed to support the new translation project that produced the Authorized Version of 1611. Certainly inspired by the Geneva Bible, early editions of the King James Bible appeared not only in large, folio format, but also in smaller formats, printed in roman as well as black letter (the first quarto and octavo editions appeared in 1612, and both were printed in roman).

In the early 1650s, the orientalist, philologist, and biblical scholar Brian Walton decided to undertake a monumental work of biblical scholarship: the so-called London Polyglot, printed by Thomas Roycroft from 1654 to 1657. The greatest of the Renaissance polyglot Bibles, the London Polyglot presented the texts in the original languages of the oldest and best manuscripts, requiring fonts for no fewer than nine languages. Ironically, this monument of English typography contains no English-language text. New types, specifically Hebrew, Syriac, Samaritan, Arabic, and Ethiopic, had to be cut for the Polyglot (though all but perhaps the Hebrew were based on French models). The complexity of the editorial project benefited greatly from the layout of the page, which, though crowded and sometimes criticized by connoisseurs of typography, allows a scholar to compare the texts efficiently. Oliver Cromwell supported the project—apparently at the urging of John Milton[4]—by allowing the paper (some seven thousand reams) to be imported duty-free. Walton thanked the Protector in the original preface, but when Cromwell died a year later, Walton quickly cancelled the last three leaves of the preface and added a dedication to Charles II instead. The University of Illinois copy shown here contains the original Cromwellian preface.

The first volume of the London Polyglot is open to Walton's *Prolegomenon,* the last part of the set published. (Subscribers were advised not to bind the first volume when it was delivered in 1654, but to wait for this part, which would be printed at the end.) The typographic bravura reaches its apex here in a three-and-a-half page spread of characters to which Walton refers in a rather speculative discussion of the development of the alphabet. The nine languages of the *Polyglot* are represented in majuscule and minuscule and with variants for three Syriac scripts and rabbinical Hebrew. In addition, woodcut letters were cut for Armenian, Coptic, Illyrian, Cyrillic, Georgian, Gothic, and Chinese characters in this section.[5]

Literature: Barker 2002a and 2002b; Barnard 2001, 10; A. Johnson 1936; *ODNB* ("Walton, Brian" by D. S. Margoliouth, revised by Nicholas Keene); Reed and Johnson 1952, 153–63; Turner 1949.

## 6.6 Ranulf Higden (d. 1364). *Polycronicon.*
## Westminster: Wynkyn de Worde, 13 April 1495.

BMC xi 195; *ESTC* S106488; Goff H-268; *GW* 12469; *ISTC* ih00268000; *STC* 13439. Shelfmark: UIUC Incunabula Q. 909 H53p:Et1495.

6.6, fol. 101ʳ

6.7, fol. K4<sup>v</sup>–L1<sup>r</sup>

6.7    Richard Alison (fl. 1588–1606). *The Psalmes of Dauid
in meter, the plaine song beeing the common tunne to be sung
and plaide vpon the lute, orpharyon, citterne or base violl,
seuerally or altogether, the singing part to be either tenor
or treble to the instrument, according to the nature of the
voyce, or for fowre voyces: with tenne short tunnes in the
end.* London: William Barley, the assigne of Thomas
Morley, 1599.

*ESTC* S107043; *STC* 2497. Shelfmark: UIUC IUA00101.

Music presents special challenges for printers. It can be set, with difficulty, in special fonts, produced with woodcuts, or engraved (after about 1600 in England), but any of these techniques requires painstaking preparation and execution. Moreover, the market for printed music was limited, and manuscript transmission of music was just as important, if not more, for circulating musical works in the Renaissance. Complicating matters further, the field of music printing in sixteenth-century England was controlled largely by patents, in particular, one for Psalm books and a separate one for secular music and ruled paper. Despite all this, England excelled in the area of music printing, particularly from the mid-sixteenth to the mid-eighteenth century.

The earliest example of printed music in England appears in Wynkyn de Worde's 1495 edition of Ranulf Higden's *Polycronicon*. Caxton had printed the same work in 1482, but left blank spaces for the music to be filled in by hand. De Worde took up the challenge, using rules and quadrats (upside-down pieces of type) to make up a brief example of eight notes. Clearly, he had not hit upon a satisfactory solution for printing music. Fewer than a dozen books with music were printed in England before 1530.

The typographic challenges of music printing were significant, but apparently worth the trouble in England after the mid-sixteenth century. William Seres had the lucrative psalter license in 1552, but John Day and his son Richard held the patent longer, from 1559 until 1603. The printers Thomas Vautrollier, John Wolfe, and Henry Bynneman were also involved in music printing, but toward the end of the sixteenth century, the patents for this specialized type of printing shifted to composers and musicians. In 1575, for example, Queen Elizabeth granted William Byrd and Thomas Tallis, both musicians, a patent for printing music and for the importation of music books from the Continent. The composer Thomas Morley (1556 / 57–c. 1602), perhaps best known as the creator of the English madrigal, took over the patent for ruled paper (an important component of music printing) from William Byrd, his teacher, in 1598 and soon became the leading publisher of music in England. In 1599, he produced this "tablature book," a lute-book psalter in which five parts are typographically arranged for performers gathered around a table. As Krummel notes, "the lute [citern] part and the top voice appear on the verso or the bottom two-thirds of [the page], presumably so that the neck of the instrument, protruding to the left, would not interfere with other singers."[6] Though a charming and clever layout—and obviously the work of a musician with printing interests (Morley)—the format did not outlive its publisher.

Literature: Krummel 1975, 103–6; Steele 1903, no. 178.

6.8    John Norden (c. 1547–1625?). *Specvlvm Britanniae*. [London: Eliot's Court Press, 1593.]

*ESTC* S113229; *STC* 18635. Shelfmark: UIUC IUB00182.

6.9    John Speed (1551 / 52–1629). *The theatre of the empire of Great Britaine: presenting an exact geography of the kingdomes of England, Scotland, Ireland, and the iles*

*adioyning.* London: [William Hall] for John
Sudbury & Georg Humble, 1611 [i.e., 1612].

*ESTC* S117917; *STC* 23041. Shelfmark: UIUC F. 941 Sp32t.

The sixteenth century was a pioneering age for cartography in Europe. Sebastian Münster (1489–1552), Christopher Saxton, Abraham Ortelius (1527–98), and Gerard Mercator (1512–94) produced their grand maps and atlases in this period. Maps also appear within a variety of printed books in England; in histories and Bibles, for example, one finds both woodcut and engraved maps. England can lay claim to the first national atlas, a work published in 1579 with maps by the father of English cartography, Christopher Saxton.

Saxton's younger contemporary, John Norden, is known for his panorama of London, *The View of London Bridge from East to West* (1597).[7] He was a surveyor by trade and his *Speculum Britanniae* of 1593 includes important maps of Middlesex and useful plans of the cities of Westminster and London. These are original works—not based on earlier maps—and invaluable for understanding the topography of Elizabethan England. In most cases, maps were drawn by the cartographer and then engraved by someone else. Norden's engraver was Pieter van der Keere. In Norden's *Speculum Britanniae* a marginal index with a key of letters and numbers is used for the first time in an English map. This innovation makes sense in a work like the *Speculum,* which is not a grand atlas, but more of a guidebook, complete with foldout maps and information pertinent to the traveler to London, such as a summary of the city's history, a list of parishes, descriptions of noteworthy landmarks, and praise of its merits as a city "most sweetly scituate upon the Thamis" (F2ᵛ). The University of Illinois copy includes a presentation inscription in Norden's hand.

Norden's project to map all the counties of England in this way did not come to fruition, but some of his maps appear in the 1607 edition of William Camden's *Britannia.* Norden's maps of Middlesex, Westminster, and London were also included in John Speed's *Theatre of the Empire of Great Britaine* (1611 / 12).

Speed's atlas is an amalgam of the work of the Elizabethan cartographers Christopher Saxton, John Norden, and William Camden, though the maps were freshly and expertly cut by Jodocus Hondius (1563–1612), a Dutch map engraver, who worked on the project from Amsterdam. (The map of Ireland is based on one made by Hondius in 1591.) *The Theatre of the Empire of Great Britaine* contains the first complete set of individual county maps of England and Wales, as well as maps of Ireland and Scotland. Indeed, the atlas seems to have served an imperial function. James I had declared himself "King of Great Britain" in 1604, and on the initial map in Speed's atlas (dated 1610) the designation "Great Britaine and Ireland" appears for the first time.

The bookshop of the publishers John Sudbury and George Humble specialized in engravings and maps that were sold as separate prints. Speed's atlas must have sold well because it appeared in at least a dozen editions—printed by various assigns—before 1650. It should be noted that the maps were probably not colored when sold; some hand-coloring of Speed maps dates from the seventeenth century, but many were colored as late as the twentieth century.

Literature: Lynam 1950; *ODNB* ("Norden, John" by Frank Kitchen, and "Speed, John" by Sarah Bendall); Worms 2002.

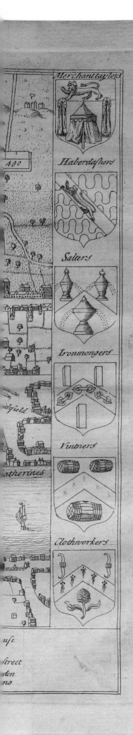

*Kenton*, E. 10.
*Knightesbridge*, G. 18.
*Kensington*, G. 16.

*Kingstonwyke*, K. 14. It is a Hamlet neere *Kingstone* vpon *Thamis*, standing in MYDDLESEX, and is so called, for that it is a rowe of houses leading into *Kingstone*, which rowe of houses in Lattine is called *Vicus*, in our toong *Vyke* or *Wyke*, of the Saxons ꝓýc. *Vadianus* an excellent Geographer, saith that *Vicus in opido via est domorum seriem complexa*, *Vike* is a way or passage in a towne being orderly compact of houses, which we also cal a streete. In *Rome* are divers of these streetes, as *Vicus affricus*, *Vicus ciprius*, & *Vicus celeratus*, *Vicus sceleratus Roma*.

*Kenton*, K. 10.

*Wike whence deriued.*

*Vadian Cosmo.*

## L.

*London*, F. 20. the most famous Citie in all *Brytaine*, which *Erasmus* vpon the Prouerbe *Rhodi sacrificium*, saith, is deducted of *Lindus* a citie of the Ile of *Rhodes*, *Stephanus* calleth it *Lyndonium*, the Saxons Londenᵹeaᵹꞇen, Londenbýꞃᵹ Londenꝓýc, *Ptolomey*, *Cornelius Tacitus*, and *Antonius*, *Londiniũ*, and *Longidinium*, *Amianus Londinum* : the Welchmen *Lundayne*, we call it *London* : *Ieffrey of Monmouth*, *Troia noua*, or *Ternouantum* Newe Troy; some call it *Luddes-Towne* of *Ludde* the eldest sonne of *Helie*: *Leland* taketh it ro be *Trenouant*, new Towne, for that in the british toong *Tre* signifieth a towne: M. *Camden* seemeth, in some sort, to yeelde that it should be called *London* of the British word *Lhwn*, which signifieth a woode, or else he will haue it *London* or *Londinum* of the British word *Lhong*, which signifieth ships or shipping, in regarde that our *Thamis* yeeldeth such apt accesse for ships euen to the citie.

There is great varietie among writers, who first founded this Citie: Some will haue *Brute* the Troian to be first builder of it, but *Brute*, and his historie, is meerely reiected of manie in our daies. It was reedefied by *Lud*, in the yeere of the worlds creation 5131. who builded the wals about it, and erected *Ludgate*, who also changed the name of *Trenouant* into *Luddestowne*, now *London*, for which alteration of *Troye* to *Luddestowne*, great contention arose among the *Britons*, as reporteth *Gildas* and others. But our late writers will not consent heereunto: Insomuch as this famous Citie lacketh the truth of it foundation, as many other famous monuments also do. But it nowe reteineth the name of *London*, famous through the whole worlde. A Citie of great Marchandize, populous, rich, and beautifull;

This Citie was burned and greatly wasted by the host of the pagan *Danes*, in the time of king *Alphred*, as reporteth *Gregory* in his

*Bale.*

*Gildas.*
*Galfrid. Monuni. pomicus Bris. hiss. lib. 1.*

*Greg. in past.*
*London burned.*

E 2

THE DEUCALIDON

LONDON

Thames fluuius

SEMPER IDEM

THE WEST OCEAN

BRITANNIA

Performed by John Speede

The Scale of Miles

6.9, map of Great Britain and Ireland from Speed's atlas (1612)

6.10    Gossuin de Metz, attributed (thirteenth century).
        *Hier begynneth the booke callyd the Myrrour of the worlde.*
        [Westminster: William Caxton, 1489–90.]

        BMC xi, 170; *ESTC* S109670; Goff M-884; *GW* 10967; *ISTC* im00884000;
        *STC* 24763. Shelfmark: UIUC Incunabula 034 Im11 1490.

6.11    *William Dugdale (1605–86). The history of St. Pauls
        Cathedral in London, From its foundation untill these times:
        extracted out of originall charters, records, leiger books, and
        other manuscripts. Beautified with sundry prospects of the
        church, figures of tombes, and monuments. London:
        Thomas Warren, 1658.*

        *ESTC* R16413; Wing D2482. Shelfmark: UIUC Q. 942.1 D87h copy 2.

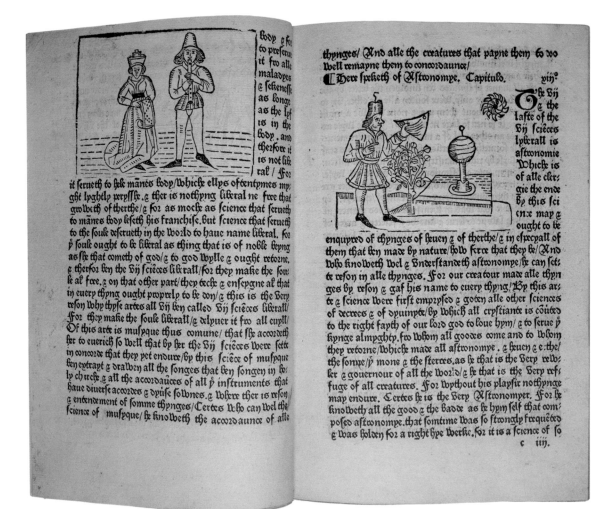

6.10, fol. C3$^v$–C4$^r$

6.11, engraving of Old St. Paul's by Wenceslaus Hollar, 1658

6.12    Aesop. *Æsop's fables with his life: in English, French &
        Latin. The English by Tho. Philipott Esq; the French and
        Latin by Rob. Codrington M.A. Illustrated with one hundred
        and twelve sculptures by Francis Barlow.* London: William
        Godbid for Francis Barlow, and are to be sold by Ann
        Seile and Edward Powell, 1666.

        *ESTC* R21542; Wing A696. Shelfmark: UIUC IUQ00243.

The English, like everyone else, like picture books. Caxton attempted illustration in a book
for the first time in 1481 in the *Myrrour of the worlde.* His second edition of 1491, with all
but one of the same woodcuts, is shown here. The twenty-eight illustrations, which are the
work of an English artist, are simple but may not deserve the scorn heaped upon them by

A lazy Tortoyze slighted by a Hare
Does to a race his active rivall dare,
And both 'fore they y̆ solemne course ingage
Submit to the sage Foxes vmpirage
Who the adjusted lists waſ to divide
And who atcheiv'd y̆ conquest to decide,

The Tortoyze gravely glides along y̆ lists,
Nor from his speede till he had gaind desifts
The Hare who much on his quick pace rely'd,
First slept and then himselfe to run aply'd
But seeing y̆ dull Tortoyze victor said,
This loſs y̆ price of his contempt hath paid.

Mean parts by industry those things doe Act

Which greater wan'd, soyld by theyr dull neglect.

F AB. LXX.

6.12, p. 141 (detail)

the twentieth-century authority on English woodcuts, Edward Hodnett, who (as mentioned earlier) called them "some of the poorest cuts ever inserted between covers."[8] The woodcuts are meant to illustrate Caxton's translation of this work of medieval science. These early "scientific" images present some rather intriguing subjects, including the spherical world with four figures; the orbits of the sun, moon, and planets; the position of the sun relative to the earth (not Copernican); the stages of an eclipse; the creation of Eve; and a woman singing from notes while a man plays the flute.

In all, Caxton illustrated nineteen of his books with a total of 381 woodcuts. Wynkyn de Worde illustrated nearly every book he printed after 1500 with at least one image. Some of the woodcuts used by the earliest printers were cut by English artists, while others were imported from France and the Low Countries. John Day was perhaps the most significant publisher of illustrated books in the sixteenth century. For example, his *Book of Martyrs* (item 3.4), by John Foxe, boasts of nearly 150 compelling (and anonymous) woodcuts, and his Euclid (item 4.5) contains complex diagrams. For Day and other printers in the sixteenth century, however, the Continent generally remained the source for illustrations. Not only woodblocks and engraved plates came to England, but also the artists who made them.

The artist Wenceslaus Hollar (1607–77) was Czech by birth, but he lived for many years in London (1636–44 and again 1652–77). An engraver with a remarkable eye for detail, Hollar worked with the antiquarian Sir William Dugdale and the printer John Ogilby on a massive project to record the monastic architecture of England. For Dugdale's *Monasticon Anglicanum* (1655–73), Hollar produced 566 plates. He also captured images of court festivals, coronations, public spectacles, art collections, and contemporary fashion in minute detail, giving historians and art historians much valuable information about England in the tumultuous seventeenth century. In Dugdale's *History of St. Paul's Cathedral* in London, published by Ogilby some eight years before the great fire, Hollar preserved Old St. Paul's in ink. The provenance of the University of Illinois copy shown here is interesting; its first owner was apparently Oliver Cromwell, whose signature appears on the title page.

The first native English book illustrator of note is Francis Barlow (c. 1626–1704). Barlow recorded English life through sporting scenes, naturalist drawings, and political cartoons. He was also a landscape painter. Barlow's skill as a naturalist served him well in his illustrated edition of Aesop. The densely illustrated work appeared in 1666 (though Barlow engraved 1665 on the ornamental title page) with the text in French and English. Copies of the 1666 edition are rare because, unfortunately, most of the print run was lost in the Great Fire of London of that year. It was reprinted in a second edition in 1687 with a new illustrated life of Aesop for which Aphra Behn (1640?–89) wrote poetic captions (bound with the 1666 edition in the University of Illinois copy).

Literature: Duff 1968; Hodnett 1978, 166.

6.13    Abraham Cowley (1618–67). *Navfragivm iocvlare, comaedia.* London: [Thomas Cotes?] for Henry Seile, 1638.

*ESTC* S108968; Greg L15(a); *STC* 5905. Shelfmark: UIUC IUA03436.

6.14    Nicolaus de Lyra (c. 1270–1349). *Postilla.* Lyon: J. Mareschal, 19 July 1529. Bound by John Reynes (d. 1545).

Shelfmark: UIUC IUQ03519.

NAVFRAGIVM
IOCVLARE,
*Comædia* :

Publicè Coram Academicis
Acta, in Collegio S S. et in-
dividuæ Trinitatis.

4°. Nonas *Feb*. An. Dom. 1638.

✢✢✢✢✢✢✢✢✢✢✢✢✢✢✢✢✢✢✢✢

Authore *Abrahamo Cowley*.

✢✢✢✢✢✢✢✢✢✢✢✢✢✢✢✢✢✢✢✢

Mart.————— *Non displicuisse meretur*
*Festinat, Lector, qui placuisse tibi.*

LONDINI,
Impensis Henrici Seile. 1638.

6.13, title page
(stab-stitched
binding)

6.15    William Gouge (1575–1653). *The whole-armor of God:
        or A Christians spiritval furniture, to keepe him safe from
        all the assaults of Satan.* London: John Beale, 1619. Bound
        by John and Abraham Bateman (active 1580–1635).

        *ESTC* S103304; *STC* 12123. Shelfmark: UIUC 248 G725p 1619.

6.16    *The whole booke of Psalmes. Collected into English meeter by
        T. Sternhold, I. Hopkins, and others.* London : Printed for
        the Company of Stationers, 1631. Embroidered binding.

        Not in *STC*. Shelfmark: UIUC MINI00513.

6.14, binding
by John Reynes,
c. 1529

6.17    Simon Patrick (1626–1707). *Advice to a friend.*
London: Printed for R. Royston, book-seller to
His most Sacred Majesty, 1673. Bound by Samuel
Mearne (1624–83).

*ESTC* R10347; Wing P738. Shelfmark: UIUC 248 P275a.

Many of the books described in this exhibition were bound in England soon after they
were printed (items 1.4, 2.13, 3.4, 4.6, and 6.6, for example). By closing the covers of these
few books, we highlight some aspects of the broad field of English bookbinding. For the
most part, binding styles in England in this period imitate those of the Continent. Indeed,
like early English printers, bookbinders at work in England often came from France, Germany, and the Low Countries. New books imported from the Continent usually arrived

6.15, binding
by John and
Abraham
Bateman, c.
1619

in gatherings and were bound by their owners. The centers for English bookbinding were London and, not surprisingly, the university towns of Oxford and Cambridge.

In the fifteenth through mid-seventeenth centuries, new books, whether imported from the Continent or printed in England, usually arrived at the stationer's shop in gatherings to be bound after purchase. Thus, each copy of the same edition of a book might have a different binding, depending on the needs and means of its owner. A small book or pamphlet often received no binding at all; it might be wrapped in a sheaf of paper or old vellum or stab-stitched, like the Latin school play by Abraham Cowley shown here (item 6.13). Though we are accustomed to finding the now precious quartos of Elizabethan and Stuart playwrights bound in fine nineteenth-century gold-tooled bindings, the fact is that they probably looked more like this little playbook when they were first read.

In sixteenth-century England, the most common binding for more "substantial" works (i.e., classical literature, histories, Bibles, and so on) was tanned calfskin, often with blind-stamped rolls or panel stamping. The example shown here (item 6.14) was bound at the productive bindery of John Reynes in London. Reynes (born Jan Rijens) came to London in 1510 from Wageningen in Holland and worked as a stationer and bookbinder in St. Paul's Churchyard until his death in 1544. His shop used blind-stamped rolls of flowers, thistles, bees, birds, and animals, as well as panel stamps with the Tudor rose, religious scenes, and allegorical figures. This 1529 Lyon edition of Nicholas of Lyra's biblical commentaries (item 6.14) is stamped in blind with a roll incorporating a pelican, dog, bee, and the monogram IR (John Reynes). The center is divided into lozenge-shaped compartments each with a pineapple ornament.

The nobility had special bindings to distinguish their books, often incorporating their arms, mottos, or initials into the design. The binding on this 1619 religious tract (item 6.15) was specially done for King James and is probably the work of the royal bookbinders John and Abraham Bateman (active 1580–1635). By the early seventeenth century, gold tooling is more common, as here in the arabesque corner pieces on a field studded with gilt cinquefoil blossoms. A center stamp shows James's arms with the motto of the Order of the Garter: Honi soit qui mal y pense.

Materials other than leather could be used to bind books, as in the embroidered psalter binding from the seventeenth century (item 6.16). The text is the psalter of Stern-

6.16, embroidered
binding, c. 1631

hold and Hopkins (in an otherwise unrecorded edition of 1631). One might imagine a woman personalizing her Psalter in this way as a public display of both her devotion and her artistic handiwork. The well-preserved binding is embroidered with flowers, leaves, and branches using silk and silver thread and sequins and protected with a piping of silver thread.

G. D. Hobson has called the second half of the seventeenth century the "golden age of English binding," a time when there is less influence from the Continent, allowing a more independent development of a British bookbinding aesthetic.[9] Samuel Mearne (1624–83) was an important figure in bookbinding in the Restoration period. Mearne served Charles II and James II as official bookbinder from 1660 to 1674. His workshop created bookbindings that have been ranked "amongst the finest ever produced in England."[10] This binding of dyed goatskin (item 6.17, shown opposite page 175) is meticulously tooled with a red, blue, and gold floral pattern reminiscent of Persian carpets, which were beginning to be imported into England at that time.

Literature: Abbey 1940; Davenport 1906; Foot 1993, 148, 312, 340–51; Foot 2002, 630; Nixon 1974.

6.18    Ludwig Lavater (1527–86). *Of ghostes and spirites walking by nyght, and of strange noyses, crackes, and sundry forewarnynges, whiche commonly happen before the death of menne, great slaughters, [and] alterations of kyngdomes.* London: Henry Bynneman for Richard Watkyns, 1572.

*ESTC* S108369; *STC* 15320. Shelfmark: UIUC 133.1 L38d:Eh.

In this exhibition, printers have spoken through their books. In prologues and epilogues, title pages and colophons, errata lists and prayers, and, above all, in the sign language of typography, printers reveal much about the circumstances of a book's production. Almost everything we know about Caxton derives from his prologues and epilogues.[11] Wynkyn de Worde provided valuable information about early English printing in his colophons and, on more than one occasion, used that place to offer prayers for Caxton's soul.[12] The printers Richard Pynson and Robert Redman (d. 1540) traded insults in their imprints.[13] Some printers complain of misuse at the hands of pirates (see item 5.8), while others, patent holders like John Wayland (item 3.2) and Thomas Morley (item 6.7), for example, tried to preempt such infringement by printing dire warnings or even the text of their patent in their works. Still others used the book's circulation to advertise their wares, giving their shop address in the imprint or including more fulsome advertisements about forthcoming books (item 2.4, for example).

Perhaps most appealing across the centuries are printers' apologies. An errata list is an admission of faults, of course, though both printer and author may be culpable. A note from the printer, however, can elicit a sympathetic reaction and cause the reader to consider the time, effort, and skill that go into making a book. Suddenly, readers used to thinking

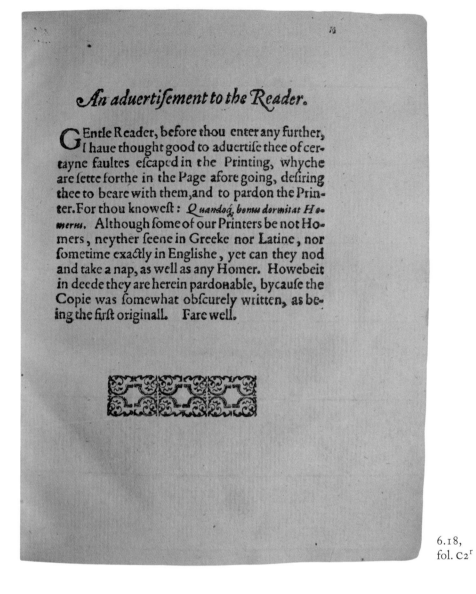

An aduertiſement to the Reader.

GEntle Reader, before thou enter any further, I haue thought good to aduertiſe thee of certayne faultes eſcaped in the Printing, whyche are ſette forthe in the Page afore going, deſiring thee to beare with them, and to pardon the Printer. For thou knoweſt : *Quandoꝗ bonus dormitat Homerus.* Although ſome of our Printers be not Homers, neyther ſeene in Greeke nor Latine, nor ſometime exactly in Engliſhe, yet can they nod and take a nap, as well as any Homer. Howebeit in deede they are herein pardonable, bycauſe the Copie was ſomewhat obſcurely written, as being the firſt originall. Fare well.

6.18,
fol. c2ʳ

only of the author as creator may appreciate the craftspeople who put authors' ideas into words—quite literally—by printing them.

In a 1572 English translation of Ludwig Lavater's work on ghosts, the printer Richard Watkyns wins our pardon in his humorous apology for typographic errors, forging a bond of humanity between readers and makers of books:

For thou knowest: *Quandoque bonus dormitat Homerus* [Even good Homer nods sometimes]. Although some of our Printers be not Homers, neyther seene in Greeke nor Latine, nor sometimes exactly in Englishe, yet they can nod and take a nap, as well as any Homer. (c2ʳ)

# NOTES

## INTRODUCTION

1. Griffiths and Pearsall 1989; Hanna 2005. Of course copying of books by hand did not cease abruptly with the appearance of the first printed book. Scribes continued to ply their trade, and printing presses and scriptoria coexisted for many years.
2. Blake 1989, 412.
3. Ibid., 404.
4. Eisenstein 1979.
5. Comenius 1659, 190–91.
6. Updike 1962, 119.
7. Clair 1965, 24.
8. Morison 1957.
9. Goodman 2006, 102.
10. From the preface to *Eneydos* (1490).
11. Painter 1976, 108–20.
12. Bennett 1969, 16.
13. Carlson 2006, 35–68.
14. Blake 1973a, 57 and 126.
15. Carlson 2006, 58–59.
16. Bennett 1969, 188.
17. Clair 1965, 29.
18. Moran 1960, 9.
19. Bennett 1969, 191.
20. Neville-Sington 1999; BMC xi, 264–300.
21. Pallotta 1991, 22.
22. This book exists in only one copy and is held by the Elizabethan Club (*STC* 7589.5).
23. Cressy 1980.
24. Jones 1953.
25. Ibid., 83–89.
26. Bennett 1969, 174–75.
27. Ibid., 156.
28. Price and Ryrie 2004.
29. From Foxe's *Gospels of the fower euangelistes* (London, 1571), ¶2ʳ, also printed by Day.
30. Jones 1953, 112.
31. See Price and Ryrie 2004, 116.
32. Bennett 1969, 66.
33. Ibid., 65.
34. Stone 1964, 41–80.
35. Quoted in Cressy 1980, 4.
36. Ibid., 44.
37. Bennett 1969, 154.
38. Cressy 1980, 176.
39. Jones 1953, 205.
40. Baugh and Cable 2004, 226.
41. Starnes 1954, 8–18.
42. Ibid., 5.
43. Ibid., 184–217.
44. Starnes and Noyes [1946] 1991.
45. See Price and Ryrie 2004, 11–24, for a discussion of the Wycliffite Bible.
46. *STC* 7865.
47. See Clegg 2001, 26–27, for a discussion of the 1586 order.
48. See Clegg 1997b and 2001.
49. Arber [1875–94] 1950, 1:xxiii.
50. Clair 1965, 107.
51. See Arber [1875–94] 1950.
52. Wilson 1969, 51.
53. Chambers [1923] 1974, 183.
54. Blayney 1997, 386.
55. Ibid., 385.
56. Straznicky 2006, 14.
57. Erne 2002, 11 (first quote), 14 (second quote).

58. Blayney 1997, 398.
59. Erne 2002, 6–9.
60. Sauer 2006, 80–95.
61. Wilson 1969, 83.
62. Blayney 1997, 414. It should be noted that *ABC* books sometimes introduced children to roman type by providing an alphabet in that font next to the black-letter alphabet (item 2.1).

63. Mish 1953, 627–31.
64. Lesser 2006, 99–126.
65. Blayney 1997, 415.
66. Shirley 1991, v, vii.
67. Ibid., vii.
68. Clair 1965, 51.

## CHAPTER 1: Early English Printing

1. There is evidence that Stephen Scrope, Fastolf's stepson, may have translated *De Senectute*, and that it was afterward edited by Fastolf's secretary William Worcester, whose name may have caused some confusion with the Earl of Worcester. Most scholars believe that the other two pieces, however, are indeed the work of John Tiptoft, Earl of Worcester. See Painter 1976, 111–13.
2. Caxton (English), Lettou (Lithuanian?) De Machlinia (Belgian), Pynson and William Faques (French), De Worde (Dutch), and Julian Notary (probably from Brittany).
3. *Statuta ap[u]d westmonasteriu[m] edita anno primo Regis Ricardi tercij* [London: William de Machlinia, 1484?]. *STC* 9347.
4. Leadam 1903–11, 1:cxxxvii–cxxxviii and 111–14.
5. Henry VIII, *An acte concerning straungers, artificers for tasking of apprentices, iourneymen & couenaunt seruauntes,* 1523. In *Anno xiiii et anno xv Henrici VIII statuta* [London]: Richard Pynson, [1523?], a2ᵛ–a4ʳ. *STC* 9362.9.
6. See Bregman 2005, for a complete description of the manuscript and its contents.

## CHAPTER 2: A World of Words

1. Hornbooks were made by pasting pages (printed only on one side) to pallets of horn or wood for use in the classroom. See Tuer [1897] 1968.
2. The earliest printing of the Lord's Prayer in English appeared, unauthorized, in a 1523 Latin primer printed by Wynkyn de Worde (*STC* 15934) and is based on another outlawed English translation, the Wycliffite Bible. The prayer also appears in early Latin–English *ABCs* and primers and even in Lily's grammar, with variations until 1545 when an "authorized" version—without the doxology—is established in the 1545 primer of Henry VIII.
3. Stein 1985, 142–43.
4. It went through four editions from 1604 to 1617. One copy exists of the second edition, one of the fourth edition, and two copies of the third. See Starnes and Noyes [1946] 1991, xiv.
5. Fol. A2ʳ. According to Starnes and Noyes [1946] 1991, 42, Blount borrowed most heavily—some 58 percent of his entries—from Thomas Thomas's *Dictionarium Linguae Latinae et Anglicanae* (1632 edition) and Francis Holyoke's *Dictionarium Etymologicum* (1639 edition).

## CHAPTER 3: "For the Regulating of Printing"

1. The act is printed in E. Peters 1980, 214.
2. Blagden 1960, 75.
3. Henry VIII 1521. Translated by O'Donovan 1908.
4. Chambers 1930, 2:327.
5. Arber [1875–94] 1950, 3:677–78. The other works ordered confiscated are: John Marston's

*Pygmalion* (1598) and *The Scourge of Vilanie* (1598), Edward Guilpin's *Skialetheia or A Shadow of Truth* (1598), Thomas Middleton's *Microcynicon* (1598), John Davies's *Epigrammes,* Ercole and Torquato Tasso's *Of Marriage and Wyving* (1599) and *15 Joyes of Marriage,* and two works by Joseph Hall and Thomas Cutwode that were later removed from the list. See Clegg 1997b, 198–217, for an extensive discussion of the ban.

6. Boose 1994.
7. Patterson 1984.
8. Duncan-Jones 1985.
9. Greg 1928 and Brettle 1928 offer conflicting views on the matter.
10. Clare 1990a, 209 n. 89.
11. £1,500 is an enormous sum when one considers that in 1595 Philip Henslowe wrote that a good day's take for a performance was 4 pounds, 6 shillings. We do not know how many spectators the Globe could hold in 1625, but even if the highest estimate, three thousand, is assumed with an average ticket price of 5 pence, the gate gross per performance could only be 62 pounds. Perhaps the players offered multiple performances per day.

## CHAPTER 4: The Place of Translation in Early English Printing

1. The figures vary somewhat since there is evidence that he printed some titles that do not survive. See Blake 1991, 72–73. For lists of Caxton's editions, see Painter 1976, 211–15; De Ricci's *Census of Caxtons* [1909] 2000; and Needham 1986.
2. See Hellinga and Trapp 1999, 3:17, on English incunabula: "those in Latin (120) account for about 33%, in English (214) 59%; in Law French (30) 8%. This compares with an overall figure for European incunabula of something over 70% in Latin and under 30% in the various vernacular languages."
3. Ibid., 3:43.
4. Hodnett [1935] 1973, 1.
5. Blake 1971, 63.
6. Hodnett [1935] 1973, 9.
7. The apparent grammatical flaw (*Vitas* instead of *Vitae*) may hark back to a full title of *Liber Vitas Patrum,* with *vitas* acting as a genitive singular, as in the term *paterfamilias.* See Rosenthal 1936, 11 n. 5.
8. Blake 1973a, 79–80, gives the text of the prologue.
9. On the varieties of English, Caxton says: "Certainly it is harde to playse every man bycause of the dyversite and change of langage." See Blake 1973a, 80.
10. Caxton mentions his translation in the prologue to his *Golden Legend* (1483–84) and a manuscript of it survives in the British Library. If the work was indeed printed, it has not survived. See Painter 1976, 114.
11. Quoted in Bate 1993, 29, from Pound's *ABC of Reading* (London, 1934).
12. Baldwin 1967, 125.
13. See Bate 1993, 8, for a discussion of Shakespeare's use of both the Latin and the English translation by Golding.
14. See Woolley 2001, 4–19.
15. In *The Cambridge History of English and American Literature,* 4:4, as quoted in Bennett 1965, 90.
16. Lord 1958, 328–29.
17. Nicoll 1956.
18. Recorded by Collier 1856, xxxii.
19. See Matthiessen [1931] 1965, 10–11.
20. Boswell 1934–50, 5:276.
21. See fol. A2¹: "Nowe at the length (gentle reader) through the diligence of Maister Hoby in penninge, and mine in printing, thou hast here set forth unto thee, the booke of the Courtier: which

for thy benifite had bene done longe since, but that there were certain places in it whiche of late yeares beeing misliked of some, that had the perusing of it . . . the Authour thought it much better to keepe it in darknes a while, then to put it in light vnperfect and in peecemeale."

22. See Price and Ryrie 2004, 115–43.
23. Pollard 1911, 297–98.
24. Pelikan and Hotchkiss 2003, 2:823.
25. See Price and Ryrie 2004, 109–10.
26. The Vulgate reads "panem supersubstantialem" for Martin's "supersubstantial bread."

## CHAPTER 5: From the Stage to the Page

1. On Colwell, see Arber [1875–94] 1950, 1:239, 315, 421. Creede was fined for pirating George Wither's *Abuses Stript and Whipt*, 1613 (STC 25893). Danter printed illegal copies of Lily's grammar and other schoolbooks; see McKerrow 1910.
2. Yamada 1994, 241–43.
3. Matthews 1932 and 1933 rejected the idea of shorthand transmission of plays. Davidson 1996 reconsiders the issue.
4. Arber [1875–94] 1950, 2:835; McKerrow 1929, 123.
5. Hanson 1938, 363–64.
6. Meres 1598, 282$^r$ (STC 17834).
7. Wells and Taylor 1986, 349.
8. Baldwin 1957. See also Bald 1958 for corrections.
9. Heywood, *The English Traveller*, 1633 (STC 13315), A3$^r$.
10. Ibid.
11. STC 13360, A2$^r$.
12. See Matthews 1932 and 1933, Duthie 1949, and Davidson 1992 and 1996.
13. Davidson 1996, 427–35. An example is an imprint of a sermon by Stephen Egerton (STC 7539) that states on the title page that it was "taken by characterie."
14. Buc 1615, Ooooi$^v$, cap. 39, cited in Davidson 1996, 425.
15. *Henry VI*, parts 2 and 3, are entitled *The Whole Contention betweene the two Famous Houses, Lancaster and Yorke . . . Divided into two parts* in this imprint. The two quartos of *The Whole Contention* are bound together in both the Illinois and the Elizabethan Club copies, whereas both institutions' copies of the 1619 *Pericles* are bound separately, though contiguous in signatures with *The Whole Contention*.
16. Neidig 1910, 146.
17. Berger and Lander 1999, 404.
18. On the quality of Shakespeare imprints, Plomer 1906, 151, says, "pick up what one you will and its distinctive features will probably be bad paper, wretched type, and careless and slovenly press-work."
19. Kernan 1995, 61, 69–70.
20. The exchange takes place in the "Induction" and appears in the third issue of the 1604 imprint, shown here, with King's Men players Burbidge, Condell, and Lewin appearing briefly as characters (A3$^r$–A4$^v$).
21. J. Loewenstein 1985, 101.
22. Drummond [1923] 1969, 51.
23. Marston, *The Parasitaster*, 1606 (STC 17484), "To my equall Reader," A2$^r$ (first quote); Marston, *The Malcontent*, 1604 (STC 17481), "To the Reader," A2$^r$ (second and third quotes).
24. Black and Shaaber 1937.
25. Black 1936, 714.

## CHAPTER 6: Making English Books

1. See Bowers 1948 and Mulryne 1975, for more information about half-sheet imposition for Renaissance quartos. Incunabular printers in England also used half sheets for quartos (BMC xi, 23–34).

2. It should be noted, however, that both black letter and roman have a common root in the Carolingian minuscule hand that was developed in the eighth century.

3. Barker 2002a, 604–6.

4. Turner 1949, 345.

5. Volume 1, *Prolegomena,* 11–14.

6. Krummel 1975, 106.

7. *STC* 18643.3.

8. Hodnett [1935] 1973, 1.

9. Abbey 1940, viii.

10. Foot 2002, 630.

11. Blake 1973a.

12. In his 1495 edition of Bartholomaeus Anglicus's *De proprietatibus rerum,* De Worde writes, "And also of your charyte call to remembraunce, / The soule of William Caxton, the fyrste printer of this book, / In Laten at Coleyn, himself to avaunce, / That every well disposed man may thereon look."

13. Redman had implied that Pynson's *Yearbooks* were inaccurate, and Pynson, in a 1525 edition of Littleton's *Tenures,* criticized Redman's skills, saying he should be called Rude-man not Redman because of his shoddy workmanship. See Timperley 1839, 246.

# BIBLIOGRAPHY

Abbey, J. R. 1940. *English Bindings, 1490–1940, in the Library of J. R. Abbey.* Edited by G. D. Hobson. London: Chiswick Press.

Adams, Robert Martin. 1953. "Reading Comus." *Modern Philology* 51:18–32.

Adams, Robert P. 1979. "Despotism, Censorship, and Mirrors of Power Politics in Late Elizabethan Times." *Sixteenth Century Journal* 10:5–16.

Albright, Evelyn May. 1927. *Dramatic Publication in England.* New York: D. C. Heath.

Arber, Edward, ed. [1875–94] 1950. *A Transcript of the Registers of the Company of Stationers of London, 1554–1640.* 5 vols. Reprint. New York: Peter Smith.

Armstrong, Elizabeth. 1979. "English Purchases of Printed Books from the Continent, 1465–1526." *English Historical Review* 94:268–90.

Auchter, Dorothy. 2001. *Dictionary of Literary and Dramatic Censorship in Tudor and Stuart England.* Westport, Conn.: Greenwood Press.

Bald, R. C. 1958. Review of *Shakespeare's "Love's Labor's Won": New Evidence from the Account Book of an Elizabethan Bookseller,* by T. W. Baldwin. *Modern Philology* 55:276–79.

Baldwin, T. W. 1944. *William Shakspere's Small Latine and Lesse Greeke.* Urbana: University of Illinois Press.

———. 1957. *Shakspere's "Love's Labor's Won": New Evidence from the Account Book of an Elizabethan Bookseller.* Carbondale: Southern Illinois University Press.

———. 1967. Review of *Ovid's Metamorphoses: The Arthur Golding Translation, 1567,* edited by John F. Nims. *Journal of English and Germanic Philology* 66:124–27.

Barker, Nicolas. 1976. "Caxton's Typography." In "Papers Presented to the Caxton International Congress, 1976." Special issue, *Journal of the Printing Historical Society* 11:114–43.

———. 2002a. "The Old English Letter Foundries." In Barnard and McKenzie 2002, 602–19.

———. 2002b. "The Polyglot Bible." In Barnard and McKenzie 2002, 648–51.

Barnard, John. 1999. "The Survival and Loss Rates of Psalms, ABCs, Psalters and Primers from the Stationers' Stock, 1660–1700." *The Library,* 6th ser., 21:148–50.

———. 2001. "London Publishing 1640–1660: Crisis, Continuity, and Innovation." *Book History* 4:1–16.

Barnard, John, and D. F. McKenzie, eds. 2002. *The Cambridge History of the Book in Britain.* Vol. 4, 1557–1695. Cambridge: Cambridge University Press.

Baskervill, C. R. 1916. "John Rastell's Dramatic Activities." *Modern Philology* 13:557–60.

Bate, Jonathan. 1993. *Shakespeare and Ovid.* Oxford: Oxford University Press.

Baugh, Albert C., and Thomas Cable. 2004. *A History of the English Language.* 5th ed. Englewood Cliffs, N.J.: Prentice Hall.

Bennett, H. S. 1965. *English Books and Readers, 1558–1603.* Cambridge: Cambridge University Press.

————. 1969. *English Books and Readers, 1475–1557.* 2nd ed. Cambridge: Cambridge University Press.

————. 1970. *English Books and Readers, 1603–1640.* Cambridge: Cambridge University Press.

Berger, Thomas L., and Jesse M. Lander. 1999. "Shakespeare in Print, 1593–1640." In Kastan 1999, 395–413.

Bergeron, David M. 1974. "The Deposition Scene in Richard II." *Renaissance Papers* 1974:31–37.

Bidwell, John. 2002. "French Paper in English Books." In Barnard and McKenzie 2002, 583–601.

Birchenough, Edwyn. 1938. "The Prymer in English." *The Library,* 4th ser., 18:177–94.

Black, Matthew W. 1936. "Shakespeare's Seventeenth Century Editors." *Proceedings of the American Philosophical Society* 76:707–17.

Black, Matthew W., and Matthias A. Shaaber, eds. 1937. *Shakespeare's Seventeenth-Century Editors, 1632–1685.* New York: Modern Language Association of America.

Blagden, Cyprian. 1955. "The English Stock of the Stationers' Company." *The Library,* 5th ser., 10:163–85.

————. 1960. *The Stationers' Company: A History, 1403–1959.* Stanford: Stanford University Press.

Blake, Norman F. 1966. "Investigations into the Prologues and Epilogues by William Caxton." *Bulletin of the John Rylands Library* 49:17–46.

————. 1969. *Caxton and His World.* London: Deutsch.

————. 1971. "Wynkyn de Worde: The Early Years" *Gutenberg Jahrbuch* 1971:62–69.

————. 1972. "Wynkyn de Worde: The Later Years." *Gutenberg Jahrbuch* 1972:128–38.

————, ed. 1973a. *Caxton's Own Prose.* London: Deutsch.

————, ed. 1973b. *Selections from William Caxton.* Oxford: Clarendon.

————. 1989. "Manuscript to Print." In *Book Production and Publishing in Britain, 1375–1475,* 403–32. Edited by Jeremy Griffiths and Derek Pearsall. Cambridge: Cambridge University Press.

————. 1991. *William Caxton and English Literary Culture.* London: Hambledon Press.

Bland, Mark. 1999. "The Book Trade in 1600." In Kastan 1999, 450–63.

Blayney, Peter. 1991. *The First Folio of Shakespeare.* Washington, D.C.: Folger Library Publications.

————. 1997. "The Publication of Playbooks." In *A New History of Early English Drama,* 383–422. Edited by John Cox and David Scott Kastan. New York: Columbia University Press.

————. 2003. *The Stationers' Company before the Charter, 1403–1557.* London: Worshipful Company of Stationers and Newspapermakers.

————. 2005. "The Alleged Popularity of Playbooks." *Shakespeare Quarterly* 56:33–50.

Bodleian Library. 1978. *Printing and Publishing at Oxford: The Growth of a Learned Press, 1478–1978.* Oxford: Bodleian Library.

Boffey, Julia, and John Scattergood, eds. 1997. *Texts and Their Contexts: Papers from the Early Book Society.* Dublin: Four Courts Press.

Boose, Lynda E. 1994. "The 1599 Bishops' Ban, Elizabethan Pornography, and the Sexualization of the Jacobean Stage." In *Enclosure Acts: Sexuality, Property, and Culture in Early Modern England,* 185–202. Edited by Richard Burt and John Michael Archer. Ithaca, N.Y.: Cornell University Press.

Boswell, James. 1934–50. *Boswell's Life of Johnson, Together with Boswell's Journal of a Tour of the Hebrides and Johnson's Diary of a Journey into North Wales.* Edited by George Birkbeck Hill and Lawrence Powell. 6 vols. Oxford: Clarendon.

Bowers, Fredson 1948. "Running-Title Evidence for Determining Half-Sheet Imposition." *Studies in Bibliography* 1:200–202.

Bracken, James K., and Joel Silver. 1996. *The British Literary Book Trade, 1475–1700.* Vol. 170 of the *Dictionary of Literary Biography.* Detroit: Gale Research.

Braden, Gordon, ed. 1978. *The Classics and English Renaissance Poetry: Three Case Studies.* New Haven: Yale University Press.

Bregman, Alvan. 2005. "A Gabriel Harvey Manuscript Brought to Light." *Book Collector* 54.1:61–81.

Brettle, R. E. 1928. "Eastward Ho, 1605 by Chapman, Jonson, and Marston: Bibliography and Circumstances of Production." *The Library*, 4th ser., 9:287–302.

Britland, Karen. 2006. *Drama at the Courts of Queen Henrietta Maria.* Cambridge: Cambridge University Press.

Bruce, F. F. 1978. *History of the Bible in English: From the Earliest Versions.* 4th ed. Cambridge: Lutterworth Press.

Brusendorff, Aage. 1925. *Chaucer Tradition.* London: Oxford University Press.

Bühler, Curt F. 1944. "The Bindings of Books Printed by William Caxton." *Papers of the Bibliographical Society of America* 38:1–8.

Burke, Peter. 1995. *The Fortunes of the Courtier: The European Reception of Castiglione's Cortegiano.* University Park: Pennsylvania State University Press.

Butterworth, Charles C. 1949. "Early Primers for the Use of Children." *Papers of the Bibliographical Society of America* 43:374–82.

———. 1953. *The English Primers, 1529–1545: Their Publication and Connection with the English Bible and the Reformation in England.* Philadelphia: University of Pennsylvania Press.

Camden, Carroll, Jr. 1931. "Elizabethan Almanacs and Prognostications." *The Library*, 4th ser., 12:83–108.

Carlson, David R. 1993. *English Humanist Books: Writers and Patrons, Manuscript and Print, 1475–1525.* Toronto: University of Toronto Press.

———. 2006. "A Theory of the Early English Printing Firm: Jobbing, Book Publishing, and the Problem of Productive Capacity in Caxton's Work." In Kuskin 2006, 35–68.

Cathcart, Charles. 2006. "John Marston, *The Malcontent*, and the King's Men." *Review of English Studies* 57:43–63.

Chambers, E. K. [1923] 1974. *The Elizabethan Stage.* 4 vols. Reprinted with corrections. London: Oxford University Press.

———. 1930. *William Shakespeare: A Study of Facts and Problems.* 2 vols, Oxford: Clarendon.

Charlton, Kenneth. 1965. *Education in Renaissance England.* London: Routledge and Kegan Paul.

Christianson, C. Paul. 1989. "A Community of Book Artisans in Chaucer's London." *Viator* 20:207–18.

———. 1990. *A Directory of London Stationers and Book Artisans, 1300–1500.* New York: Bibliographical Society of America.

———. 1999. "The Rise of London's Book Trade." In Hellinga and Trapp 1999, 128–47.

Clair, Colin. 1965. *A History of Printing in Britain.* London: Cassell.

Clare, Janet. 1990a. *"Art made tongue-tied by authority": Elizabethan and Jacobean Dramatic Censorship.* Manchester, Eng.: Manchester University Press.

———. 1990b. "The Censorship of the Deposition Scene in Richard II." *Review of English Studies,* n.s., 41:89–94.

Clegg, Cyndia. 1996. "The Stationers' Company of London." In *The British Literary Book Trade, 1475–1700,* Vol. 170 of the *Dictionary of Literary Biography,* 275–91. Edited by James K. Bracken and Joel Silver. Detroit: Gale Research.

———. 1997a. "'By the Choise and Inuitation of al the Realme': Richard II and Elizabethan Press Censorship." *Shakespeare Quarterly* 48:432–48.

———. 1997b. *Press Censorship in Elizabethan England.* Cambridge: Cambridge University Press.

———. 2001. *Press Censorship in Jacobean England.* Cambridge: Cambridge University Press.

Collier, J. Payne. 1856. *Seven Lectures on Shakespeare and Milton.* London: Chapman and Hall.

Comenius, Joannes Amos. 1659. *Orbis sensualium pictus. Joh. Amos Commenius's Visible world. Or, A picture and nomenclature of all the chief things that are in the world, und of mens employments therein.* Translated by Charles Hoole. London: For J. Kirton, at the Kings-Arms, in Saint Paules Church-yard.

Corsten, Severin. 1976. "Caxton in Cologne." In "Papers Presented to the Caxton International Congress, 1976." Special issue, *Journal of the Printing Historical Society* 11:1–18.

Cressy, David. 1980. *Literacy and the Social Order: Reading and Writing in Tudor and Stuart England.* Cambridge: Cambridge University Press.

Crotch, W. J. B. [1928] 1971. *The Prologues and Epilogues of William Caxton.* Early English Text Society 176. Reprint. New York: Burt Franklin.

Daniell, David. 1994. *William Tyndale: A Biography.* New Haven: Yale University Press.

Davenport, C. 1906. *Samuel Mearne: Binder to King Charles II.* Chicago: Caxton Club.

Davidson, Adele. 1992. "Shakespeare and Stenography Reconsidered." *Analytical and Enumerative Bibliography,* n.s., 6:77–100.

———. 1996. "'Some by Stenography?' Stationers, Shorthand, and the Early Shakespearean Quartos." *Papers of the Bibliographical Society of America* 90:417–49.

Daye, Anne. 1998. "Torchbearers in the English Masque." *Early Music* 26:246–62.

Dee, John. 1975. *The Mathematicall Preface to the Elements of Geometrie of Euclid of Megara (1570).* New York: Science History Publications.

De Hamel, Christopher. 1983. "Reflexions on the Trade in Books of Hours at Ghent and Bruges." In *Manuscripts in the Fifty Years after the Invention of Printing: Some Papers Read at a Colloquium at the Warburg Institute on 12–13 March 1982,* 29–33. Edited by J. B. Trapp. London: Warburg Institute, 1983.

DeMolen, Richard. 1991. *Richard Mulcaster (c. 1531–1611) and Educational Reform in the Renaissance.* Nieuwkoop: De Graaf.

De Ricci, Seymour. [1909] 2000. *A Census of Caxtons.* Reprint. Mansfield Center, Conn.: Martino Publishing.

Doyle, A. I. 1993. "English Books in and out of Court from Edward III to Henry VII." In *English Court Culture in the Later Middle Ages,* 163–81. Edited by John Scattergood and J. W. Sherborne. New York: St. Martin's.

Drummond, William. [1929] 1953. *Ben Jonson's Conversations with William Drummond of Hawthornden.* Edited by R. F. Patterson. Folcroft, Pa.: Folcroft Press.

Duff, E. Gordon. [1895] 1913. *Hand-Lists of English Printers, 1501–1556.* London: Blades, East, and Blades, for the Bibliographical Society.

———. [1905] 1948. *A Century of the English Book Trade.* Reprint. London: Bibliographical Society.

———. 1906. *The Printers, Stationers and Bookbinders of Westminster and London from 1476 to 1535.* Cambridge: Cambridge University Press.

———. 1917. *Fifteenth-Century English Books.* Oxford: Bibliographical Society.

———. 1968. "England." In *Early Illustrated Books: A History of Decoration and Illustration of Books in the 15th and 16th Centuries,* 222–49. By Alfred W. Pollard. 2nd ed. New York: Haskell House.

Duncan-Jones, Katherine. 1985. "Jonson's Epitaph on Nashe." *TLS* 4814 (7 July 1985): 4–6.

Duthie, George Ian. 1949. *Elizabethan Shorthand and the First Quarto of King Lear.* Oxford: Blackwell.

Dutton, Richard, ed. 1981. *Jacobean and Caroline Masques.* 2 vols. Nottingham: Nottingham Drama Texts.

———. 2004. "Thomas Middleton's *A Game at Chess*: A Case Study." In *The Cambridge History of British Theatre,* 424–38. Edited by Jane Milling and Peter Thomson. Cambridge: Cambridge University Press.

Edwards, A. S. G. 1991. "From Manuscript to Print: Wynkyn de Worde and the Printing of Contemporary Poetry." *Gutenberg Jahrbuch* 1991:143–48.

———. 1995. "Continental Influences on London Printing and Reading in the Fifteenth and Early Sixteenth Centuries." In *London and Europe in the Later Middle Ages,* 229–56. Edited by Julia Boffey and Pamela M. King. London: University of London, Queen Mary and Westfield College, Centre for Medieval and Renaissance Studies.

Edwards, A. S. G., and Carol M. Meale. 1993. "The Marketing of Printed Books in Late Medieval England." *The Library,* 6th ser., 15:95–124.

Eisenstein, Elizabeth. 1979. *The Printing Press as an Agent of Change.* 2 vols. Cambridge: Cambridge University Press.

Erne, Lukas. 2002. "Shakespeare and the Publication of His Plays." *Shakespeare Quarterly* 27:1–20.

———. 2003. *Shakespeare as Literary Dramatist.* Cambridge: Cambridge University Press.

———, ed. 2006. *The First Quarto of Romeo and Juliet.* Cambridge: Cambridge University Press.

Fanger, Claire, ed. 1998. *Conjuring Spirits: Texts and Traditions of Medieval Ritual Magic.* University Park: Pennsylvania State University Press.

Farmer, Alan B., and Zachary Lesser. 2000. "Vile Arts: The Marketing of English Printed Drama, 1512–1660." *Research Opportunities in Renaissance Drama* 39:77–165.

Feather, John. 1998. *A History of British Publishing.* London: Routledge.

Fisher, John H. 1977. "Chancery and the Emergence of Standard Written English in the Fifteenth Century." *Speculum* 52:870–99.

Flynn, Vincent Joseph. 1943. "The Grammatical Writings of William Lily, 1468?–1523?" *Papers of the Bibliographical Society of America* 37:85–113.

Foot, Mirjam. 1993. *Studies in the History of Bookbinding.* Brookfield, Vt.: Ashgate.

———. 2002. "Bookbinding." In Barnard and McKenzie 2002, 620–31.

Ford, Margaret Lane. 1999. "Importation of Printed Books into England and Scotland." In Hellinga and Trapp 1999, 179–201.

Fox, Harold G. 1947. "Copyright in Relation to the Crown and Universities with Special Reference to Canada." *University of Toronto Law Journal* 7:98–136.

France, Peter, ed. 2000. *The Oxford Guide to Literature in English Translation.* Oxford: Oxford University Press.

Friedman, John. 1991. "Remedies for Fortune in Some Late Medieval Magic Manuscripts." *Journal of English and Germanic Philology* 90:311–23.

French, Peter. 1972. *John Dee: The World of an Elizabethan Magus.* London: Routledge and Kegan Paul.

Gallagher, Joseph E., ed. 1993. *The Doctrinal of Sapience of William Caxton.* Heidelberg: C. Winter.

Gomori, George. 2004. "A Memorable Wedding: The Literary Reception of the Wedding of the Princess Elizabeth and Frederick of Pfalz." *Journal of European Studies* 34:215–25.

Goodman, Jennifer. 2006. "Taking Advice from a Frenchman: Caxton, Pynson and Christine de Pizan's Moral Proverbs." In Kuskin 2006, 101–27.

Grasden, Antonia. 1982. *Historical Writing in England.* 2 vols. Ithaca, N.Y.: Cornell University Press.

Greg, W. W. 1908. "On Certain False Dates in Shakespearean Quartos." *The Library,* 2nd ser., 9:113–31 and 381–409.

———. 1928. "Eastward Ho, 1605." *The Library,* 4th ser., 9:303–4.

———. 1944 "Entrance, License, and Publication." *The Library,* 4th ser., 24:1–22.

———. 1956. *Some Aspects and Problems of London Publishing between 1550 and 1650.* Oxford: Clarendon.

Greg, Walter, and Charlton Hinman. 1975. *Othello: 1622.* Oxford: Oxford University Press.

Griffiths, Jeremy, and Derek Pearsall, eds. 1989. *Book Production and Publishing in Britain, 1375–1475.* Cambridge: Cambridge University Press.

Hadfield, Andrew, ed. 2001. *Literature and Censorship in Renaissance England.* New York: Palgrave.

Halasz, Alexandra. 1997. *The Marketplace of Print: Pamphlets and the Public Sphere in Early Modern England.* Cambridge: Cambridge University Press.

Hale, David G. 1964. "Thomas Colwell: Elizabethan Printer." *The Library,* 5th ser., 19:223–26.

Hamilton, Frederick. 1918. *A Brief History of Printing in England.* Chicago: Committee on Education, United Typothetae of America.

Hanna, Ralph. 2005. *London Literature, 1300–1380.* Cambridge: Cambridge University Press.

Hanson, Laurence. 1938. "English Newsbooks, 1620–1641." *The Library,* 4th ser., 18:355–84.

Harman, Marian. 1979. *Incunabula in the University of Illinois Library at Urbana-Champaign.* Urbana: University of Illinois Press.

Havens, Earle. 2001. *Commonplace Books: A History of Manuscripts and Printed Books from Antiquity to the Twentieth Century.* New Haven: Beinecke Rare Book and Manuscript Library.

———. 2006. *Gloriana: Monuments and Memorials of the Reign of Queen Elizabeth I.* New Haven: Elizabethan Book Club of Yale University.

Hawkyard, Alasdair, and Nigel Nicolson. 1988. *The Counties of Britain: A Tudor Atlas by John Speed.* London: Pavilion/The British Library.

Hellinga, Lotte, and J. B. Trapp, eds. 1999. *The Cambridge History of the Book in Britain.* Vol. 3, 1400–1557. Cambridge: Cambridge University Press.

Hills, Richard Leslie. 1988. *Papermaking in Britain, 1488–1988: A Short History.* London: Athlone Press.

Hirsch, Rudolf. 1967. *Printing, Selling, and Reading, 1450–1550.* Wiesbaden: Harrassowitz.

Hodnett, Edward. [1935] 1973. *English Woodcuts, 1480–1535.* Reprint. London: Bibliographical Society.

———. 1978. *Francis Barlow: First Master of English Book Illustration.* London: Scolar Press.

Hornblower, Simon, and Antony Spawforth, eds. 1996. *The Oxford Classical Dictionary.* Oxford; New York: Oxford University Press.

Hotchkiss, Valerie R., and Charles C. Ryrie. 1998. *Formatting the Word of God.* Dallas: Bridwell Library, Southern Methodist University.

Howard-Hill, T. H. 1991. "The Unique Eye-Witness Report of Middleton's *A Game at Chess.*" *Review of English Studies* 42:168–78.

———, ed. 1993. *A Game at Chess: Thomas Middleton.* Manchester, Eng.: Manchester University Press.

Hunt, Arnold. 1997. "Book Trade Patents, 1603–1640." In *The Book Trade and Its Customers, 1450–1900: Historical Essays for Robin Myers,* 27–54. Edited by Arnold Hunt, Giles Mandelbrote, and Alison Shell. New Castle, Del.: Oak Knoll.

Jackson, William A., ed. 1957. *Records of the Court of the Stationers' Company, 1602–1640.* London: Bibliographical Society.

Johns, Adrian. 1998. *The Nature of the Book: Print Knowledge in the Making.* Chicago: University of Chicago Press.

———. 2002. "Science and the Book." In Barnard and McKenzie 2002, 274–303.

Johnson, A. F. 1936. "Sources of Roman and Italic Types Used by English Printers in the Sixteenth Century." *The Library,* 4th ser., 17:70–82.

Johnson, Gerald D. 1992. "Thomas Pavier, Publisher, 1600–1625." *The Library,* 6th ser., 14:12–50.

Jones, Richard Foster. 1953. *The Triumph of the English Language: A Survey of Opinions Concerning the Vernacular from the Introduction of Printing to the Restoration.* Stanford: Stanford University Press.

Judge, Cyril Bathurst. 1934. *Elizabethan Book-Pirates.* Cambridge, Mass.: Harvard University Press.

Kastan, David Scott, ed. 1999. *A Companion to Shakespeare.* Oxford: Blackwell.

Kawanami, Ayako 1996. "'Pleasing All': Thomas Heywood's Preservation of the Bases of Elizabethan Theatre." *Shakespeare Studies* 34:27–48.

Kelen, Sarah A. 1996. "'It Is Dangerous (Gentle Reader)': Censorship, Hollinshed's Chronicle, and the Politics of Control." *Sixteenth Century Journal* 27:705–20.

Kerling, Nelly J. M. 1955. "Caxton and the Trade in Printed Books." *Book Collector* 4:190–199.

Kernan, Alvin. 1995. *Shakespeare, the King's Playwright: Theater in the Stuart Court, 1603–1613.* New Haven: Yale University Press.

Kibbee, Douglas A. 1987. "Bilingual Lexicography in the Renaissance: Palsgrave's English–French

Lexicon (1530)." In *Papers in the History of Linguistics*, 179–88. Edited by Hans Aarsleff, L. G. Kelly, and Hans-Josef Niederehe. Amsterdam: John Benjamins.

King, John N. 2006. *Foxe's Book of Martyrs and Early Modern Print Culture*. Cambridge: Cambridge University Press.

Kirschbaum, Leo. 1955. *Shakespeare and the Stationers*. Columbus: Ohio State University Press.

———. 1959. "Copyright of Elizabethan Plays." *The Library*, 5th ser., 14:231–50.

Klaassen, Frank. 1998. "English Manuscripts of Magic, 1300–1500." In *Conjuring Spirits: Texts and Traditions of Medieval Ritual Magic*, 3–31. Edited by Claire Fanger. University Park: Pennsylvania State University Press.

Knowles, David, and R. Neville Hadcock. 1971. *Medieval Religious Houses, England, and Wales*. New York: St. Martin's.

König, Eberhard. 1987. "The History of Art and the History of the Book at the Time of the Transition from Manuscript to Print." In *Bibliography and the Study of 15th-Century Civilization*, 154–84. Edited by Lotte Hellinga and John Goldfinch. London: Warburg Institute und British Library.

Krummel, Donald W. 1975. *English Music Printing, 1553–1700*. London: Bibliographical Society.

Kuskin, William, ed. 2006. *Caxton's Trace: Studies in the History of English Printing*. Notre Dame: University of Notre Dame Press.

Lathrop, H. B. 1922. "The First English Printers and Their Patrons." *The Library*, 4th ser., 3:69–96.

———. 1967. *Translations from the Classics into English from Caxton to Chapman (1477–1620)*. New York: Octagon Books.

Leadam, I. S. 1903–11. *Select Cases before the King's Council in Star Chamber, Commonly Called the Court of Star Chamber, A.D. 1477–1544*. London: Quaritch.

Lelong, Jacques. 1713. *Discours historique sur les principales des Bibles Polyglottes*. Paris: [s.n.].

Lerer, Seth. 1993. *Chaucer and His Readers: Imagining the Author in Late Medieval England*. Princeton: Princeton University Press.

Lesser, Zachary. 2004. *Renaissance Drama and the Politics of Publication: Readings in the English Book Trade*. Cambridge: Cambridge University Press.

———. 2006. "Typographic Nostalgia: Play-Reading, Popularity, and the Meaning of Black Letter." In Straznicky 2006, 99–126.

Levenson, Jill. 1999. "Show Business: The Editor in the Theater." In *Shakespeare: Text and Theater: Essays in Honor of Jay L. Halio*, 248–65. Edited by Lois Potter and Arthur Kinney. Newark: University of Delaware Press.

Livingstone, E. A., ed. 1997. *The Oxford Dictionary of the Christian Church*. New York: Oxford University Press.

Loewenstein, David A. 1988. "Areopagitica and the Dynamics of History." *Studies in English Literature, 1500–1900* 28:77–93.

Loewenstein, Joseph. 1985. "The Script in the Marketplace." *Representations* 12:101–14.

———. 2002. *The Author's Due: Printing and the Prehistory of Copyright*. Chicago: University of Chicago Press.

Lord, George deF. 1958. Review of *Chapman's Homer: The Iliad, the Odyssey, and the Lesser Homerica*, by Allardyce Nicoll. *American Journal of Philology* 79:328–31.

Love, Harold. 1993. *Scribal Publication in Seventeenth-Century England*. Oxford: Clarendon.

———. 2002. "Oral and Scribal Texts in Early Modern England." In Barnard and McKenzie 2002, 97–121.

Lowry, Martin J. C. 1987. "Diplomacy and the Spread of Printing." In *Bibliography and the Study of 15th-Century Civilisation*, 124–37. Edited by Lotte Hellinga and John Goldfinch. London: British Library.

Lynam, Edward. 1950. "English Maps and Map-Makers of the Sixteenth Century." *Geographical Journal* 116:7–25.

Lyne, Raphael. 2001. *Ovid's Changing Worlds: English Metamorphoses, 1567–1632*. New York: Oxford University Press.

Madan, Falconer. 1895–1931. *Oxford Books: A Bibliography of Printed Works Relating to the University and City of Oxford.* 3 vols. Oxford: Clarendon.

———. 1904. *A Chart of Oxford Printing, "1468"–1900.* Oxford: Oxford University Press.

Maguire, Laurie E. 1999. "The Craft of Printing (1600)." In Kastan 1999, 434–49.

Marotti, Arthur. 1995. *Manuscript, Print, and the English Renaissance Lyric.* Ithaca, N.Y.: Cornell University Press.

Martin, Henri Jean. 1993. *Print, Power, and People in 17th-Century France.* Translated by David Gerard. Metuchen, N.J.: Scarecrow Press.

Matheson, Lister M. 1985. "Printer and Scribe: Caxton, the *Polychronicon,* and the *Brut.*" *Speculum* 60:593–614.

———. 1998. *The Prose Brut: The Development of a Middle English Chronicle.* Tempe, Ariz.: Medieval and Renaissance Texts and Studies.

Matthews, William. 1932. "Shorthand and the Bad Shakespeare Quartos." *Modern Language Review* 27:243–62.

———. 1933. "Shorthand and the Bad Shakespeare Quartos." *Modern Language Review* 28:81–83.

Matthiessen, F. O. [1931] 1965. *Translation, an Elizabethan Art.* Reprint. New York: Octagon.

Mayhew, A. L. 1908. *The Promptorium parvulorum: The First English–Latin Dictionary.* London: Kegan Paul, Trench, Trübner.

McCabe, Richard A. 1981. "Elizabethan Satire and the Bishops' Ban of 1599." *Yearbook of English Studies* 11:188–93.

McKenzie, D. F. 2002. "Printing and Publishing, 1557–1700: Constraints on the London Book Trades." In Barnard and McKenzie 2002, 553–67.

McKerrow, Ronald B., et al. 1910. *A Dictionary of Printers and Booksellers in England, Scotland, and Ireland, and of Foreign Printers of English Books, 1557–1640.* London: Bibliographical Society.

———. 1929. "Edward Allde as a Typical Trade Printer." *The Library,* 4th ser., 10:121–62.

McMillin, Scott. 1987. *The Elizabethan Theatre and the Book of Sir Thomas More.* Ithaca, N.Y.: Cornell University Press.

Meersch, Polydore Charles van der. 1856. *Recherches sur la vie et les travaux des imprimeurs Belges et Néerlandais.* Gand, France: L. Hebbelynck.

Mendle, Michael. 1995. "De Facto Freedom, De Facto Authority: Press and Parliament, 1640–1643." *Historical Journal* 38.2:307–32.

Meres, Francis. 1598. *Palladis tamia.* London: P. Short, for Cuthbert Burbie.

Middleton, Bernard C. 1996. *A History of English Craft Bookbinding Technique.* New Castle, Del.: Oak Knoll, 1996.

Miller, Peter N. 2001. "The 'Antiquarization' of Biblical Scholarship and the London Polyglot Bible (1653–57)." *Journal of the History of Ideas* 62:463–82.

Mish, Charles C. 1953. "Blackletter as a Social Discriminator in the Seventeenth Century." *PMLA* 68:627–31.

Molinaro, Julius A. 1959. "Castiglione and His English Translators." *Italica* 36:262–78.

Moore, Helen. 2004. *Amadis de Gaule Translated by Anthony Munday.* Aldershot, Hants, Eng.: Ashgate.

Moore, John Robert. 1935. "The Contemporary Significance of Middleton's *Game at Chess.*" *PMLA* 50:761–68.

Moran, James. 1960. *Wynkyn de Worde: Father of Fleet Street.* London: Wynkyn de Worde Society.

Morison, Stanley. 1957. *Four Centuries of Fine Printing: Two Hundred and Seventy-Two Examples of the Work of Presses Established between 1465 and 1924.* New York: Farrar, Straus, and Cudahy.

Mozley, J. F. 1953. *Coverdale and His Bibles.* London: Lutterworth Press.

Mulryne, J. R. 1975. "Half-Sheet Imposition and Running-Title Transfer in *Two New Plays* by Thomas Middleton, 1657." *The Library,* 5th ser., 30:222–28.

Myers, Robin, and Michael Harris, eds. *The Stationers' Company and the Book Trade, 1550–1990.* New Castle, Del.: Oak Knoll.

Needham, Paul. 1986. *The Printer and the Pardoner: An Unrecorded Indulgence Printed by William Caxton for the Hospital of St. Mary Rounceval, Charing Cross*. Washington: Library of Congress.

———. 1999. "The Customs Rolls as Documents for the Printed Book Trade in England." In Hellinga and Trapp 1999, 148–63.

Neidig, William J. 1910. "The Shakespeare Quartos of 1619." *Modern Philology* 8:145–63.

Nelson, Holly Faith, and Jim Daems. 2006. *Eikon Basilike: The Portraiture of His Sacred Majesty in His Solitudes and Sufferings: With Selections from Eikonoklastes by John Milton*. Petersborough, Ont.: Broadview Editions.

Neville-Sington, Pamela. 1999. "Press, Politics and Religion." In Hellinga and Trapp 1999, 576–607.

Nicholson, Watson. 1912. "Notes on Milton." *Modern Language Notes* 27:252–53.

Nicoll, Allardyce, ed. 1956. *Chapman's Homer. The Iliad, the Odyssey, and the Lesser Homerica*. 2 vols. New York: Pantheon Books.

Nims, John Frederick, ed. 2000. *Ovid's Metamorphoses: The Arthur Golding Translation, 1576*. With a new essay by Jonathan Bate. Philadelphia: Paul Dry Books.

Nixon, Howard M. 1974. *English Restoration Bookbinding: Samuel Mearne and His Contemporaries*. London: British Museum.

———. 1978. *Five Centuries of English Bookbinding*. London: Scolar Press.

Norton, David. 2005. *A Textual History of the King James Bible*. Cambridge: Cambridge University Press.

O'Connor, John J. 1970. *Amadis de Gaule and Its Influence on Elizabethan Literature*. New Brunswick, N.J.: Rutgers University Press.

O'Donovan, Louis, ed. 1908. *Henry VIII's Assertio septem sacramentorum or Defence of the Seven Sacraments*. Translated by Louis O'Donovan. New York: Benziger Brothers.

Orme, Nicolas. 1996. "John Holt, Tudor Grammarian." *The Library*, 6th ser., 18:283–305.

Osgood, Charles G. 1945. "*Areopagitica*—1644." *Proceedings of the American Philosophical Society* 89:495–98.

Pace, Richard. 1967. *De fructu qui ex doctrina percipitur· The Benefit of a Liberal Education*. Edited and translated by Frank Manley and Richard Sylvester. New York: Published for the Renaissance Society of America by Ungar.

Pafort, Eloise. 1946. "A Group of Early Tudor School-Books." *The Library*, 4th ser., 26:227–61.

Painter, George D. 1976. *William Caxton: A Quincentenary Biography of England's First Printer*. London: Chatto and Windus.

Pallotta, Augustus. 1991. "Venetian Printers and Spanish Literature in Sixteenth-Century Italy." *Comparative Literature* 43:20–42.

Pantzer, Katharine F. 1983. "Printing the English Statutes, 1484–1640: Some Historical Implications." In *Books and Society in History*, 69–114. Edited by Kenneth E. Carpenter. New York: Bowker.

Parks, Stephen. 1986. *The Elizabethan Club of Yale University and Its Library*. New Haven: Yale University Press.

Parrot, Thomas Marc, and Hardin Craig, eds. 1938. *The Tragedy of Hamlet: A Critical Edition of the Second Quarto, 1604, with Introduction and Textual Notes*. Princeton: Princeton University Press.

Partridge, Stephan. 2007. "Wynkyn de Worde's Manuscript Source for the Canterbury Tales: Evidence from the Glosses." *Chaucer Review* 41.4:325–59.

Patterson, Annabel. 1984. *Censorship and Interpretation: The Conditions of Writing and Reading in Early Modern England*. Madison: University of Wisconsin Press.

Pearson, David. 2005. *English Bookbinding Styles, 1450–1800*. London: The British Library.

Pelikan, Jaroslav, and Valerie Hotchkiss, eds. 2003. *Creeds and Confessions of the Faith in the Christian Tradition*. 3 vols. New Haven: Yale University Press.

Pelikan, Jaroslav, with David Price and Valerie Hotchkiss. 1996. *The Reformation of the Bible / The Bible of the Reformation*. New Haven: Yale University Press.

Peters, Edward 1980. *Heresy and Authority in Medieval Europe.* Philadelphia: University of Pennsylvania Press.

Peters, Julie Stone. 2000. *Theatre of the Book, 1480–1880: Print, Text, and Performance in Europe.* Oxford: Oxford University Press.

Pinciss, G. M. 1970. "Thomas Creede and the Repertory of the Queen's Men, 1583–1592." *Modern Philology* 67:321–30.

Pitcher, John. 2002. "Literature, the Playhouse and the Public." In Barnard and McKenzie 2002, 351–75.

Plomer, H. R. 1900. *A Short History of English Printing, 1476–1898.* London: Kegan Paul, Trench, Trübner.

———. 1906. "The Printers of Shakespeare's Plays and Poems." *The Library,* 2nd ser., 7:149–66.

———. 1922. "Richard Pynson: Glover and Printer." *The Library,* 4th ser., 3:49–51.

———. 1923 / 24. "The Importation of Books into England in the Fifteenth and Sixteenth Centuries: An Examination of Some Customs Rolls." *The Library,* 4th ser., 4:146–50.

———. 1925. *Wynkyn de Worde and His Contemporaries from the Death of Caxton to 1535.* London: Grafton.

———. 1928 / 29. "The Importation of Low Country and French Books into England, 1480 and 1502–3." *The Library,* 4th ser., 9:164–68.

Pollard, Alfred W., ed. 1911. *Records of the English Bible: The Documents Relating to the Translation and Publication of the Bible in English, 1525–1611.* London: Oxford University Press.

———. 1916a. "Authors, Players, and Pirates in Shakespeare's Day." *The Library,* 3rd ser., 26:73–101.

———. 1916b. "Regulation of the Book Trade." *The Library,* 3rd ser., 7:20.

———. 1926. *Early Illustrated Books: A History of the Decoration and Illustration of Books in the 15th and 16th Centuries.* 3rd ed. London: Kegan Paul, Trench, Trübner.

———. 1964. *Fine Books.* New York: Cooper Square Publishers.

Pollard, Graham. 1937. "The Company of Stationers before 1557." *The Library,* 4th ser., 18:1–38.

———. 1978. "The English Market for Printed Books (The Sandars Lectures, 1959)." *Publishing History* 4:7–48.

Pope, Hugh. 1952. *English Versions of the Bible.* St. Louis: Herder.

Pound, Ezra. 1934. *ABC of Reading.* New Haven: Yale University Press.

Price, David, and Charles C. Ryrie. 2004. *Let It Go among Our People: An Illustrated History of the English Bible from John Wyclif to the King James Version.* Cambridge: Lutterworth Press.

Rasmussen, Eric. 1997. "The Revision of Scripts." In *A New History of Early English Drama,* 441–60. Edited by John D. Cox and David Scott Kastan. New York: Columbia University Press.

Raymond, Joad. 2002. "Milton." In Barnard and McKenzie 2002, 376–87.

Reed, A. W. 1917. "The Regulation of the Book Trade before the Proclamation of 1538." *Transactions of the Bibliographical Society* 15:157–84.

Reed, Talbot Baines, and A. F. Johnson. 1952. *A History of the Old English Letter Foundries; with Notes, Historical and Bibliographical, on the Rise and Progress of English Typography.* Edited and Revised by A. F. Johnson. London: Faber and Faber.

Richardson, H. G. 1934. "Dives and Pauper." *The Library,* 4th ser., 15:31–37.

Richardson, Malcolm. 1980. "Henry V, the English Chancery, and Chancery English." *Speculum* 55:726–50.

Romano, Antonella. 1999. *La contre-réforme mathématique: Constitution et diffusion d'une culture mathématique jésuite à la Renaissance (1540–1640).* Rome: Ecole française de Rome.

Rosenthal, Constance Lowengrund. 1936. *The Vitae Patrum in Old and Middle English.* Philadelphia: University of Pennsylvania.

Rosier, James L. 1977. "A New Old English Glossary: Nowell upon Huloet." *Studia Neophilologica* 49:190–94.

Sage, Lorna. 1971. "The Coherence of 'Comus'" *Yearbook of English Studies* 1:88–99.

Sauer, Elizabeth. 2006. "Closet Drama and the Case of *Tyrannicall-Government Anatomized*." In Straznicky 2006, 80–95.

Shaaber, M. A. 1943–44. "The Meaning of the Imprint in Early Printed Books." *The Library*, 4th ser., 24:120–41.

———. 1966. *Some Forerunners of the Newspaper in England, 1476–1622.* New York: Octagon Books.

Shawcross, John T. 2004. *The Arms of the Family: The Significance of John Milton's Relatives and Associates.* Lexington: University Press of Kentucky.

Sherman, William H. 1995. *John Dee: The Politics of Reading and Writing in the English Renaissance.* Amherst: University of Massachusetts Press.

Shirley, Rodney. 1991. *Early Printed Maps of the British Isles, 1477–1650.* Revised edition. Somerset, Eng.: Castle Cary Press.

Shohet, Lauren. 2006. "The Masque in/as Print." In Straznicky 2006, 176–202.

Siebert, Fred S. 1952. *Freedom of the Press in England, 1476–1776: The Rise and Decline of Government Controls.* Urbana: University of Illinois Press.

Simmons, R. C. 2002. "ABCs, Almanacs, Ballads, Chapbooks, Popular Piety, and Textbooks." In Barnard and McKenzie 2002, 504–13.

Simpkins, Diana M. 1966. "Early Editions of Euclid in England." *Annals of Science* 22:225–49.

Spencer, T. J. B., ed. 1964. *Shakespeare's Plutarch.* Harmondsworth, Eng.: Penguin.

Spivack, C. K. 1967. *George Chapman.* New York: Twayne.

Sprunger, Keith L. 1994. *Trumpets from the Tower: English Puritan Printing in the Netherlands, 1600–1640.* Leiden: E. J. Brill.

Starnes, DeWitt T. 1951. "Richard Huloet's Abcedarium." *Studies in Philology* 48:717–37.

———. 1954. *Renaissance Dictionaries: English–Latin and Latin–English.* Austin: University of Texas.

Starnes, DeWitt T., and Gertrude E. Noyes. [1946] 1991. *The English Dictionary from Cawdrey to Johnson, 1604–1755.* Philadelphia: John Benjamins.

Steele, Robert. 1903. *The Earliest English Music Printing: A Description and Bibliography of English Printed Music to the Close of the Sixteenth Century.* London: Bibliographical Society.

Stein, Gabriele. 1985. *The English Dictionary before Cawdrey.* Tübingen: Max Niemeyer Verlag.

———. 1987. "Peter Levins: A 16th-Century English Word Formationalist." In *Neuere Forschungen zur Wortbildung und Historiographie der Linguistik: Festgabe für Herbert E. Brekle zum 50. Geburtstag,* 287–302. Edited by Brigitt Asbach-Schnitker and Johannes Roggenhofer. Tübingen: G. Narr.

———. 1997. *John Palsgrave as Renaissance Linguist: A Pioneer in Vernacular Language Usage.* Oxford: Clarendon.

———. 2006. "Richard Huloet as a Recorder of the English Lexicon." In *Selected Proceedings of the 2005 Symposium on New Approaches in English Historical Lexis,* 24–33. Edited by R. W. McConchie, et al. Somerville, Mass.: Cascadilla Proceedings Project.

Stern, Tiffany. 2004. *Making Shakespeare: From Stage to Page.* London: Routledge.

Stern, Virginia F. 1979. *Gabriel Harvey: His Life, Marginalia, and Library.* Oxford: Clarendon.

Stoddard, Roger E. 1985. *Marks in Books.* Cambridge, Mass.: Houghton Library, Harvard University.

Stone, Lawrence. 1964. "The Educational Revolution in England, 1560–1640." *Past and Present* 42:41–80.

Straznicky, Marta, ed. 2006. *The Book of the Play: Playwrights, Stationers, and Readers in Early Modern England.* Amherst: University of Massachusetts Press.

Summit, Jennifer. 2000. *Lost Property: The Woman Writer and English Literary History, 1350–1589.* Chicago: University of Chicago Press.

Sutton, Anne F., and Livia Visser-Fuchs. 1997. *Richard III's Books: Ideals and Reality in the Life and Library of a Medieval Prince.* Stroud, Gloucester, Eng.: Sutton Publishing.

Thomas, Sidney. 1976. "The Myth of the Authorized Shakespeare Quartos." *Shakespeare Quarterly* 27:186–92.

Timperley, C. H. 1839. *A Dictionary of Printers and Printing.* London: H. Johnson.

Treadwell, Michael. 1992. "Printers on the Court of the Stationers' Company in the Seventeenth and Eighteenth Centuries." *Journal of the Printing Historical Society* 21:29–43.

Tuer, Andrew. [1897] 1968. *History of the Horn Book.* New York: B. Blom.

Turner, Arthur W. 1949. "Milton's Aid to the *Polyglott Bible.*" *Modern Language Notes* 64:345.

Updike, Daniel Berkeley. 1962. *Printing Types, Their History, Forms, and Use: A Study in Survivals.* 3rd ed. Cambridge, Mass.: Belknap Press.

Veevers, Erica. 1989. *Images of Love and Religion: Queen Henrietta Maria and Court Entertainments.* Cambridge: Cambridge University Press.

Wall, Wendy. 1993. *The Imprint of Gender: Authorship and Publication in the English Renaissance.* Ithaca, N.Y.: Cornell University Press.

Warner, Christopher J. 1998. *Henry VIII's Divorce: Literature and the Politics of the Printing Press.* Woodbridge, Suffolk, Eng.: Boydell Press.

Watson, Foster. 1908. *The English Grammar Schools to 1660: Their Curriculum and Practice.* Cambridge: Cambridge University Press.

Watson, Nicholas. 1995. "Censorship and Cultural Change in Late-Medieval England: Vernacular Theology, the Oxford Translation Debate, and Arundel's Constitutions of 1409." *Speculum* 70:822–64.

Webster, John. 1985. *The White Devil.* Edited by Elizabeth H. Brannan. London: A and C Black.

———. 1996. *The White Devil.* Edited by John Russell Brown. Manchester, Eng.: Manchester University Press.

Weiss, Susan Forscher. 2003. "Didactic Sources of Musical Learning in Early Modern England." In *Didactic Literature in England, 1500–1700: Expertise Constructed,* 40–62. Edited by Natasha Glaisyer and Sara Pennell. Burlington, Vt.: Ashgate.

Weller, Barry, and Margaret W. Ferguson, eds. 1994. *The Tragedy of Mariam, the Fair Queen of Jewry.* Los Angeles: University of California Press.

Wells, Stanley W., and Gary Taylor, eds. 1986. *William Shakespeare: The Complete Works.* Oxford: Clarendon.

West, Anthony James. 2001–3. *The Shakespeare First Folio: The History of the Book.* 2 vols. Oxford: Oxford University Press.

Wheale, Nigel. 1999. *Writing and Society: Literature, Print, and Politics in Britain, 1590–1660.* New York: Routledge.

Wheatley, H. B., ed. [1867] 1937. *Manipulus Vocabulorum: A Rhyming Dictionary of the English Language.* Reprint. London: Oxford University Press.

Willoughby, Edwin Elliott. 1934. *A Printer of Shakespeare: The Books and Times of William Jaggard.* London: P. Allan.

Wilson, F. P. 1969. *The English Drama, 1485–1585.* Oxford History of English Literature. Vol. 4, part 2. Oxford: Claredon Press.

Woodhouse, J. R. 1978. *Baldesar Castiglione: A Reassessment of "The Courtier."* Edinburgh: Edinburgh University Press.

Woolley, Benjamin. 2001. *The Queen's Conjurer: The Science and Magic of Dr. John Dee, Adviser to Queen Elizabeth I.* New York: Henry Holt.

Worms, Laurence. 2002. "Maps and Atlases." In Barnard and McKenzie 2002, 228–45.

Wright, George T. 1992. "An Almost Oral Art: Shakespeare's Language on Stage and Page." *Shakespeare Quarterly* 43:159–69.

Yamada, Akihiro. 1994. *Thomas Creede, Printer to Shakespeare, and His Contemporaries.* Tokyo: Meisei University Press.

Zetterberg, J. Peter. 1980. "The Mistaking of 'the Mathematicks' for Magic in Tudor and Stuart England." *Sixteenth Century Journal* 11:83–97.

# INDEX

licensing works of, 26–28; proofs corrected by, 22; rights to plays, 32

of, 118–19; imprisonment of, 96; masques of, 35, 160; Plutarch used by, 118; typefaces of, 179; works: *Caesar and Pompey,* 118; *Eastward Ho* (with Jonson and Marston), 96–97, *97,* 118; Homer (trans.), 118–20, *119,* 179; *The Memorable Maske* (with Jones), 158–61, *159*

Charles I (1600–1649; king, 1625–49): beheading of, 105; masques and, 35, 160; parody of, 97–99, *98, 99;* printing restrictions under, 28–29

Charles II (1630–85; king, 1660–85): Bible dedicated to, 181; bookbinder of, 198; Milton's works suppressed by, 1, 30, *82,* 105

Charles V (1500–1558; Holy Roman Emperor, 1519–56), 12

Charlewood, John (d. 1593), 31

Chaucer, Geoffrey (c. 1340–1400): context of, 127; glossary of words used by, 22–23; Ovid used by, 112; works: *Canterbury Tales* (two editions), 5, *50,* 51–53; *House of Fame,* 5; *Parliament of Fowls,* 5; *Troilus and Criseyde,* 5

Chetwind (Chetwinde), Philip (fl. 1656–74): works printed for: Shakespeare Third Folio, 170–73, *171*

Chichester Cathedral School, 54

Children of the Queen's Revels, 118, 163

Christianity: Bible reading and, 16; educational expansion and, 16; practical magic book on, 57, *57;* upheavals in, 15. *See also* Catholicism and Catholic Church; Church of England; Reformation, Protestant; religious works

Christine de Pisan (Pizan) (c. 1364–c. 1431), 5

Christ's College (Cambridge), 16

*Chronicles of England (The Brut):* Higden's *Polycronicon* bound with, 53; Holinshed's version, 175; manuscript and book compared, *46,* 47–49, *48*

Church of England: Bible of, 13–14; Elizabeth's restoration of, 25; establishment of, 10, 24, 87; tracts against, 25–26

Cicero, Marcus Tullius (106–43 B.C.E.): *De senectute,* 5; *De Senectute* and *De amicitia,* 49, *50,* 51

Clair, Colin, 43

classical works: Baret's trilingual dictionary and, 21–22; Elyot's bilingual dictionary and, 18–20; imports of, 114; translations of, 12–13. *See also specific authors*

coats of arms, *196,* 197

Cockeram, Henry (fl. 1623–58), 23

codex, 3

Codrington, Rob.: Aesop's *Fables* (trans.), 191–93, *192*

Coleridge, Samuel (1772–1834), 118, 120

Colet, John (1467–1519): Lily's Latin grammar and, 16, 61; works: *Aeditio,* 61

collectors: books and manuscripts undistinguished by, 3; books imported and bound by, 195–98

College of Douai (Flanders), 92

College of Edinburgh, 16

Coloma, Carlos de (1573–1637), 98

colophons, *178,* 198

Colwell, Thomas (fl. 1561–75): legal difficulties of, 139; works printed by: *A Comedy Concernyng Thre Lawes* (Bale), 137–41, *138*

Comenius, Joannes (1592–1670): educational publications of, 16; on handpress printing, 3; works: *Orbis sensualium pictus, 4*

commonplace books, *56,* 56–57

Condell, Henry (bap. 1576?–1627), 34, 172–73

Convocation of Coventry, 14

Cooper, Thomas (1517–94): Elyot's *Dictionary* and, 20, 22; works: *Thesaurus Linguae Romanae et Britannicae* (comp.), 22, 66–67

Coote, Edmund (d. 1609), 63

copyright, 53

Corro, Antonio de (1527–91), 79

Cotes, Thomas (d. 1641): works printed by: *Mathematicall recreations* (Leurechon), *124,* 124–25; *Navfragivm iocvlare, comaedia* (Cowley), 193–98, *194;* Shakespeare Second Folio, *169,* 169–73, *170*

Council of Trent (1546), 14, 132

Coverdale, Miles (1488–1569): Bible translation of, 13, 24, 60, 85, 128; prohibited works of, 25. *See also* Great Bible (1539)

Cowley, Abraham (1618–67): *Navfragivm iocvlare, comaedia,* 193–98, *194*

*Crafte of conjureynge and howe to rule ye ffierye spiritts of ye planets, The* (c. 1590), 56–57, *57*

Creede, Thomas (c. 1554–1616): legal difficulties of, 139; works printed by: *Locrine* (attributed to Shakespeare), 137–41, *139; The London Prodigal,* 141; *Romeo and Juliet* (Shakespeare), 155–57, *156; The Tragedie of Mariam* (Cary), 162–64, *163*

Crom, Matthew (1505/10–46?): works printed by: Matthew Bible, 128, *129*

Cromwell, Oliver (1599–1658), 30, 181, 193

Cromwell, Thomas (c. 1485–1540), 85

"cum privilegio regali": use of phrase, *84,* 85

Curtain Theatre (Moorfields), 31

Cutwode, Thomas (bap. 1561–1602/3), 203n5

Daniel, Roger (fl. 1627–66): works printed by: Shakespeare Third Folio, 170–73, *171*

Elizabeth (James I's daughter), 158–61, *159*

Elizabeth I (1533–1603; queen, 1558–1603): astrological charts for, 116; Bible translations and, 13, 128, *130*, 130–32, *131*; books dedicated to, 116; censorship under, 25–26, 95–96; executions under, 92; fondness for masques, 35; injunctions of, 26, 92, *93*; Lily's grammar endorsed by, 61; political and religious context of, 90–92, *91*; privileges and patents under, 26, 87, 114, 180, 184; on Richard II, 93–94; theatrical companies under, 31

Elyot, Thomas (c. 1490–1546): on borrowing foreign words, 12; spying by, 128; works: *The Book named the Governour*, 16, 19, 67; *Castel of Helth*, 67; *Dictionary* (later, *Bibliotheca Eliotae*), 18–20, *19*, 22, 26, 27, 66–67, *67*

English language: Caxton's influence on, 5–7; Chapman's praise for, 120; deficiencies in, 12; elementary introduction to, 16, 17, *62*, *63*; English stage as improving, 167; first book printed in, 54; flexibility and changes in, 72, 203n9; foreign words in, 12, 14, 23, 108, 111; prohibition of circulation of Bible in, 13, 24, 60, 83, 128; translators' style as influence on, 11–12; Tyndale's influence on, 128; typefaces for, 10; vowel shift in, 6. *See also* dictionaries; English orthography; Middle English; Old English; vernacular texts

English orthography: Butler's revision of, 64, *64*; Caxton's influence on, 6–7; fitting text to page space and, 37, *38*; Levens's rules for, 69–70

English Stock: almanac of, 87

engravings: of maps, *41*, 41–42, 185; of music notation, 41; of solutions to scientific problems, 125; of St. Paul's Cathedral, *191*, 193; woodcuts replaced by, 43

Erasmus, Desiderius (d. 1536): educational model of, 63; Lily's Latin grammar and, 16; works: *Adagia*, 19, 22

errata, 198–99, *199*

Essex, earl of (Robert Devereux, 1566–1601): military news report on, 120–22, *121*; rebellion of, 93–94

Estienne (Stephanus), Robert (1559–1630), 18–19, 20, 22

Etten, Hendrick van (pseud.). *See* Leurechon, Jean (1591–1670)

Euclid (c. 325–c. 250 B.C.E.): *The Elements of Geometrie*, 114, *115*, 116, 193

*Everyman* (play), 30

*Every Woman in Her Humor* (anon.), 142–44, *143*

Faques, William (fl. 1504–8), 10, 85

Farrant, Richard (c. 1528–80), 31

Fastolf, John (1380–1459), 49

Fleming, Abraham, 22

Flemish scribes: bâtarde characters of, 2

Flesher, Miles (d. 1664): works printed by: *The Fair Maid of the West* (Heywood), 165–67, *166*

Fletcher, John (1579–1625), 160

Florio, John (1553–1625), 79

Fogny, John (1561–87): Bible printed by, 132–34, *133*

folios: explanation of, 36–37, *38*, 39; Jonson's *Workes* as, 164, *165*. *See also* Shakespeare First Folio (1623)

Fortune Theatre, 31

Foxe, John (1516/17–87): *Acts and Monuments* (or *Book of Martyrs*), 25, 87–89, *88*, *89*, 114, 193; *The Gospels of the fower Euangelistes* (translation), 13

Frampton, John (fl. 1559–81): works translated by: *Ioyfull nevves out of the newe founde worlde* (Monardes), *123*, 123–25

France: Bibles printed in, 85; books smuggled to England from, 92; courtly literature of, *106*, 127; popular scientific work in, 125; spread of printing in, 4

Frederick V (1596–1632), 160

freedom of speech: Milton on, 1, 29–30, 102, *103*, 105; opportunity for, 30, 101–2

French language: dictionaries of, 20, 21–22, 79–81, *80*; reflected in Caxton's translation, 108, 111

Fulke, William (1536/37–89), 14

Gardiner, Stephen (c. 1495–1555): text linked to: *De vera obediencia*, 89, *90*, 90–92

Garland, John (c. 1195–1258), 18

Gataker, Thomas (1537–1654), 146

Gaultier, Thomas (fl. 1550–53), 26

gender: literacy and, 16; reading of plays and, 164

Geneva Bible: alternative to, 130, 181; Book of Samuel in, *179*; description of, 177–81; King James Bible compared with, 134; shortcomings of, 14; typeface of, 10, 181

Geoffrey of Monmouth (d. 1154), 47

Germany: spread of printing in, 3–4

Gerson, Jean (1363–1429), 107

Globe Theatre: establishment of, 31; income of, 203n11; Middleton's *Game at Chess* at, 97–99, *98*, *99*; *Othello* performed at, 158

glossaries: in Douai-Rheims Bible, 14, 133–34. *See also* dictionaries

Godbid, William (fl. 1656–77): works printed by: Aesop's *Fables*, 191–93, *192*

*Golden Legend, The* (1483–84), 5

Golding, Arthur (1535/36–1606): works trans-

Holinshed, Raphael (1525–80), 48, 175
Hollar, Wenceslaus (1607–77): career of, 193;
  works: St. Paul's Cathedral, *191*
Holme, William (fl. 1600), 144
Holt, John (d. 1504): *Lac puerorum,* 54, *55,* 61
Holyoke, Francis, 203n5
Homer (c. 8th cen. B.C.E.): *Iliad,* 118–20, *119;*
  *Odyssey,* 119
Hondius, Jodocus (1563–1612), 185
honeymoon: etymology of, 72, *73*
Hopkins, John (1520/21–70): Psalter, 114, *197,*
  197–98
hornbooks: construction of, 202n1; contents of,
  59–61, *60;* typefaces for, 39–40, *40*
Hugo of Pisa (d. 1210), 18
Huloet (Howlet), Richard (fl. 1552): *Abcedarium
  anglico-latinvm pro tyrunculis,* 20, 21, *68,*
  68–69
Humble, George (d. 1640): works printed for:
  *The Theatre of the Empire of Great Britaine*
  (Speed), 184–85, *188–89*
Hunt, Thomas (fl. 1483), 9

illuminators, 2
illustrations: early printing of, 2, 40–43; in
  English–Latin dictionary, 68; in Plutarch's
  *Lives of the Noble Grecians and Romans, 117,*
  118. *See also* engravings; woodcuts
*Imitation of Christ, The,* 12, 53
incunables: characteristics of, 2–3, 53; English vs.
  European, 203n2; half sheets used in, 205n1
indexes, 185
informational works: on manners, 125–27, *126;*
  on mathematics, *124,* 124–25; on military
  news and activities, 120–22, *121, 122;* translations of, 12–13
inkhorn terms: use of phrase, 12
interludes: monopolies absent for, 138–39; printing of, 30–31
Italian language: dictionary of, 76, *78,* 79–81

Jackson, John (fl. 1584–96): works printed by:
  *Bibliothecæ Hispanicæ* (Perceval), *78,* 79–81
Jacobus de Voragine (c. 1229–98), 52
Jaggard, Isaac (d. 1627): works printed by:
  Shakespeare First Folio, *168,* 168–73
Jaggard, William (1568–1623): Okes compared
  with, 167; works printed by and/or for: Shake-
  speare First Folio, *168,* 168–73; Shakespeare's
  plays (Pavier Quartos), 150–54, *151, 152, 153,
  154, 155*
James I (1566–1625; king of Great Britain,
  1603–25, and king of Scotland as James VI,

1567–1625): Bible translation under, 14–15,
  134–35, *135,* 181; bookbinding for, *196, 197;*
  College of Edinburgh founded under, 16;
  fondness for masques, 35; as "King of Great
  Britain," 185; masque presented at daughter's
  marriage, 158–61, *159; Othello* performed
  for, 158; parody of, 97–99, *98, 99;* printing privileges under, 87; satire of, 96–97, *97;*
  swearing in plays prohibited by, 157, 158;
  theatrical companies under, 31; works: *Essays
  of a Prentise,* 118
James II (1633–1701; king, 1685–88), 198
Jerome (saint, d. 419/420): Latin Vulgate Bible
  and, 132–33; works (Pseudo-Jerome): *Vitas
  Patrum,* 5, 109, *110,* 111
jobbing: concept of, 141; income from, 8
Johnson, Fabian (fl. 1591): *Trve intelligence,*
  120–22, *121*
Johnson, Samuel (1709–84), 126
Jones, Inigo (1573–1652): *The Memorable Maske*
  (with Chapman), 158–61, *159; The Temple of
  Love* (with Davenant), *35,* 158–61, *160*
Jones, R. F., 17
Jonson, Ben (1572–1637): collected plays of,
  34; imprisonment of, 96; masques of, 35, 36,
  160; Ovid used by, 113; Plutarch used by, 118;
  references to Lily's grammar by, 61; works:
  *Cataline,* 118; *Eastward Ho* (with Chapman
  and Marston), 96–97, *97,* 118; *Epigrammes,*
  164; *Every Man out of His Humor,* 141–44,
  *143; Isle of Dogs* (with Nashe), 96; "To the
  Reader," *172,* 173; *Workes,* 36, 164, *165*
Judson, Thomas (fl. 1584–99): works printed by:
  *Nashes Lenten stuffe* (Nash), *95,* 95–96
Jugge, Richard (c. 1514–77): Bible printed by,
  13, 128, *130,* 130–32, *131;* royal privileges
  of, 26

Keats, John (1795–1821), 118, 120
Keere, Pieter van der (c. 1571–c. 1624), 185
Kersey, John (c. 1660–c. 1721), 76
King James Bible (1611): context and translation
  of, 13–15, 134–35; influences on, 128, 131,
  134–35; Psalms in, 134–35, *135;* size of, 181;
  typefaces of, 10, 179, 181
King's Men: Marston's play performed by,
  *161,* 161–64; Middleton's play performed
  by, 97–99, *98, 99;* printing of plays and,
  154; Shakespeare's *Richard II* performed by,
  93–94, *94*
King's Players. *See* King's Men
King's Printer (Printer to the King): Berthelet
  as, 10, 67; designation as, 9, 10; Faques as, 85;

Martin, Gregory (1542?–82): Allen's relationship to, 92; Bible translated by, 14, 132–34, *133*

Martin, John (fl. 1649–80): works printed for: *A world of errors discovered in the New World of Words* (Blount), 74–76, *75*

Mary I (1516–58; queen, 1553–58): censorship under, 25, 114; executions under, 89; fondness for masques, 35; Geneva Bible and, 130; plays published in reign of, 140; political and religious context of, *90*, 90–92; printing monopolies and privileges under, 86–87; reestablishment of Catholicism under, 15, 25; Stationers' Company established by, 61, 87

masques: description of, 35–36, 158–61; monopolies absent for, 138–39; music for, 161; title pages of, *159, 160*

mathematical works: Euclid's *Elements of Geometrie,* 114, *115,* 116; as vernacular text, *124,* 124–25

Matthew, Thomas (pseud.), 13, 128. *See also* Rogers, John (c. 1500–1555)

Matthew Bible (1537): context and translation of, 13, 128; Gospel of John in, *129;* import and sale of, 15; publisher of, executed, 89; revision of, 85

Matthews, Augustine (fl. 1619–53): works printed by: *A Game at Chess* (Middleton), 99; *A Maske presented at Ludlow Castle* (Milton), 159–61, *160*

Mearne, Samuel: bookbinding of, *174,* 198

medical works: translations of, 13, 67, *123,* 123–25

*Medula Grammatica* (Marrow of Grammar; 15th cen.), 18

Medwall, Henry (1462–c. 1501), 30

Meighen, Richard (fl. 1615–41): works printed for: Shakespeare Second Folio, *169,* 169–73, *170; Workes* (Jonson), 164, *165*

Melanchthon, Philipp (1497–1560), 25

Mercator, Gerardus (1512–94), 185

Mercers' Guild, 49

Merchant Taylors' School (London), 30, 63

Meres, Francis (1565/66–1647), 144

Middle English: Bible in, 128; *Brut* in, 47–48; English spelling based on, 6–7; in *Promptorium paruulorum,* 64–66, *65. See also* Chaucer, Geoffrey (c. 1340–1400); Gower, John (c. 1325–1408); Lydgate, John (c. 1370–1449/50?)

Middlesex: map of, *41,* 184–85, *188–89*

Middleton, Thomas (bap. 1580–1627): imprisonment of, 98, 99; works: *A Game at Chess,* 34, 97–99, *98, 99,* 164; *Microcynicon,* 203n5

military: reports on, 120–22, *121, 122*

Milton, John (1608–74): family of, 74; on intellectual freedom, 1, 29–30, 102; London Polyglot Bible and, 181; Plutarch used by, 118; regicide defended by, 105; suppression of books of, 1, 30, *82,* 105; warrant to search Prynne's rooms, 102, *104,* 105; works: *Areopagitica,* 1, 29–30, 102, *103,* 105; *Discourse of the Poets and Poetry* (attributed), 75; "An Epitaph . . . Shakespeare," 173; *A Maske presented at Ludlow Castle,* 36, 159–61, *160; Of Education,* 16; *Samson Agonistes,* 34

Minsheu, John (1559/60–1627): *Ductor in linguas,* 22, 79–81, *81*

*Missale Sarum* (music; 1500 ed.), 40

misspelling: use of term, 7

Monardes, Nicolás (c. 1512–88): *Ioyfull nevves out of the newe founde worlde, 123,* 123–25

monopolies, patents, and privileges: *ABC* and schoolbooks, 26, 87; almanacs, 26, 86, 87; Bibles, 26, 85; catechisms, 26; dictionaries, 26, *27;* disputes over, 26–27; government documents, 85; legal books, 26, 85, 86; music printing, 26, 184; prayer books, 85; primers, 85, 86–87; psalters, 86, 87, 114, 184; service books, 26, 86; warnings about, 198. *See also* King's Printer (Printer to the King)

morality plays, 30–31

More, Thomas (1478–1535): correspondents of, 54; educational model of, 63; interludes of, published, 30; reading of, 87; Tyndale's translation denounced by, 24, 128

Morison, Stanley, 5

Morley, Thomas (1556/57–c. 1602): printing patents of, 184, 198; works printed for: *The Psalms of David in meter* (Alison), *183,* 183–84

Morris, William (1834–96), 49

Morton, John (d. 1500), 54

Moseley, Humphrey (c. 1603–61): books for sale by: *Glossographia* (Blount), 72, *73*

Mulcaster, Richard (1531/32–1611): educational model of, 63; on spelling, 6, 17; works: *Elementarie,* 16, 17, *62,* 63

Munday, Anthony (1560–1633): theater denounced by, 167; works translated by: *Amadis de Gaule, 106,* 127

*Mundus et Infans* (play), 30

Münster, Sebastian (1489–1552), 185

Murray, James (d. 1658), 96

music: in masques, 36; monopolies for printing, 26, 184; printing notation of, 40–41, *182,* 182–84, *183*

ton's comments on becoming a printer in, 107; Caxton's translation of, 4, 5, 49, 54; context of printing, 127

Redman, Robert (d. 1540), 198

Reformation, Protestant: Bible reading and, 16; translations of Bible and, 11

Regnault, François (d. c. 1540), 85

regulations: for actors and theaters, 31–32, 157, 158; church motivations for, 24–25; governmental role in, 26–29; Parliamentary acts on, 83, 100–102, *101;* petitions for increased, 29–30; royal injunction concerning, 26, 92, *93;* for texts before printing, 83. *See also* censorship; monopolies, patents, and privileges; Star Chamber

religious works: *ABC* book combined with, 59–61, *60;* audience of, 9, 11; chosen for translation, 12–13; current events and, 120–22, *122;* guide for priests, 107–9, *108;* on lives of saints, 109, *110,* 111; market for, 15; royal license to print, 26. *See also* Bibles; primers

*Return from Parnassus, The* (1606), 138–41, *140*

*Reynard the Fox* (1481), 5, 8

Reynes, John: bookbinding of: *Postilla* (Nicolaus de Lyra), *195,* 196–97

Reynolds, John (1549–1607), 134

Rheims New Testament, 132–34, *133*

Rich, Jeremiah (d. 1666/69): shorthand revised by, *147,* 148

Richard II (1367–1400; king, 1377–99): Shakespeare's play about, 93–94, *94*

*Riche and Pore (Dives et Pauper),* 53–54, *55*

Riddel, William (fl. 1552–60): works printed by: *Abcedarium anglico-latinvm pro tyrunculis* (Huloet), *68,* 68–69

Roberts, James (c. 1540–1618?): royal privileges of, 26; works printed by: *Hamlet* (Shakespeare), *149,* 149–50; *The Merchant of Venice* (Shakespeare), 151, *152; A Midsummer Night's Dream* (Shakespeare), 153–54, *155*

Robinson, Humphrey (d. 1670): works printed for: *A Maske presented at Ludlow Castle,* 159–61, *160*

Rogers, John (c. 1500–1555), 13, 89, 128

Rood, Theodoric (fl. 1478–86), 9

Roper, Abel (bap. 1665–1726): works printed for: *A world of errors discovered in the New World of Words* (Blount), 74–76, *75*

Rose Theatre, 31, 118

*Royal Book, The,* 8

Roycroft, Thomas (d. 1677): works printed by: *Biblia sacra polyglotta* (ed. Walton), 178–81, *180*

Roye, Gui de (1345–1409): works attributed to: *The Doctrinal of Sapyence,* 12, 107–9, *108*

Royston, Richard (1601–86): works printed for: *Advice to a friend* (Patrick), *174,* 195–98; *The Fair Maid of the West* (Heywood), 165–67, *166*

running heads, 2

Ryckes, John (d. 1532), 88

Salesbury, William (c. 1520–c. 1580): *Dictionary in Englyshe and Welshe,* 22, 76, *77,* 79–81

Salmasius, Claudius (1588–1653), 30

satire: anti-Spanish, 97–99, *98, 99;* of James and Scots, 96–97, *97;* linked to Wolsey, 31; in praise of red herring, *95,* 95–96

Sawbridge, George (the elder, c. 1621–81): books for sale by: *Glossographia* (Blount), 72, *73*

Saxton, Christopher (c. 1542–c. 1610), 42, 185

schoolbooks: grammars as, 16, 17, 62, *63;* Holt's *Lac puerorum* as, 54, *55;* monopolies for printing, 26, 87. *See also* dictionaries; education; grammars; hornbooks

Scrope, Stephen, 202n1

Seile, Ann (d. 1678): works printed for: Aesop's *Fables,* 191–93, *192*

Seile, Henry (d. 1661): works printed for: *Navfragivm iocvlare, comaedia* (Cowley), 193–98, *194*

Seres, William (d. 1578/80): monopolies and patents of, 86–87, 184; partner of, 114; works printed by: *The Courtier* (Castiglione), 125–27, *126; Metamorphoses* (Ovid), 111–14, *113*

service books: monopolies for printing, 26, 86

Shakespeare, William (1564–1616): on *ABC* books, 60; allusion to, 97; circumstances of publishing plays of, 32–34; court performances of works, 158, 160; lost plays of, 144, 146; masques incorporated in plays of, 36; Ovid used by, 112, *113*–14; Plutarch used by, 118; possible reference to Mulcaster by, 63; references to Lily's grammar by, 61; works: *Antony and Cleopatra,* 118; *Coriolanus,* 118; *Errors,* 144; *Gentlemen of Verona,* 144; *Hamlet,* 33, 34, *149,* 149–50; *Henry IV,* 155–57, *157; Henry V,* 141, 152–54, *154; 1 Henry VI,* 37, *38,* 153; *2 Henry VI,* 141, 153; *3 Henry VI,* 153; *Julius Caesar,* 118; *King John,* 60; *King Lear,* 152–54, 153; *Locrine* (attributed), 137–41, *139; Love's Labour's Lost,* 63, 144; *Love's Labour's Won,* 144, *145,* 146; *The Merchant of Venice,* 144, 151–54, *152; The Merry Wives of Windsor,* 61, 151–54, *152; A Midsummer Night's Dream,* 113, 144, 153–54, *155; Othello,* 33, *158,* 159; Pavier

Quartos of plays, 150–54, *151, 152, 153, 154, 155,* 172; *Pericles, Prince of Tyre,* 150–54, *151,* 173; *The Rape of Lucrece,* 114; *Richard II,* 93–94, *94; Richard III,* 175–76, *176; Romeo and Juliet,* 32, 33, 34, 141, 155–57, *156; Sir John Oldcastle* (attributed), 154; *The Tempest,* 37, 39, 114, 116; *Timon of Athens,* 118; *Titus Andronicus,* 61, 113, 141, 146; *Troilus and Cressida,* 146; *A Yorkshire Tragedy* (attributed), 154; *As You Like It,* 95. *See also* King's Men
Shakespeare First Folio (1623): description of, 168–73; fitting text on pages of, 37, *38;* format of, 36–37; *Hamlet* in, 150; motives in publishing, 33; note to reader in, *168; Othello* in, 158; Pavier Quartos compared with, 154; printers of, 154; *Richard II* in, 94; signatures in, 37, 39; *Troilus and Cressida* omitted from, 146
Shakespeare Second Folio (1632): description of, 169–73; epitaph in, *170;* title page of, *169*
Shakespeare Third Folio (1664): description of, 170–73; *Locrine* in, 141; *Pericles* in, 173; title page of, *171*
Shakespeare Fourth Folio (1685): description of, 171–73; title page of, *172*
Shirley, Rodney, 42
Short, Peter (d. 1602): works printed by: *Richard III* (Shakespeare), 175–76, *176*
shorthand: New Testament in, *147;* piracy of plays via, 33, 148; sermons recorded via, 148, 204n13
Sidney, Philip (1554–86), 127
signatures (marks): explanation of, 37, 39
Simmes, Valentine (fl. 1585–1622): works printed by: *The Malcontent* (Marston and Webster), *161,* 161–64; *Nashes Lenten stuffe* (Nash), *95,* 95–96; *Richard III* (Shakespeare), 175–76, *176*
Skelton, John (c. 1460–1529), 31
Slater, Thomas (d. 1653?): works printed for: *Pleasant Dialogves and Drammas* (Heywood), *146,* 146–48
Smethwicke (Smithweeke), John (d. 1641): works printed for: Shakespeare First Folio, *168,* 168–73; Shakespeare Second Folio, *169,* 169–73, *170*
Spanish language: dictionary of, 22, *78,* 79–81
*Speculum vitae Christi,* 109
Speed, John (1551/52–1629): *The Theatre of the Empire of Great Britaine,* 42, 184–85, *188–89*
Speght, Thomas (d. 1621), 22–23
spelling. *See* English orthography
Spenser, Edmund (1552?–99), 12, 57, 63, 127
St. John's College (Cambridge), 16, 138–41

St. John's College (Oxford), 16
St. Paul's School (London), 61, 63
Stafford, Simon (fl. 1596–1626): works printed by: *Summers Last Will and Testament* (Nashe), 141–44, *142*
Stanbridge, John (1463–1510), 9, 61
Stanhope iron press, 3
Stansby, William (bap. 1572–1638): works printed by: *Ductor in linguas* (Minsheu), 79–81, *81; Workes* (Jonson), 164, *165*
Star Chamber: disbanding of, 101; on licensing and registration (1637), 28–29, *29,* 99–102, *100;* on orders in printing (1586), 26, 28
stationer: definition of, 28–29
Stationers' Company of the City of London: almanac printed for, *86,* 86–87; Elizabeth's injunction to, 26, 92, *93;* establishment of, 61, 87; on Lily's grammars, 61; petitions of, 29–30; raids by, 139; regulations and powers of, 28–29, 100–102, *101;* royal charter for, 27–28
Stationers' Guild, 61
Stationers' Register, 28, 92, 94, 102
Stein, Gabriele, 67
Stephanus (Estienne), Robert (1559–1630), 18–19, 20, 22
Sternhold, Thomas (d. 1549): psalter, 114, *197,* 197–98
Stoddard, Roger E., 39
Stone, Lawrence, 15–16
Straten, Dirik Van der (fl. 1546–48), 31
Stubbes, Philip (c. 1555–c. 1610), 167
Sudbury, John (fl. 1610–15): works printed for: *The Theatre of the Empire of Great Britaine* (Speed), 184–85, *188–89*
Swan Theatre, 31
Swinburne, Algernon Charles (1837–1909), 118

Tallis, Thomas (c. 1505–85), 26, 184
Tasso, Ercole (d. 1613), 203n5
Tasso, Torquato (1544–95), 203n5
Tate, John (c. 1448–1507/8), 52
Taverner, Richard (1505?–75), 85
Taylor, Gary, 144, 146
Terence (d. 159 B.C.E.), 30
theaters: attacks on, 28, 167; closed due to plague, 167; establishment of, 31–32; Heywood's defense of, *136,* 167; income of, 203n11; variety of performances in, 34–36. *See also* actors and acting companies; drama (plays); *specific theaters*
Theatre, The (Shoreditch), 31
*Theatrum poetarum* (1675), 74–75

VALERIE HOTCHKISS is the head of the Rare Book and Manuscript Library and professor of medieval studies at the University of Illinois at Urbana-Champaign. Her publications include *Clothes Make the Man: Female Transvestism in Medieval Europe* and the four-volume *Creeds and Confessions of Faith in the Christian Tradition*, edited in collaboration with Jaroslav Pelikan.

FRED C. ROBINSON is Douglas Tracy Smith Professor Emeritus of English and a librarian of the Elizabethan Club at Yale University. He is the author of *Beowulf and the Appositive Style, The Tomb of Beowulf,* and *The Editing of Old English* and coauthor of *A Guide to Old English.*

THE UNIVERSITY OF ILLINOIS PRESS IS A
FOUNDING MEMBER OF THE ASSOCIATION
OF AMERICAN UNIVERSITY PRESSES.

This book is typeset in Adobe Caslon Pro, designed by
Carol Twombly in 1990 for Adobe Systems Inc.,
part of the Adobe Originals library.
Her design was based on specimen pages
printed by William Caslon in London
between 1734 and 1770.
Designed by Copenhaver Cumpston.
Typeset by Jim Proefrock and
Copenhaver Cumpston at the
University of Illinois Press.
Printed on 70# Matte
by Bang Printing.

UNIVERSITY OF ILLINOIS PRESS
1325 South Oak Street
Champaign, IL 61820–6903
www.press.uillinois.edu